the *Gentle* art of *Domesticity*

the Gentle art of Domesticity

STITCHING, BAKING, NATURE, ART & THE COMFORTS OF HOME

jane brocket

STC Craft | A Melanie Falick Book
Stewart, Tabori & Chang
New York

Published in 2008 by Stewart, Tabori & Chang
An imprint of Harry N. Abrams, Inc.

Copyright © 2007 by Jane Brocket
First published in Great Britain in 2007 by Hodder & Stoughton
An Hachette Livre UK company

Library of Congress Cataloging-in-Publication Data

Brocket, Jane.
  The gentle art of domesticity / by Jane Brocket.
    p. cm.
  "STC Craft/A Melanie Falick book."
  ISBN 978-1-58479-736-4
  1. Home economics. 2. Handicraft. I. Title.
  TX147.B76 2008
  640--dc22
                              2008007819

Interior design: Ashley Western
Cover design, STC edition: Alissa Faden
Design Production, STC edition: Shawn Dahl
Production Manager, STC edition: Jacquie Poirier

The text of this book was composed in Parisine Clair and
Pendulum.

Printed and bound in China
10 9 8 7 6 5 4 3 2 1

HNA
harry n. abrams, inc.
a subsidiary of La Martinière Groupe

115 West 18th Street
New York, NY 10011
www.hnabooks.com

For Simon

Contents

Introduction

Domesticity, not domestication

There is a world of difference between domesticity and domestication. This book is about domesticity and the pleasures and joys of the gentle domestic arts of knitting, crochet, baking, stitching, quilting, gardening and homemaking. It is emphatically not about the repetitive, endless rounds of cleaning, washing, ironing, shopping and house maintenance that come with domestication. Domesticity rises above the bossiness of cleaning products and media exhortations to keep our houses pristine and hygienic, and focuses instead on creativity within the domestic space.

Domesticity gives us the opportunity to express ourselves, and the gentle arts are the most satisfying and achievable means of doing so. Domesticity frees our minds and hands and eyes to enjoy often-neglected and undervalued skills, textiles, color, textures, patterns and comforts, all of which can bring pleasure to both the domestic artist and those around her.

It took me many years to realize that I was thoroughly domestic, and only grudgingly domesticated. I accept that chores must be accomplished in order to maintain a clean and manageable living environment, but that's where it stops. I may not be on a level with the writer, wit and English eccentric Quentin Crisp, who famously declared that after four years the dust doesn't get any worse, but I can ignore moldings and food cupboards when there are so many more wonderfully satisfying domestic arts I can practice.

The path to enlightenment

I am the eldest of four children and in my teens was something of a bedroom recluse. However, this was no normal bedroom. It had been rented out to a university student before it became my creative domain and was large, painted lime green and purple (my choices) and, as well as the usual bedroom furniture, it contained a sofa, a gas fireplace, a tiny stove and a sink. It was a self-contained domestic paradise for a teenager whose passions ran from chemistry experiments one moment, to tie-dyeing and candle-making the next, taking in windowsill herb growing, macramé, gold-sprayed pasta collages, leather-belt production, egg painting, clothes making and all sorts of textile dabbling along the way.

But I hated tidying up, and I never classed myself as a budding domestic diva. Instead, I fell in with the expectations of my fiercely academic girls' school and went along with wanting, and preparing for, some brilliant career. I was banned from the art room, even though I argued that some downtime from Russian irregular verbs could only be good for a girl. The few who did dare to follow their artistic bent were seen as rebels and likely to come to no good. And this, may I remind you, was the 1970s, not the 1870s, but I cannot recall a single mention of the three Ms: Men, Marriage and Motherhood. No heed was paid to the fact that we were all women, most of us likely to have relationships with the opposite sex and make babies, and inhabit a domestic space of some sort. And yet there we were, educated at the height of the second wave of the

feminist movement, in collective denial about one immensely significant aspect of our future lives.

Even when I went to university to study Russian and French, the Chekhovian subtext of my enjoyment of domesticity sat uneasily with academic expectations—my own and those of others. While I was there, I mastered the gentle arts of knitting, baking birthday cakes and making blue rock cakes—small little pastries similiar to scones—but I came away from Bristol still confused. Goodness knows why my next move was to Sheffield University to train to be a teacher; the only lasting memory I have of this time is knitting a ghastly mohair sweater night after night in my tiny room. Needless to say, I never wore it, imbued as it was with misery and frustration.

The real world

As soon as I had picked up my teaching qualification, I made a dash for the life I thought I would enjoy: travel, languages, expense account, company car. I sold synthetic textiles to the Soviet Union, then marketed upholstery fabrics to Belgium, France and Holland, and later traveled all over Europe as a brand manager for an international wine and spirits company. The apex of my corporate life was marketing a portfolio of champagnes in the UK, and it was this role that set me on the path to becoming a Master of Wine (MW) in 1992.

In the meantime, I'd met Simon through a university friend (I'd always known the Russian would be useful one day). Simon taught me everything I know about housekeeping; while I knitted and cooked and used the garage to force bulbs in pots, he was the domesticated partner. He was, and still is, handy with a vacuum cleaner and adept with an iron, while I see them as instruments of torture, and this excellent balance of interests meant I was free to concentrate on the finer pleasures of domesticity. Reader, of course I married him.

Not long after I became Mrs. Brocket, I renounced office life completely to work from home as a freelance wine consultant. It was only then that I realized what a homebody I truly was: I grew tomatoes on the windowsill in front of my desk, baked in the afternoons, and tasted wine for my exams in the evenings. Even though my status and income were drastically reduced, I loved this way of life and was far happier and more fulfilled.

Life got even better when our first attempt at IVF was successful and we were utterly delighted to find I was expecting boy/girl twins just as we were moving to Germany with Simon's work.

Giving up and in

Full-blown domesticity was now finally forced upon me and I admit I gave in willingly. Instead of fighting the glaringly anachronistic corporate-wife lifestyle, I realized I didn't have to kowtow to that particular set of expectations. Instead, I saw that enforced domesticity could be tremendously liberating and would allow me to do all the things I had loved for so long and yet had felt guilty about practicing. Knitting, baking, buying flowers and bread, exploring a different domestic culture, reading the Victorian novelist Elizabeth Gaskell—all this suddenly became worthwhile, and a way of being *me* in the face of impending motherhood and, that dreadful label, a trailing spouse.

After three years in Germany, Simon, Tom, Alice and I moved to Belgium, and Phoebe, our surprise bonus baby, was born. Now I had the family I'd longed for, a supportive network of women friends in similar situations, the space to make red-currant jam and grow vegetables, and the time to enjoy the children. I even managed to exploit my MW qualification by running wine courses for expats and wine tastings for groups in the evenings. I was often tired, but happily tired.

We returned to England in 1998. For several years I carried on the wine work while the children were at school but, eventually, it became more and more difficult to fit it in with their schedules and, anyway, I realized I wanted a new challenge. The obvious solution was something academic so, in my early forties, I went back to university, to Royal Holloway College (University of London) to study for an MA in Victorian Art and Literature. I was so motivated by academia that I even began a PhD. This time, however, the conflict between the intellectual and the creative life was too great, and after one year I decided to shelve my thesis.

It hasn't always been easy to see my brilliant career go bung on several occasions.* But I have been incredibly fortunate, and have managed to combine my work with wine, an MA, knitting, baking, textiles, literature and art with family life. As a result of all this practical experience, I am convinced that variety and choice are the keys to understanding the values and pleasures of the gentle domestic arts.

The gentleness of the gentle arts

For the gentle arts are just that: gentle. They do not demand to be practiced. No one is obliged to pursue them. They have not been taken up by any government department and regulated and repackaged with health and safety messages and warnings. They are a matter of individual and personal choice. They can be enjoyed by anyone with an interest and the ability to thread a needle, break an egg, choose a color or wield a pair of scissors. They don't require complicated skills, qualifications, training or equipment. They don't

take up much space, create dirt and mess (although you may find yourself leaving the house covered in little threads or fibers) or impinge on others' lives.

What they do require, though, is a conscious choice to do something "old-fashioned" and "quaint," to choose not to buy and consume endlessly, but to make and create for a change.

The gentle arts are not an all-or-nothing decision, though. Fortunately, there are no legal guidelines about how much is good for you. So you can consider yourself a practitioner whether you decide to bake a cake or knit a sock once in a while, or live a life packed with quilting and stitching. It's the awareness of the worth of the gentle arts that counts, the ability to see that the feminists of the 1970s were misguided when they thought that teaching young girls to devalue domesticity constituted progress.

Just as it's possible to combine the gentle arts with all sorts of lifestyles—full-time work, part-time work, unpaid work—so it's also possible to combine a range of skills. Many how-to craft books categorize readers as knitters or quilters or embroiderers, without considering the possibility that they may be all of these, and more. Anyone who likes knitting may enjoy crochet, those who work with a needle may love hand-quilting or hand-embroidering, a machine-embroiderer may want to bake cakes as a subject for a textile piece. And so the connections go on to create a world of colorful, tactile possibilities that are limited only by your reluctance to try something new.

And that is the second important message of this book. If it inspires anyone to take a shot at making something, to discover or rediscover the delights of domesticity, to try something new, then it will fulfill its purpose. As a domestic artist with absolutely no artistic background or training, I can say with complete confidence that there are no right or wrong ways when it comes to the gentle arts, and that the only way you will learn is to give them a try.

The art of the possible

If you do feel encouraged to make or bake or grow something, the wonderful thing about the gentle domestic arts is that they are totally manageable and achievable.

There is constant pressure in today's society to have the perfect house/body/children/relationship, and we can only fail because the standards set in the

---

* As in *My Brilliant Career* and *My Career Goes Bung* by Miles Franklin (Virago).

media are so ridiculously unrealistic. But the joy of knitting or stitching or baking or homemaking lies in the fact that there are no rules, there are no levels of perfection that we need to attain. The whole point about the gentle arts is that they are noncompetitive, soothing and utterly pleasurable. Anyone who tells you otherwise should be tied up with acrylic yarn and deprived of her knitting needles for a long time.

The gentle art of domesticity is also the art of the possible. We no longer *need* to knit socks, exhaust ourselves on "baking day," stitch quilts to keep ourselves warm or sew aprons to wear in the kitchen, and we are no longer judged on the quality of our hemming, pastry or heel-turning. The gentle arts have moved into a new realm in contemporary life, a realm we can choose to enter should we wish, and one in which the act of doing is as important as the result. Ignore all calls for perfection and focus instead on what you can achieve, and the pleasures of the gentle arts will be yours for the taking.

yarnstorm

It still isn't easy to come out as a practitioner of the gentle arts. I know, because I tried, and failed, for many years. I was embarrassed about the knitting and my obsessions with beads, sequins and general textile gorgeousness. I could get away with baking as there are always willing consumers for the results, but knitting, what on earth would a Master of Wine/Master of Arts want with knitting? So I knitted and quilted and stitched in isolation. I still have numbers of unframed machine embroideries that I felt weren't worth displaying and yet I continued to make them.

This muddled approach—great private pride in my ability to knit and sew and bake, plus a personal recognition of their value, combined with a public silence about my cherished activities—finally came to an end when I discovered the world of knitting and craft

blogs. I was immediately drawn into this mostly female community of domestic artists who shared their creations and wrote articulately about the values and processes. Here, at last, was the opportunity to unite my creative and intellectual interests, and I joined the blogworld with yarnstorm in February 2005.

Initially I wrote about knitting only, but it didn't take long for the content to reflect all my eclectic interests. I started photographing my domestic world and writing not just about what I had made, but why I made it, examining the thoughts that accompany creativity and the act of making.

yarnstorm has allowed me to explore not only the hows but, just as importantly, the whys of the gentle arts. If we no longer *have* to knit socks, make quilts, bake bread, why would we want to do so? What do we lose if we no longer value these skills and arts? What is their true significance beyond the usefulness and visual pleasure of the end product?

In keeping with the gentleness of the gentle arts, I would hate to think that anyone reading the following pages felt obliged or bossed into taking up needles or spatulas, or that I considered this to be the only desirable outcome of the book. Many readers of yarnstorm tell me that, even though they don't knit or sew, make or bake, they enjoy the colors, the pictures and the text, and that this peek into a world of domesticity brightens their days and gently alters their perspectives. I would be delighted, therefore, if the act of considering the subject of contemporary creativity simply gives you greater confidence in your individual style, suggests new ways of looking at traditional skills and encourages you to be proud of, and see the worth in, your own domestic space.

Read on, domestic artist, read on.

Inspiration

A habit of seeing

I used to assume inspiration was the province of artists and poets, architects and designers, scientists and inventors. Inspiration could surely visit only those with a higher purpose in life, with a greater sensitivity than the rest of us, with a more refined awareness than the average mortal.

I was wrong. Inspiration is inspiration, whether the end result is a painted masterpiece, a soul-searching sonnet, a richly colored homemade quilt or a batch of freshly baked scones. We shouldn't diminish our creativity by despising the results of our inspiration, but instead celebrate and exploit the wonderful feeling of elevated energy and enthusiasm we experience when we feel inspired. That quickening of the senses and the heightening of the imagination are, I'm sure, just the same for the Matisses and Wrens and Brownings as they are for the rest of us. It's just that they can do different things with their inspired talents.

Inspiration is the opposite of expiration, a drawing in, as opposed to a letting out. We can walk through life without seeing, without taking in the details, the words, the colors, the pictures, and miss the whole point of inspiration. Or, we can adopt an approach that allows us to stop a while and look and listen and reflect and enjoy. We can learn to sift through the mass of stimuli we encounter every day and to focus on what inspires us as individuals and, in doing so, create a way of seeing, a way of being receptive to inspiration.

For the one thing that sets creative people apart is that they have all acquired the habit of being receptive to inspiration, actively seeking it or even simply recognizing it. Some may have to travel to the ends of the earth to find inspiration, others may find it hiding in libraries, at the tops of mountains, buried under the earth. But the domestic artist is in the glorious position of being able to find inspiration in daily, domestic life.

Writing yarnstorm has made me focus each day on something positive so that I have a subject for my posts. When I started photographing the details of my domestic life, I was quite sure I would run out of material in a matter of weeks. But, instead of exhausting all possibilities, I actually found myself unearthing more and more sources of inspiration, all within the confines of a quite ordinary, domestic life.

The more I realized I was surrounded by inspiration, the more I felt I could do with it. Some days are more passive and ruminative, and I may feel inspired by something as simple as noticing a new flower in the garden or reading a short story, but on other days I am inspired to think up a whole quilt design, take up crochet or imagine a pineapple tea cozy.

Even if I had all the free time in the world, I would not feel compelled to create endlessly. Making things would then become mechanical and mindless, and there would be no room to contemplate inspiration and to work out how to incorporate it into my life as a unique form of self-expression. For the more willing you are to let yourself be inspired, the more you can store away in your creative resources. This way, you can call on them when you do have the time and inclination to turn the personal stash of colors, details, patterns, textures into something tangible. And it will be all the richer in meaning as a result of this habitual and highly individual accumulation.

Framing domesticity

Domesticity is, in truth, an abstract concept. We think we know what we understand by the word, but it turns out there are all sorts of interpretations. As many interpretations as there are domestic artists, I'd guess. And this makes it a pretty difficult concept to pin down.

I think this is why paintings of domestic scenes and details never cease to fascinate me; they bring together one person's vision or concept of a particular aspect of domesticity within a single frame. A frame puts a border and a boundary on something that otherwise remains difficult to quantify.

Domestic paintings have always been underrated, but I am drawn to their charm, their ordinariness, their variety. I find that many artists who may be better known for their grand paintings often display a greater warmth, sincerity and humanity in the paintings of domestic scenes. No matter where I am, whether visiting the imposing national galleries of London, Paris or New York, or in some small, modest, provincial gallery, it is the domestic paintings that draw me. In fact, some of the very finest and most unexpected treasures are to be found in lesser known galleries that have never been able to afford the "masterpieces."

This type of painting inspires me because it tells me that domesticity can be what we want it to be. It tells me how other people frame their domesticity, how they organize their domestic spaces, what they do there and how they live. I like the way all sorts of things that would be excluded from "serious" paintings can be included in domestic works. Kettles, pans, washing lines, teapots, cushions, rugs, taps, colanders, comfy chairs, kitchen stools, calendars, pincushions, work baskets are there, together with the rest of the clutter and jumble of everyday life. When the people who live in these places are added to this realism, a wonderful narrative opens up before your eyes.

I am particularly fond of older domestic paintings. It's almost as if we have to wait until an era has ended and is framed in a context before we can see the significance of the paintings of everyday life. They acquire more resonance when we know the end of the story. That's why I enjoy Victorian and Edwardian domestic paintings and those up to the 1950s; after that, the contemporary story, my story, starts and hasn't yet ended. I suppose you could say that domestic art is a little like a visual obituary for ordinary people.

A Life Well Spent
James West Cope (1878)

This (pictured opposite) is a favorite painting. I don't care that it's not great feminist thinking and that many women would be appalled by this portrayal of the mid-Victorian feminine ideal, because I believe that for some women this has been and still is, indeed, a life well spent.

It's ironic that I first came across it when I was studying for my MA in Victorian Art and Literature. I'd needed to get out of the house and face a new intellectual challenge, something that would fit in with the children's schools and holidays, and it was clear that the best option was something academic. So I studied Dickens, Elizabeth Gaskell and the Pre-Raphaelites while the children did their times tables, spelling and gym class, and I could still be there to take them to, and pick them up from, school.

In time the MA turned into a PhD and the essays into a thesis. And then, when I realized that a PhD demanded a whole life, I was faced with a major decision. On the one hand, I had Dickens and fairy tales, libraries and conferences, critics and theories, individual fulfilment. On the other, I had domesticity and creativity, baking and making, kitchens and sewing machines and family fulfillment. In the end, I decided to give up my studies and enjoy domesticity in all its glory and chaos.

I wrote about A Life Well Spent for an MA essay, bringing out all the usual theories and arguments about this type of Victorian painting. And yet, despite this cleverness, my true response was to see that this mother was doing something incredibly valuable *and* enjoyable. Although the painting is loaded with symbols and evidence of Victorian thinking, I see past those to a pivotal maternal figure, a relaxed but attentive son, a daughter who is already multitasking and just a little touch of happy disorder with books and yarn left on the carpet. And I reckon that any mother who knits red-and-white-striped socks while listening to her son's catechism must have hidden depths.

Summer in Cumberland
James Durden (1925)

When I was a teenager, I spent hours in the Manchester City Art Gallery gazing at its wonderful collection of Pre-Raphaelite paintings, wishing I, too, could be a languid (or "bored" as Simon says) Rossetti beauty. I still go back whenever I can, revisit the bored ladies and examine the altogether more energetic *Work* by Ford Madox Brown. I also go to look at one particular domestic painting that shines out—almost literally.

Summer in Cumberland (pictured opposite, top) is a domestic idyll. It glows with golden light and gilded youth. It's the kind of domesticity I would be happy to experience, but could not necessarily maintain. I am charmed by the gentility of it, the son in his cricket or tennis whites, the daughter in her pale linen dress, the mother with lilac-grey hair that matches the cushion and delphiniums. I am entranced by the informality that is nevertheless elegant—the delicate china, the silver tea service, the closeness of the family and the inclusion of the cat. I covet this tall-ceilinged, paneled room in yellow, and would not settle for anything less than these beautiful chintz, velvet and linen upholstery fabrics. It's all so beautiful that even the Lake District obligingly matches the color scheme.

This painting conjures up the domestic novels of Angela Thirkell with their tennis parties, rectories and lovely mothers, but without the irony. It captures a moment of Englishness through a domestic scene, with the boy on the outside of the house and the women within, order restored after a world war, but the coziness of domesticity still threatened by distant forces. It reminds me that I should value the apparently casual domestic moments because you never know what's coming next.

A Knitting Party
Evelyn Dunbar (1940)

If you look carefully, it is possible to find plenty of knitting paintings, but the majority are painted by men keen to stress the picturesque and pastoral. As a result, there are many paintings of women knitting socks up mountains, by harbors, outside cottages and hovels, in doorways, on balconies, and in fields. Some male artists obviously think of knitting as a hearty, outdoor pursuit.

So when I find a scene of women knitting painted by a woman artist, I am delighted. I was a lone knitter for years, until I discovered the knitting group at Foyles (see Sharing, page 214), and hadn't experienced the pleasures of knitting with others. This is why I feel an immediate connection with any realistic painting of knitters; these people negate my isolation and make me part of a much greater and wider domestic art.

Evelyn Dunbar was an illustrator and muralist who worked with delightfully domestic subjects, and was appointed an official war artist in 1940. Instead of painting heroes and heroic exploits, though, she recorded women's domestic war efforts. So her documentary, factually correct paintings are of *Women's Land Army Dairy Training*; *Milking Practice with Artificial Udders*; *A Canning Demonstration* and *Potato Sorting, Berwick*. But of all her war paintings, my favorite is *A Knitting Party* (pictured opposite, below).

These women are contributing to the war effort by knitting with drab colors (khaki, airforce blue, English cloud grey), and the picture exudes calmness and a sense of purpose. I am intrigued by the way the knitters all space themselves out, with their eyes lowered and their backs upright, so that they can keep their thoughts private. While the men fight, the women will not slacken, and socks and sweaters *will* be knitted. There is an unspoken sense of camaraderie and feminine solidarity. Beneath that English reserve and those intransigent hats lie sympathy and fellow feeling. And, crucially, Evelyn Dunbar has caught the details of knitting perfectly; the various ways needles are held, the different looks of concentration and even, at the back, the way one woman is winding a skein of yarn from her knees.

Looking at *A Knitting Party*, I am inspired to value knitting not just as a craft, but as a shared activity. It makes me realize just how lucky we are to have lattes and raspberry and white chocolate muffins to accompany our own gossipy, laughter-filled knitting parties.

Vicarious Kitchen pleasures

Some days my creative output is zero; life is more a matter of holding everything together until relief arrives in the form of Simon/a glass of wine/a child taken out of the equation/bedtime. On days like these, I have to live out my need to create through my children. Instead of swimming against a very strong current, I find it easier to go with the flow and let them do the making. What I never expected though, was to discover that they would be such a rich and entertaining source of inspiration to me. Especially in the kitchen.

Tom, Alice and Phoebe all love baking and decorating, just as I did when I was a child, but they take the media of cookies, cakes and icing to new levels of incandescence and extravagance. They acknowledge no boundaries when it comes to baking, and their ingenuity and invention with the sculptural qualities of baked goods and the painterly qualities of icing are untrammelled and uninhibited. Many would see this as an inherently childish approach, but Tom, Alice and Phoebe have inspired me to see that adults could have a lot more fun if, every so often, they forgot about good taste and sophistication.

In the early days of our joint kitchen adventures, my role was to set up—tie on aprons, deal with the oven, put out bowls of icing, candy, iced flowers and silver balls—and then retire as they did the decorating. But now they can do everything themselves, and with fantastic results.

When they were little, the children suggested that I convert our wide kitchen window into a shop front through which I could sell my baked goods under the banner of "Jane Brocket Stores." These days, I can feel my own retirement looming as the next generation is poised to take over and soon the sign will read "Jane Brocket & Son & Daughters."

Bizarre baking

The initial idea for the cupcakes pictured below came from one of Donna Hay's food magazines for children. It featured cakes with a nautical theme, and this appealed to Alice, who has a fascination with the gruesome and gory, and with sharks in particular.

It wasn't long before a gentle marine tale turned into a blood-and-guts horror story. She made little shark attack scenes on each cake with blue buttercream frosting for the sea, red for blood, partially eaten Jelly Babies (little gummy figures) for victims and jagged pieces of chocolate for sharks' fins. The top cake is a lovely piece of iced drama—note the happy, unsuspecting pair out for a jaunt in a boat with an octopus bobbing nearby. Not for long.

For a whole afternoon, the kitchen work surface was a vast ocean of sugar and sweets. That is, until Alice and her siblings could contain their own hunger no longer, and ate the sharks themselves.

Gingerbread architecture

I have always associated gingerbread houses with Hansel and Gretel and forests, but it seems we have moved into an urban gingerbread fantasy where we live. Last Christmas, Phoebe attended a gingerbread house workshop and came away with the wonderful piece of architecture pictured opposite, which was entirely her own work. Every detail was carefully thought out in the manner of great architects such as Voysey or Lutyens whose work this obviously so closely resembles, especially in the pitched roof, traditional materials, landscaped surroundings, the chocolate bar fence. . . .

Phoebe's house was flavored with cinnamon, and this prompted Tom and Alice, who love everything flavored with ginger, to consider building their own alternative edible residences. At one point, when their imaginations were whirring wildly, I thought we would end up with a Coronation Street terrace or a whole Gotham City, or even a parallel universe made out of cake. I could almost smell the surfeit of gingerbread before we'd even sifted the ground ginger.

Surfeit

When I first met Simon, something that always made us laugh was the fact that King Henry I is reputed to have died from a "surfeit of lampreys," a kind of eel once considered a delicacy. This phrase was one of our early in-jokes, so he knew how I felt at the end of the day we made the houses, when I claimed I was in danger of succumbing to a "surfeit of gingerbread."

It turns out that gingerbread houses are one of those little secrets no one ever tells you about until it's too late, like the pain of childbirth or the whole dinner-party thing. My goodness, they take some making. I spent an entire day mixing gingerbread, chilling it, baking it, cooling it in the tray and repeating the process until we had sufficient ends, sides, roofs and chimneys for three houses. The kitchen may have smelled great, but I didn't feel fragrant.

After the construction of the materials, you then have the ordeal that is the assembly of your structure. This is the cue for industrial quantities of royal icing, all sorts of improvised scaffolding and supports, emergency measures, dark mutterings and not a little swearing. The upshot was an ever-diminishing level of success, from the first completed edifice, which was Alice's Three Little Pigs cottage, to Phoebe's roofless Gothic structure (which, until she added a bungalow roof, looked like the bombed-out church at the end of *Mrs. Miniver*), to the last—Tom's hovel/bus shelter, which only ever had two ends and was a work in progress until the bulldozers moved in.

This was quite enough gingerbread architecture for a whole year, or maybe even a lifetime. After all, I don't want to end up like King Henry.

My goodness, they take some making. I spent an entire day mixing gingerbread, chilling it, baking it, cooling it in the tray and repeating the process until we had sufficient ends, sides, roofs and chimneys for three houses.

The domestic library

In my more lightly morbid moments, I stop to wonder which of my five senses I would least like to lose. And the answer is always sight: I would hate to be like Milton's Samson Agonistes and condemned never to read a book on my own again. The reading habit has been ingrained in me since I was very young. I was the only child in my primary school class of forty who stopped off at the library on the way home, and I am still grateful to my best friend, Janet, who waited for me patiently outside instead of skipping off to the penny tray at the candy shop.

In my time, I have worked my way through the great French, Russian and English classics, given a cursory glance to modern literature, avoided beach books, sci-fi, fantasy and thrillers, and have always come back to the domestic novel. Domestic literature is both gentle and gently rewarding. It gives a story to so many untold lives, and a meaning and significance to generations of women who were expected to live quietly domestic lives, but who were often far from dull and domesticated. Domestic novels reveal the textures of women's lives and the infinite possibilities and permutations of the domestic space. They also give contemporary women the chance to reflect that we are fortunate in not being compelled to live in that way unless we choose to do so, which makes domesticity a potentially enriching way of life, not a reductive one.

As I get older, I find I am happier to reread rather than spend (waste?) time with unknown and possibly disappointing books. I savor remembered details, greet favorite scenes or sections with pleasure, wonder why I turned up the corner (my bad habit for marking special pages) or recall the reasons why a pencil line or exclamation mark was left. There is coziness, friendliness and reassurance in rereading beloved books and poems, the repetition of which is a welcome counterpoint to the sometimes more fraught and unpredictable nature of real life.

These are some of the books I choose to read when in need of inspiration, encouragement and laughter.

Mrs. Miniver
Jan Struther (1939)

These days the film is much better known than the book, which is a great shame. Greer Garson is far too sophisticated as Mrs. Miniver, the sets are horribly false and the propaganda element mars this very English vision of loving, happy, brightly cheerful domesticity. I prefer the printed *Mrs. Miniver* for its period domestic detail, the heroine's enjoyment of her "forties" (more than her "thirties"), her thoughts as she watches her children grow up, her appreciation of small, ordinary things. The book also contains the most wonderful, evocative description of chrysanthemums I know: "the big, mop-headed kind, burgundy coloured, with curled petals." Every autumn I look for Mrs. Miniver chrysanthemums, but none can ever match hers.

Domestic novels reveal the textures of women's lives and the infinite possibilities and permutations of the domestic space. They also give contemporary women the chance to reflect that we are fortunate in not being compelled to live in that way unless we choose to do so, which makes domesticity a potentially enriching way of life, not a reductive one.

They Knew Mr. Knight
Dorothy Whipple (1934)

Anything by Dorothy Whipple is worth reading. Once a publishing phenomenon, now largely forgotten, she writes the most compellingly readable books I have encountered since my childhood, when I often consumed a book in a day. She writes with an astounding fluency, and her novels are richly detailed, wonderfully observed, funny, warm and clever. Her imagery is subtle, her understanding of human nature is amazing, and her ability to move around her characters and see them from all angles is quite brilliant. She doesn't moralize, but is deeply ethical. *They Knew Mr. Knight* is a cautionary tale, but one with plenty of knitting, crocuses, ginger puddings and permanent waves.

Jane Eyre
Charlotte Brontë (1847)

Quite simply one of the best romantic fantasies ever. Little Charlotte Brontë, cooped up with her sisters and needlework in a windswept Yorkshire parsonage, escapes by means of an unparalleled imaginative effort to become little Jane Eyre who falls in love with, fights with, and ultimately manipulates, subdues and controls a madly passionate, frighteningly fierce Mr. Rochester. Miss Temple offers seed-cake, Mrs. Fairfax knits quietly in the "beau-ideal of domestic comfort," Grace Poole sews with waxed thread while all those around them burn and rage, until Jane finally finds "the best things the world has . . . domestic endearments and household joys." But not before she has negotiated the terms of endearment herself.

Family Roundabout
Richmal Crompton (1948)

Richmal Crompton is best known for her hilarious William books, which are worth reading for a jawbreaker-sucking boy's-eye view of middle-class English life in the 1920s and 1930s. But she also wrote a huge number of novels for adults, most of which have sunk without trace. Thankfully, *Family Roundabout* has been rescued and republished, for this gentle, perceptive, often sad, domestic saga about two families still has the power to touch contemporary readers. It's a very female book and is dominated by two matriarchs with contrasting styles—one relaxed, one controlling—and their influence on their extended families. It's full of womanly, homely detail such as sock knitting, basket mending, name-tapes, tapestry, iced cakes, party dresses and grandchildren. It's the domestic novel par excellence.

Cranford
Elizabeth Gaskell (1853)

A slight book—at first glance no more than a collection of short pieces about twittering ladies—but one which should be read by every domestic artist. Mrs. Gaskell writes with wit, intelligence and a light touch of acidity about a community of ladies in a small town and their domestic concerns. She may expose their vanities, anxieties and fears to make the reader laugh, but she does so with a great underlying fondness and sympathy. Goodness will, and does, prevail, and in the meantime we are given all the details of the ladies' frugal but creative housekeeping and outmoded dress, friendships based on "Shetland wool . . . and new knitting stitches,"

crochet commissions, potpourri and clove-stuck apples, sea green, silver-grey and maize silks, and the relative merits of plain-work, wool-work and fancywork. Fantastic.

The Diary of a Provincial Lady
E. M. Delafield (1930)

The Provincial Lady is the Bridget Jones of domesticity, complete with queries and memos to herself and a great line in self-deprecation. Her diary is laugh-out-loud funny and all the better for being based on domestic concerns such as indoor hyacinths, chemists' bills, blocked pantry sinks, her son's handkerchiefs and her husband's breakfasts. It wouldn't do for her to complain, so she contrasts her outward behavior with her inner thoughts, which creates wonderful comedy as she commits to her diary the "tart and witty rejoinders" she struggled to find earlier. Any smugness or self-satisfaction is undercut by humor; domesticity is rarely portrayed in such a richly entertaining style.

The Home-Maker
Dorothy Canfield Fisher (1924)

The story of what happens when a wife and mother puts all her efforts into the house, and not the home. Fortunately, irreparable damage is averted when Lester, the father, takes over the role of homemaker. My copy of this incredible book has more folded page corners than any other, so memorable are the observations and details. It reaffirms all the good things about having children and considers what makes a nurturing, supportive, creative, empathetic parent. Poetry, baking, cookbooks, literature, housework, egg beating and sock darning are all valued by this male homemaker, who can see the opportunities that domesticity offers to the thoughtful mind.

At Mrs. Lippincote's
Elizabeth Taylor (1945)

I haven't read an entire novelist's output, one title after the other, since I read Thomas Hardy under the desk in biology class when I was fifteen. But last year I read the thirteen novels of Elizabeth Taylor, and it was the most wonderful reading experience I've had since the days of Tess and Jude and Angel Clare. Elizabeth Taylor is an elegant, witty, perspicacious, humanistic and gently subversive writer. Her novels are of the English domestic variety rendered with a truly painterly vision and not a little bite. If I had to pick one book, it would be At Mrs. Lippincote's, with its Brontë motifs, beautifully sketched mother-and-son relationship, strangely disturbing house and Julia's excellent nonconformity. And I have a very soft spot for the wing commander who leans against the mantelpiece in the mess doing his wife's knitting, watched by the admiring wives of senior officers, who exclaim playfully, "Now, Harry, don't drop your stitches!" and later gasp when he turns the heel of a sock.

Pineapple passion

One of the best presents I ever received was a pineapple in a paper bag. It was given to me at a time when a pineapple was way beyond my student means. I was incredibly touched and thrilled when I pulled the fruit out of the bag and realized the act of generosity it constituted. I still think of this exotic, juicy, golden fruit, with its connotations of wealth and luxury, as the epitome of romance.

I was reminded of this personal pineapple passion when Alice discovered a whole, candied pineapple—leaves and all—in a very chic grocery (pictured below right). I had to buy it for her as my own act of pineapple generosity and, besides, it was quite bewitching to behold and far longer lasting than a fresh one.

Pineapple inspiration

It is amazing what a single fruit can inspire. The pineapple has wonderful sculptural qualities, brilliant colors, an amazing texture and a bold surface pattern. Put together, these details produce an inspirational natural object that can be turned into all sorts of forms. It was a symbol of domestic wealth in eighteenth- and nineteenth-century England, and is a traditional symbol of hospitality in the United States, which means it can be found on all sorts of domestic items,

such as wooden gateposts and bedposts, silverware, teapots, coffeepots and brass and ceramic jelly molds.

But it is the homely, useful, textile interpretations of the pineapple that I love. I lust after collectible pineapple quilts (a version of the log cabin design), in which the lines and fabrics cleverly form a spiky pineapple motif, but I am not quite up to making one myself. And I am fascinated by the whole branch of the gentle arts devoted to pineapple crochet with fabulously intricate, lacy repeats of fruits, not to mention scores of knitting patterns for pineapple blankets and hats.

And then there is the knitted pineapple tea cozy. I cannot afford an exquisite eighteenth-century Staffordshire creamware pineapple teapot, and I certainly don't have an exceptionally rich and generous wooer to give one to me in a paper bag, but I can have the tea cozy. As I pondered my pineapple passion, my thoughts turned to a bright, kitsch, beaded version with a burlesque topping of pointy leaves—the kind of thing that Carmen Miranda might favor. I would be able to pour tea from a lusciously clad teapot to accompany a retro Pineapple Upside-Down Cake, complete with garish red cherries. Now, wouldn't that be something to look forward to on a wet Sunday afternoon?

If you brought me diamonds,
If you brought me pearls,
If you brought me roses
Like some other gents
Might bring for other girls,
It couldn't please me more
Than the gift I see;
A pineapple for me.

("It Couldn't Please Me More" from the musical *Cabaret*)

Pineapple pinnacle

One of my favorite phrases in literature contains a pineapple. It comes in Dickens's *Martin Chuzzlewit,* when a character first beholds a fine, plump, buxom bar-lady. He exclaims that she is "the very pink and pineapple." It's a malapropism, of course, and he doesn't mean "pineapple" but "pinnacle" (and "pink" as in the "pink of perfection"). Or maybe he does, for this woman is certainly good enough to eat.

Well, the tea cozy pictured opposite is the pink and pinnacle of my pineapple passion. I thought long and hard about how best to approach knitting it. I wasn't quite ready to replicate the pineapple's Fibonacci sequence in stitches, but did consider blackberry stitch, entrelac, bobbles and braids before deciding to keep it very simple but still in the Carmen Miranda style. I also bore in mind that a tea cozy's function is to insulate the teapot, and that's why they are usually multilayered. So, in the end, I went for four ruffles and knitted what could be mistaken for a prototype skirt for Carmen.

I don't design a great deal, so I made this up as I went along, just noting down a few key numbers. The spikes were made up with double thickness yarn to prevent them flopping, because nothing could be sadder than a floppy pineapple. I even bought a real one to check the way the leaves emerged from the base and see how to put them together. I finished it off with some juicy beads with tiny sparkles to suggest the surface scales of the fruit.

What I really like about knitting fruity tea cozies is the marriage of form and function. Thankfully, there are no rules about what that form should be. As a result, the world is my fruit basket.

The last piece in the pineapple jigsaw

I suppose it was inevitable. Having been inspired by the pineapple thus far, I knew I was bound to make a Pineapple Upside-Down Cake.

Not long after the cozy was completed, I was browsing through de Cuisine, Simon's favorite website for baking surprises (see Resources, page 277), and was overcome with excitement when I came across a pineapple cake pan (pictured opposite, top right). I love many things about this ridiculously endearing pan. I love the way the bottom of each section is exactly the right size for a slice of canned pineapple (let's not have any hit-or-miss, hand-sliced circles of fresh pineapple that need trimming to fit when we can simply open a can and slot the slice in snugly). I love the beautiful pineapple details, the spiky leaves and the way it even has dedicated cherry spaces.

I read a recipe recently for a Pineapple Upside-Down Cake in which the writer said that in old recipes there was "never enough sticky fruit, too much sponge and as for those cherries. . . ." Well, call me tasteless and tacky, but I think "those cherries" are essential to this retro, canned-pineapple creation. And they fit perfectly in their own little concave seats in this brilliant tray; whoever designed it was clearly a Pineapple Upside-Down Cake connoisseur.

I couldn't find a recipe I liked, so made a very simple version of the ones I saw on the Internet. I put a little butter and soft, brown sugar at the bottom of each mold and placed the pineapple ring and cherry on top so they would caramelize. Then I made a simple cake with 1 cup each butter and soft brown sugar, 4 large eggs, ¾ cup self-rising flour, ¼ cup ground almonds and a teaspoon of baking powder.

I was amazed by the way the cakes turned out with all the surface details intact—even the pineapple crisscrosses on the outside. I didn't make a glazing syrup with sugar and pineapple juice from the can because *someone* could not wait to start eating, but I shall next time.

And opposite, bottom left, is a group photo; a testament to pineapple inspiration.

Playtime

Everyone needs time to play, and I have been inspired to do so by my children. Thanks to them, I made the happy discovery that informal play for adults is as vital a source of inspiration as any amount of formal training and process. Plus it's a lot more fun and games, to boot.

As a child I grew up very quickly and, by the time I had Tom and Alice, I was terribly out of practice when it came to play. So I started at the very beginning (if I sound like Julie Andrews in *The Sound of Music* that's fine, because she demonstrated to the whole von Trapp family the value of play, as opposed to rigid discipline) and watched how my children learned to play. It was one of the great, unexpected bonuses of being a mother; I had no inkling how much their mode of discovering the world would affect my adulthood.

We read books, played with dough and crayons, Playmobil and Lego, mud and water, but I also learned to play in a more creative, abstract way by watching these three observe life with what the Zen Buddhists call beginner's eyes. Instead of approaching creativity with a set of known guidelines, I understood from the children that it was possible to be less structured and "correct," and that this give-it-a-try attitude is often far more pleasurable, productive and satisfying than a more rule-based one.

Ludic interlude

It was during an afternoon of intense writing that I found the word "ludic" lurking at the back of my mind, as if suggesting that was what I needed to be for a while—spontaneously and aimlessly playful. Ludic is a good word and I like the idea that it is rooted in a sensible Latin word, *ludus,* which makes being ludic part of some great, classical tradition and, therefore, eminently worthy. That's my playful philosophy for you.

So I took time away from the computer and had a little playtime with a pile of fabrics, as I wanted to see how I could group them to make the best possible combination for a quilt. Like a child at play, I got down on the floor with my fabrics and then I spread them out, lined them up, made favorite groups, introduced them to each other and generally let them take on a personality, just as children do in their imaginative, role-playing games. I'd baked cupcakes that morning and found there was even more playful amusement to be had from matching cupcakes, china and fabric. In fact, I began to wonder why I don't do this sort of thing every day.

My ludic interlude had many benefits—I felt visually refreshed and revitalized, I went back to writing with a spring in my step, I reaffirmed my love of pinks, yellows and turquoises, and I was newly convinced that I no longer need fear blue textiles. In the space of thirty minutes' play, I'd put together a pleasing fabric combination, found a suitable quilt design (they will make a snowball quilt) and set my imagination bouncing once more.

Setting out

I don't know if there is a "setting-out" gene but, if there is, it's dominant in our family. I did a great deal of setting out when I was a child, lining up my toys, books, pens, papers, pasta shapes, buttons, chocolates, dolls and setting them out in neat, orderly patterns. They could be grouped by color, size, shape, value or whatever category I chose that day.

Then I became a student and chaos reigned for several years. University is a time for deconstruction, I know, but I went the whole hog and deconstructed myself, too. I rebuilt myself with gentle knitting and new patterns of life, until I met Simon and everything fell back into place.

It wasn't until many years later, when I was at a machine-embroidery weekend taught by the lovely Linda Miller, that I realized I had subconsciously rediscovered the pleasures of setting out. I was stitching a piece with rows of vegetables and Linda, who had seen other embroideries I had made, commented en passant that I appeared to be very fond of neat rows and lines of objects—teacups, cakes, meringues, doughnuts, leeks, carrots, cauliflowers, apples, pears and raspberries.

This simple observation made me think deeply about my creative tendencies, and it was as if I was seeing my own thought processes and design impulses for the first time. Linda's perceptiveness opened up a new awareness of my personal creativity; much as I always liked the idea of being freestyle, spontaneous and organic in my gentle arts, I had to face the fact that I am really an amateur who likes lines, rows and the arrangements to be found in greengrocers, garden plots, candy shops and haberdasheries. But, crucially, Linda helped me understand that this was totally fine—as long as it was fine with me.

The pleasure of setting out has also been reignited by the children, who have spent many hours with small toys, creating fabulous effects with doll handbags and shoes, Playmobil people and groceries. I have often stumbled upon some small and exquisitely formed design in the middle of a room and been enchanted by the work and thought that has gone into its making.

Now, I apply my DNA-dictated tendencies to allotment quilts (see pages 43 and 287), Jelly Bean Cushions (see Color, pages 56–9), crisscross patterns of traditional Easter hot cross buns and cake embroideries, and I am happy. Free-form is fantastic, but not when one's setting-out gene must be appeased.

Play on words

The children have also inspired me with their wordplay. I studied languages for years and had rules and grammar drummed into me, so I could never have imagined inventing words. But Tom, Alice and Phoebe take an epicurean delight in words; they savor and relish sounds and syllables, rolling them around their mouths until they begin to take on new meanings. In fact, Alice plays with language to such a degree that she now claims to speak "Diverted English," which is, quite simply, a masterly description of what she does to words; she diverts them from their original pronunciation and spelling and leads them down an imaginative brain path until they emerge fresh and new. She has invented the verb "to spatulate" as the technical term for wielding a spatula, and my favorite word in Diverted English is a noun that Alice coined when we were baking together. Something needed a pinch or a smattering of an ingredient, and so the word "itchling" came into being, as in "an itchling of vanilla extract" or "an itchling of pepper." This wonderfully expressive word deserves to be in *The Oxford English Dictionary.*

The children's wordplay always reminds me how willingly we, as adults, accept rules and constraints, and that creativity is simply a matter of rerouting our normal thought processes. That, and an itchling of play.

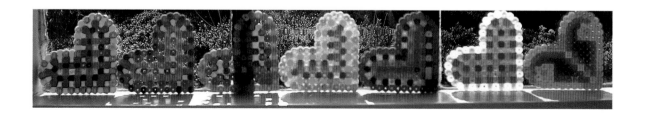

Visions of domesticity

I think we need a new category of film. There are fifteen categories in the *Time Out Film Guide*, and not one mentions domesticity. There are Horror, Gangsters, War, Swashbucklers, Epics and Fantasy among others, but nothing that remotely suggests the kind of film the gentle, domestic artist would choose to watch for inspiration and pleasure.

I wouldn't say I am a film buff, but I am passionate about films. Film buffs carry cast lists and esoteric stuff about editors, gaffers and extras in their heads, whereas I tend to recall hats, frocks, aprons, curtains and colors. I grew up with *Zulu* (1964), Elvis and Tarzan but soon graduated to the Kitchen-Table Domestic genre (to give it a proper title), and somehow managed to bypass the femme fatale phase completely.

Films can be part of every domestic artist's life. Now that there are cheap DVDs on Amazon (boxed sets are excellent because you get some unknown and unexpected treats in there—why else would you watch *You Can't Take It With You*, 1938, with James Stewart or *Flying Down to Rio*, 1933, with Fred Astaire?) and DVD rental stores on every street corner, it's much easier to watch vintage and less-well-known films than it used to be. Plus, there are some gems on TV that can be recorded and watched when you need Cary Grant or Gregory Peck to make life worth living again. Every Saturday I look in the TV listings for the coming week to see what overlooked and undervalued films are being shown. You need to search carefully; I have found classics such as *A Matter of Life and Death* (1946) or *An Affair to Remember* (1957) hidden in wickedly antisocial slots in the schedules.

I don't like many television programs and much prefer the flexibility of watching films on DVDs at home to going to a movie theater. While there may not be popcorn or a frilly usherette with a tray of ice-cream sandwiches, there is the joy of a homemade cup of tea and a cookie, the knowledge that Ben and Jerry are in the freezer, and decent lighting, which means you can multitask (eat, drink, watch, knit, quilt, sew) to your heart's content. My domestic cinema shows all the films I want to watch at a time that suits me, and all without irritating advertisements and trailers.

So what do I find to inspire me in Kitchen-Table Domestic films? Well, firstly there is a certain valida-tion of domesticity. If it's in a film, then it's already

deemed worthy of note and creative treatment. Then there's the fact that it's refreshing, comforting and challenging to see different domestic arrangements, interiors and relationships portrayed in films. These films lead the viewer to reflect on alternative values and possibilities of homemaking. And it's not all sweetness and light.

Take a look at the many subsections of my new film category. There is Cozy Domestic as seen in *Meet Me in St. Louis* (1944); Bohemian Domestic as in *Breakfast at Tiffany's* (1961), in which Audrey Hepburn's knitting spirals out of control; Heroic Domestic as in *Mrs. Miniver* (1942) and Stiff-Upper-Lip Domestic as in *This Happy Breed* (1944). Then there is the Melodramatic Domestic of *All That Heaven Allows* (1955) and anything else by Douglas Sirk, with his lush colors, overblown plots and the screen-filling Rock Hudson. The recent remake *Far From Heaven* (2002), which comes under the category of Repressed Domestic, is worth watching for a tense cake-making scene and absolutely the best 1950s-style dresses ever. For Passionate Domestic I would watch *The Bridges of Madison County* (1995) and for Destructive Domestic the Oscar would have to go to *Gone with the Wind* (1939). Musical Domestic can be found cour-tesy of Doris Day in *On Moonlight Bay* (1951) and its follow-up, *By the Light of the Silvery Moon* (1953), and my favorite Murderous Domestic film is *Mildred Pierce* (1945).

While these films offer all kinds of fascinating domestic imagery, ultimately they reaffirm the centrality of the happy, supportive home to any well-functioning community. I turn to films not only when I want to be diverted and entertained, but also when I need confirmation that domesticity is as creative a choice as I want to make it. And to be reminded that some women really do wear clothes that match their kitchen units, like Doris Day in *Pillow Talk* (1954).

Unmissable films

Sometimes, there is nothing better than a couple of hours' quilting or knitting or crochet in front of a favorite film. When I know I am going to treat myself to this luxury, I choose my film carefully. Nothing too tense, dramatic, searing or frightening (*Rear Window*,

1954, is about as far as I can go, and that's mainly so that I can be reminded of James Stewart's stunningly blue eyes and Grace Kelly's outrageously beautiful couture dress). The following films are the ones I watch over and over again. These are the ones that make me feel good about domesticity.

Brief Encounter (1945)

It is ironic that an awful lot of words have been written about this film in which the unspoken is more significant than the spoken. It is exquisitely understated, wonderfully acted, perfectly enunciated and quite heartbreaking. The small ordinary details—the station tearoom, the Kardomah Café, the drugstore lending library—underpin the great, chaste passion, and Laura returns to her semidetached house and her pipe-smoking, crossword-puzzle-solving husband while the Rachmaninov score signals what is really going on inside. It's a triumph of responsibility over personal fulfilment. It may be horribly old-fashioned for many, but decency isn't always easy.

Young at Heart (1954)

The first time I saw this, I could not believe my eyes. Hard-boiled Frank Sinatra and domestic goddess Doris Day together? Surely not. And as for Frank's behavior in the kitchen, how did she put up with it? While she dons a starched apron and ices gingerbread men, he sits on the kitchen work surface and smokes. Meanwhile, the old aunt knits while she watches the boxing on TV (with a bet on the side) and one

of the sisters wants to marry a plumber and give up family music making, for goodness' sake. It's shocking, funny, unexpected and a great exploration of different kinds of domesticity. There are a couple of good songs and a wonderfully melodramatic ending.

I Capture the Castle (2003)

The film of the book, with the added bonus of some of the most fantastic vintage-style knitwear ever filmed (sadly invisible in the book). Cassandra and her sister, Rose, wear beautiful hand-knits straight out of Needlewoman magazine circa 1935, the kind of cardigans and sweaters that everyone wore when most mothers and girls knitted. (The sisters also have a very lovely linen look in summer.) There is the spectacle of bohemian domesticity in a crumbling castle in Suffolk and a brilliant scene in which the girls and their stepmother dye every article of clothing they possess a disgusting shade of green.

Houseboat (1958)

Readers of yarnstorm know I have a thing about Cary Grant. And yet he is possibly the most undomesticated of all heartthrobs in that most of his films are about him evading or eluding marriage and domesticity until Grace Kelly/Doris Day/Audrey Hepburn/Katharine Hepburn/Rosalind Russell/Ingrid Bergman/Eva Marie Saint/Leslie Caron (the list is endless) make him see the error of his masculine ways. But in Houseboat we see the process of domestication taking place as Sophia Loren knocks him into shape. Of course,

even when fishing with his son, eating with the family or dealing with a sinking home, he never looks less than immaculate (see opposite). It's not the greatest film he ever made, but it's good for quilting while you imagine what you would do if you were in Sophia's place.

Amélie (2001)

Amélie requires the most boring knitting ever to accompany it, as I can't bear to miss a single frame of this exquisitely visual film. It is the cinematic antithesis of Brief Encounter, a riot of reds, greens and yellows, wonderfully overcrowded scenes and layer upon layer of detail. Just take a look at the greengrocer's stand; every fruit and vegetable is set out with the precision and reverence that underpins the entire presentation of domestic Paris (and the fantastic, hyper-real suburban gardens we also see). Amélie is also remarkable for its loving portrayal of the cast of eccentrics, all of whom have collections: gnomes, paintings, illnesses, photo-booth snapshots, proverbs. The film is a collection of collections in cartoon colors, and every scene is a mini masterpiece.

Little Women (1949)

My ability to cry at the mere mention of Beth has passed into family legend, and I am not alone; Phoebe once missed her lunch to sob over Beth's death. Although the 1933 George Cukor version wins all the plaudits, my favorite version is the one made in 1949 with a winningly lovely Elizabeth Taylor as Amy and a heart-wrenchingly sweet Margaret O'Brien as Beth. But I always wanted to be Jo as played by June Allyson. I wanted to read books and eat apples in the attic, vault effortlessly over gates and fences, charge around tomboyishly with a voice to match, and marry Laurie. In fact, I never really understood why she didn't do the latter. Laurie would have been perfectly good enough for me. But, that slight blip apart, this is a warm, funny, domestic film. Just don't forget the tissues.

Brodeuses (A Common Thread) (2004)

This lovely French film never received the attention it deserved on release. Its gentle pace, unshowiness and wonderfully controlled cinematography are just right for the central story of healing and the rebirth of faith and trust. Embroidery is at the heart of the beauty that redeems lives in a muddy, rural community. The

touches of gold (the heroine's wavy, auburn tresses, the sequins and threads of the embroidery, the wintry sun on the fields) contrast with the dark interiors and the bleak stories, but hint at better things to come. Even the shots of rows of cabbages on the hillside are suffused with artistry.

Sense and Sensibility (1995)

I am definitely more sensible than proud when it comes to Jane Austen. Persuasion apart, Sense and Sensibility is my favorite of her novels. I am impressed by the beautifully styled interiors in the recent version of Pride and Prejudice (2005), but much prefer the simpler, greyer Georgian settings of this film. It is amazing what excitement, plotting and planning can take place within confined domestic spaces and rigid social codes—and all without email and cell phones. I love the wit, the drama and the general sunniness of this adaptation. Alan Rickman feeling his way round the wainscoting as he droops in lovesick agony is a little unsettling, but Hugh Laurie as the brilliantly rude, hen-pecked husband (who is a fine sort underneath as we always knew he would be—when does Laurie ever play a truly bad character?) more than makes up for that.

The Sound of Music (1965)

No, I'm not being ironic. I really do love this film. Obviously it must help to have an enormous house and sufficient curtains to clothe seven children and yourself, but my spirits lift every time I see Julie Andrews getting off the bus, swinging her suitcases and clicking her heels at the prospect of looking after the seven young von Trapps. It reminds me that I really ought to try harder when I get up in the morning to face my three. The scenes of the children and Maria breaking away from naval order to ride their bikes, climb trees and fall in the lake are completely wonderful. And, after all these years, I still want a floaty, chiffony pink dress like the one Liesl wears when she celebrates being nearly seventeen.

But in *Houseboat* we see the process of domestication taking place as
Sophia Loren knocks him into shape. Of course, even when fishing
with his son, eating with the family or dealing with a sinking home,
he never looks less than immaculate.

Stockholm, not Stockport

I think there was a spelling mistake on my birth certificate, and that in actual fact I come from Stockholm, not Stockport. It was when I visited Stockholm for the first time one autumn that I began to suspect I'm actually Swedish.

The fact that I call myself a domestic artist does not preclude a little travel away from my home space. I have always traveled—with studies, wine and work—and even though domesticity curbed my tendencies, I would find it very difficult to stop altogether. Anyway, the cost in time and money is always paid back with enormous dividends in inspiration. A day away from home can be packed with lovely things—walks, galleries, shops, cafés, books, sights and architecture—so two nights away is a precious opportunity that must not be squandered.

I chose a weekend in Stockholm because I wanted to see a Kaffe Fassett exhibition at the Prins Eugens Waldemarsudde. I found cheap flights, an excellent hotel deal, packed my guide books, comfortable shoes, camera and an open mind. I returned two days later with a brain brimful with wonderful colors, impressions and ideas.

Stockholm is beautiful, calm, friendly, egalitarian and stylish. The bread is good, the cakes are better, the cafés are excellent, public transport works, there are knitters galore, and sewing is still something many women do. The only thing I'd need to bring for a longer stay is tea bags, for Stockholm is a coffee-drinker's paradise.

I still find it hard to believe that the photo below, far right, was taken in a part of central Stockholm. It is

a section of the kitchen garden that belongs to Rosendals Trädgård, a garden center on the island of Djurgården, with a brilliant organic café located in a series of greenhouses. There are masses of vegetables and flowers planted in neat rows around the buildings, and it's all quite breathtakingly lovely in a very domestic, real-life way. As it was sunny when I visited, I sat outside in the orchard to eat my lunch and then wandered around to admire the details. The apparently casual and informal arrangements on tables, in makeshift sculptures and in boxes of fruit and vegetables belie an exceptional attention to detail and sense of fun, which could be translated into pleasing and witty touches in any ordinary house or garden. (I particularly loved the way the gardening gloves and rusted fence matched the red chard in the field—see opposite, center left.)

Not far from the café, I came across the statue pictured opposite, far left, adorned with a wreath of dried flowers. It's as if he were a god of autumn, presiding over all this seasonal magnificence.

Domestic art

The Kaffe Fassett exhibition was held in a gallery just a rotary cutter's throw from the Rosendals Trädgård. Everything about it was so lovely that I went twice; once to look and once to see.

Waldemarsudde was an inspired choice of location. It is a large house at the water's edge, set in grounds full of flowers, trees and sculptures. It belonged to Prince Eugen, an artist of note, who bequeathed it to

the nation when he died in 1947. The ground floor rooms are as he left them, and visitors are given full access, so you can walk around looking at the books and paintings, getting close to the fabulous, fresh floral displays and the views, and you can even have a coffee in the old kitchen. Upstairs, in the former studio, was the exhibition.

In two large, airy rooms with white walls and bleached wooden floors, was a breathtaking display of quilts, knitting and needlepoint. It was simple, beautifully lit and quite mesmerizing. I went primarily to see the quilts, and I was not disappointed. There was enough in these rooms to inspire years of colorful fabric creativity.

There is something very special about seeing art and craft in a domestic setting. Kaffe Fassett's quilts looked completely at home in the surroundings of this former home. In fact, I think more textile artists should arrange exhibitions in less formal, more domestic locations. Historic homes such as those belonging to the National Trust, cozy hotels, smart garden centers, informal restaurants and the former homes of famous artists and writers would all be far better suited to the gentle arts than the bare walls of tall, imposing galleries.

When I wasn't looking at quilts or rows of vegetables, there was plenty to see and do in Stockholm. In between visits to cafés, such as Blooms Bageri, where I photographed the treats pictured opposite, far left, I walked from yarn shop to yarn shop looking at the alpacas and linens we don't see in England. I invested in some skeins of linen in traditional Swedish colors, woven cotton ribbons from an old-fashioned trimmings shop, bread to take home to Tom, a few buttons for a Jelly Bean Cushion, and a handful of magazines showing Swedish interiors that made me want to move there straightaway.

Swedish Allotment Quilt

But it was the inspiration that Stockholm provided that proved to be the greatest and longest-lasting souvenir of my visit.

Stockholm is on an archipelago, and the island of Djurgården was ablaze with autumnal color. It was a riot of rich and brilliant yellows, golds, greens, browns and flashes of bright pinks. The vegetables and flowers were growing in long, neat, wide rows but with a kitchen garden-style informality of mix and surrounded by trees with brilliant yellow leaves. Bright sunflowers were next to bottle-green spinach, red chard was next to pink and white cosmos. I found orange pumpkins, silvery green cardoons, rosy pink apples, cream and green gourds, chalky, pastel zinnias, vibrant nasturtiums, deep ruby dahlias. And when I stood back all I could see was a riot of vivid yellows and greens.

I'd thought of designing a quilt based on a garden allotment with sections broken up into horizontal strips, and this scene gave me the inspiration I'd been looking for in terms of color and detail. I knew I needed lots of yellows and greens, but soon saw that bright pink (as I'd seen in the cosmos, chard and zinnias) made all the difference and brought life and vitality to the mix. I chose fabrics featuring fruits, vegetables, foliage, flowers and plants in keeping with the theme, and then I simply cut random widths of each design before building up two beds with row after row of abundant allotment produce.

There must be something about the fertility of the Stockholm soil, the possibilities of this quilt design or the joy of using such rich, deep colors, but this piece grew like crazy. In fact, I had to curb its wild growth and stop it from taking over a whole room. It's large enough for a king-size bed, but I feel like a queen when I am covered in its Stockholm-inspired harvest.

Color

Coloring in the world

Color is vital to me. Color makes me feel alive—to the extent that I sometimes wonder if I resonate on the same wavelength as some of my favorite colors.

I have never studied the color wheel properly and have only looked with incomprehension at theories of color. I have tried to read books on color, but find that the combination of physics and art can be deadly to what I like to think of as one of life's greatest free pleasures. As with so many very basic pleasures—touch, taste, smell—we can destroy our natural reactions if we overintellectualize the processes and sensations.

I have to admit to loving bright colors. I don't mean simply garish and gaudy, I mean deep, rich colors that are full of themselves and not a washed-out apology for a shade: the bright colors of nature, the rich hues of textiles, the incandescent tones of colorful paintings. The colors of brightly frosted cupcakes, crazy assortments of candy, piles of ripe fruits and vegetables, balls of yarn heaped in a basket, layers of patchwork fabrics in my cupboard and drawers full of beads and embroidery threads, buttons and ribbons. I make sure that I can see wonderful colors every day by painting the walls of our rooms in emerald greens, sunflower yellows, brilliant turquoises and fiery reds, and by throwing the quilts and blankets I have made over furniture and on beds where they can be used and enjoyed all the time.

I react to pale and subtle colors in a very different way. I can appreciate them in a more impersonal, thoughtful fashion, all the while knowing that I *should* recognize how tasteful and pleasing they are. I often think how lovely and calming it must be to be surrounded by cool, gentle colors—but then remind myself that I'd be bored and hungry for color after a very short while. Give me strong, pure, jewel-like colors and I feel so much happier, even though I know that my tastes may be classed as obvious and unsophisticated.

Because I have never been "taught" about color, I don't have any hang-ups about liking it. But I realize that many people *are* fearful of color and shy away from using it. Manufacturers respond to this timidity by producing acres of bland furnishing fabrics and unspeakably pallid paint charts. This wary, conservative response to vivid color is compounded by the adult and establishment view that a love of color is somehow vulgar or childish. Most magazines would have us believe that white on white on white is the ultimate in sophisticated living—which is a nightmare of colorlessness and cleaning, as far as I can see.

The wonderful thing about playing with color in the gentle arts is that it can be done on any scale you wish. Knitting, stitching and baking offer unlimited opportunities to experiment with color and combinations, without having to overhaul your entire wardrobe or house. You may want to incorporate just the tiniest touches of color in the form of a few stitches or beads, or a button or two, or a jelly bean on a cupcake. You may want to knit a brightly colored scarf or tea cozy if the idea of a rainbow sweater brings you out in a cold sweat. Or you may want to create a huge, brilliant quilt to scorch the retinas of all who warm their eyes and feet with it. My basic color rule is that there are no rules, just what works for you. The more you experiment, the more you will develop your own tastes and ideas.

Over the next few pages, you can see the way in which I have been inspired to work with color and how I use it all the time in my creative thinking. I have been a cerise-pink and lime-green girl since I could first afford to buy twelve-inch squares of felt and matching sequins in Stockport market with my pocket money to make outfits for my dolls, but I firmly believe that it is never too late to unleash color into your domestic space.

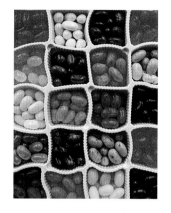

What's your favorite color?

I am always amazed when anyone answers this question with a single answer or, as they say on BBC Radio 4, without hesitation or deviation, but with a great deal of repetition.* How is it that so many mothers and pop stars (for it is generally children and teen magazines that pose the question) can be so sure? My mother invariably answered "orange," but I do wonder now whether that was to keep us quiet.

I don't usually hedge or dither, but I am stumped by this question. I can remember, when the children were young, how their eyes would glaze over before they wandered off to find someone who *did* know their mind, while I was left explaining the theory of color relativity to an empty room.

It's difficult for me to answer this question because I find that colors are at their most lovely when they are in combination with others. I have no problem liking bright pink on its own, but it's only when it's presented with something like lime green or lemon yellow or navy blue that I really *see* it. On the other hand, something like chocolate brown doesn't do a great deal for me until it's paired with, for example, duck-egg blue or coral pink and then it begins to acquire value and resonance.

* The key words in the rules of the popular radio show
Just a Minute.

Think of some fabulous color combinations. Chartreuse green and cranberry red. Silver grey and mandarin orange. Brilliant white and cerise pink. Turquoise and lemon. Iris blue and marigold orange. Burnished gold and plum violet. Shocking pink and acid lime. If you take away one half of the sum, you are left with a lot less than half of what you started with, as each color sets up, supports and enhances the other.

Working with two colors is a rewarding and easy way to begin an exploration of your personal preferences. A monochromatic piece of knitting is lifted by a single row of color at the edges (see Style, page 149), a row of contrasting buttons adds interest to a cardigan, and a traditional red and white quilt never fails to please. But you can bring instant color into your domestic life with two-color cake decorating—no lasting commitment, just a brief, colorful fling.

I came across these sugar-coated chocolate hearts in Paris but could not make up my mind which one to buy. I wanted the bittersweet lime *and* the holly red. As I held the two packs in my hand I saw that the only way I would really enjoy the color of either was to buy both. (The application of my theory of color relativity usefully and unfailingly provides a watertight justification for purchase.)

I came across these sugar-coated chocolate hearts in Paris but could not make up my mind which one to buy. I wanted the bittersweet lime *and* the holly red.

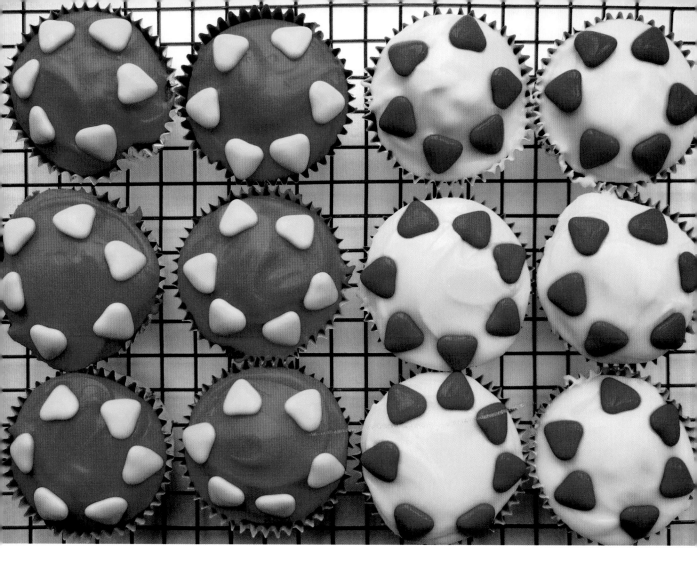

These cupcakes also reverse the color combinations to interesting effect, and when I put them out on the crisscrosses of the wire cooling rack my eyes were dancing around with delight, taking in all the movement the two colors create. In fact, I could happily spend hours rearranging cupcakes to make various "baked quilts."

Alternatively, you can take two colors of icing and play with those in a more random and less patterned way. Phoebe found some little flower decorations (the type that ruin expensive dental work) made from white icing with colored, metallic balls. Taking their cue from the blue and pink centers, she and Alice whipped up two bowls of icing—one sky blue and one ribbon pink. More pink and blue balls, sprinkles, marshmallows and colored sugar were applied liberally as each cake was decorated individually. What could

have been a free-for-all was saved by the overarching pink and blue theme that held the whole together and, indeed, made it a thing of beauty.

I would find it very difficult to work with one color only. Whitework embroidery is exquisite, but it pains me to see the white stitches disappear on the white background. I always feel the need to place a scarlet glacé cherry on a plainly iced cupcake. I used to knit cream Aran sweaters but these days much prefer the endless color permutations of Fair Isle knitting. Old-fashioned quilted, peach satin comforters do not hold my attention the way a vibrant, two-color quilt might. So I would suggest that the next time someone asks you "What's your favorite color?" you try not to take the easy, orange way out.

I warned you I always had a long-winded answer to the question.

Sweetheart

Alice was a sweet girl. When she was younger, her awareness of the candy market was on a par with that of Willy Wonka. She had an encyclopedic knowledge of brands, shapes, colors and flavors, and approached the task of candy-buying and candy-eating like a consummate professional. She used to compare and contrast and make mental notes, savoring the words, packaging and promises as much as the contents. She would have made a great proprietor of a candy shop—just like the one in Richmal Crompton's *William* books, who places customer satisfaction above profit and takes the time to discuss the merits and demerits of various brands of jawbreakers with William. She still

spends happy times on websites like A Quarter Of and Sugar Boy (see Resources, page 285) filling her fantasy basket with exciting combinations of flavors and shapes.

Her sweet tooth reopened a whole world of color I'd not noticed since I was a child. Candy pink marshmallows, pastel Love Hearts, chalky bonbons, golden pineapple cubes, tiny polka-dot suckers, black licorice wheels, lime green sour apples, and a whole palette of jelly-bean colors.

Interestingly, Alice derived almost as much pleasure from playing with sweets as eating them. She and Phoebe still enjoy creating beautiful, edible candy quilts (see left), which I now recognize are only one step away from lovely textiles such as quilts and Fair Isle knitting. I've also realized that this essentially childish and untrained sorting and arranging approach works equally well with yarns, beads, fabrics, threads and buttons and is an imaginative way to experiment and play with colors, patterns and repeats. But in this case you can eat the materials.

It is, however, possible to have too much sugar in any diet. This kind of color combination looks delicious when confined to socks, but I can't think of anyone, not even Willy Wonka himself, who could carry off a whole candy-bag sweater. This sock yarn, Lana Grossa Meilenweit Fantasy #4833, works only because it keeps to a limited palette (pink, orange, purple and white) and limited pattern variations (stripes and broken, two-color sections).

So the secret of candy-bag colors, as with sweets themselves, is moderation. And a good toothbrush.

Ripple effect

A crocheted blanket is an excellent place to start any exploration of color. The nature of the stitch construction in crochet ensures that a blanket looks good on both sides, doesn't lose its shape and requires minimal finishing apart from sewing in the ends— all of which means you can concentrate on color.

In theory, I am taken by the idea of crochet as a thrift craft, a means of using up leftover yarns or colors that didn't fit into a more coordinated project. I like the mishmash of colors in vintage crocheted blankets; the way the makers seemed to use whatever they pulled from their workbag, the way they reveled in clashes and contrasts, the way they followed the dictates of the project, not those of genteel good taste. This is free and liberated creativity in which simplicity of form gives huge possibilities for playing with color.

The idea for this blanket came when I found a charming but somewhat felted, wavy blanket on eBay. I fell for the undulations of color, the way it made my eyes bob up and down on the waves, and the use of a vast number of colors that, although they didn't all "go" next to each other, somehow worked in the overall scheme.

After finding a simple, softly rippling pattern in double crochet in *200 Ripple Stitch Patterns* by Jan Eaton (see Resources, page 281) I flew in the face of all concepts of thrift crochet and bought a pile of one hundred percent wool DK yarns. I started off with a vague color idea—bright, cheerful, Matissey shades and two-row stripes. I didn't want a strict, repeating pattern, nor did I want the blanket to be so random that it lacked cohesion. So every two or three rows I would line up the potential yarns for the next few rows to make sure that I didn't get any big gaps between colors or any noticeable pattern repeats. A second pair of eyes was needed here and Tom was consulted as he has great spatial color awareness and his intuition is always right on.

As this was my first crochet project, I hadn't quite realized just how much yarn crochet guzzles. My initial purchase turned out to be laughably meager for a decent-size blanket, and it wasn't long before I was searching out all the DK yarn in the house, which meant I'd entered into the spirit of a thrift crochet blanket after all.

Crochet is remarkably easy to pick up and put down and you don't have to sit up straight to do it. It clearly brings out the inner slob in me, as I found I could crochet when slouching, with my knees up on the sofa, on the floor—I even began to wonder if you could do yoga at the same time. But the wavy stitch is dangerously addictive, and it soon became a go-faster stripe as I wanted to see how more and more colors looked. Eventually I ran out, not of steam, but of yarn, and would have waded into murky waters if I'd carried on. The finished piece is 45" by 51", weighs two pounds, and makes everyone who uses it feel as snug as a bug in a rug.

The ripple effect does wonderful things with the colors. If you had the same colors in linear stripes, the result would still be vibrant and exciting, but it would also be rather static. The waves create a dynamism that makes your eyes bounce on the stripes and then, if your eyes move laterally, they pick out groups and wider stripes that change all the time.

You could make a wavy blanket in all sorts of color combinations, and I'm quite sure that a set repeat would look very lovely, but I really do think that bold, bright and beautiful is the easiest way to become a happy hooker.

Processing color

Although, as I've said, color theory leaves me cold, I believe that color has its own, built-in rules and that working with it is a process of discovery. It's like trying to penetrate a semi-revealed mystery with only a few, obvious clues. The more esoteric relationships and connections reveal themselves in due course, but only when you are ready to see them.

When I made the Chlorophyll Quilt, I felt I was venturing into an unknown undergrowth of exotic, jungly oranges, greens and black. It started, as usual, when I found a perfect lead fabric, a fabric that catches my eye and dictates the rest of the quilt. This was a huge, strange, leafy, David Wolverson print in an off-beat palette that worked best when mixed with more Rowan fabrics to create a dense and saturated effect.

I chose a fairly simple, square-based design called Rosy, which can be found in Kaffe Fassett's *Quilt Road* and *Glorious Patchwork* books (see Resources, page 282). It's much easier to process color within a simple block framework rather than a highly complex, intricate design, especially if, like me, you are relatively new to quilting. Simplicity of form is a perfect foil to a riot of color and is really the only way you can see all the glorious patterns and details when you are planning, unless you are as experienced as Kaffe Fassett or Liza Prior Lucy.

I collected fabrics for a couple of months and then cut out all the pieces in one weekend; I find there is a spontaneity and cohesion that is transferred to a quilt when you do one of the processes in a single, big burst of energy. Using the same process I apply to all my quilts, I cut out a huge number of smaller and larger squares *before* beginning to lay them out (yes, there are leftovers every time, but one day they will all make a huge, incandescent quilt). I use the floor area of a room and, instead of making it block by block, I arrange *all* the unsewn pieces on the floor until I am happy with the placement. I climb on furniture to get a better, aerial view, stand at each edge to make sure it works in all directions, ask Tom, my Quilting Apprentice, for his expert advice, and only then do I begin to sew.

I had many misgivings along the way with this quilt, and felt it wasn't going to work. And yet this is a quilt that worked really well when I began sewing. The deep, rich shades are more beautiful in the detail of small pieces rather than as whole lengths, and I could only appreciate them when the fabrics were in my hands. Each design has foliage and/or flowers but, far from producing an English country-garden style, they combine into a more unsettling forest with a carpet of flowers and fallen leaves. There are deep greens, russets, golds, purples and ochers. There are a few flashes of sky blue and berry pink, but these are offset by a color I rarely use: black.

As I machine-pieced and hand-quilted the fabrics together, I saw more and more cleverness, and more and more wonderful combinations I'd normally eschew. The second-fiddle fabric had to be abandoned when it simply did not work with what the rest of the colors were telling me. And this is what I mean about processing color: if you allow the quilt to communicate its own color rules rather than you imposing yours, you end up with something quite different from what you had imagined, but something with a life of its own.

I don't always add borders but this jungle needed a frame to hold it together and contain it. I used a dramatic stripe and then made a second border of the pale blue lead fabric, which gives the impression of light and space above the dense trees and flowers. Tom suggested we call it the Chlorophyll Quilt because the natural, magical process of photosynthesis is at the heart of all this lushness and growth. Just like the natural, magical process of color.

Playing with color

I have always envied artists who discover a tangible form of creative expression that can be repeated over and over but with subtle variations. Think of Monet and his paintings of lilies and haystacks, Warhol and his canvases of Campbell's soup cans, Lucy Rie and her perfect bowls. There is something magnificent in their obsessive painting and making; far from being predictable and boring, these series acquire a richness and depth of meaning by showing us the value of light or color or surface texture as we are forced to look for the differences.

I can't make any claims to great meaning or artistic vision, but I can say that I was thrilled when I stumbled across a vehicle for my very own series. What began as a single knitted cushion has now become the Jelly Bean Cushion series. Ten spotty, fluffy, squishy cushion covers later, I may not be on the same level as Monet but I have had a great deal of fun playing with color.

I always knew that working with color should be enjoyable, but I hadn't really allowed myself to acknowledge the possibilities for playful spontaneity in a medium as apparently prosaic as knitting. As Alicia, who writes the brilliant Posie Gets Cozy blog (see Resources, page 276), pointed out, once I had mastered the medium of the cushion (i.e., knowing what the pattern required in terms of skill, yarn and time), I was able to play with the other aspect, that of color, and could explore color relationships within that medium. She talked of two elements: control (the unchanging structure) and surprise (the variable colors), and it is exactly these that artists explore in their series.

Jelly Bean Cushion I

The first Jelly Bean Cushion (pictured opposite, top left) was fueled by guilt. Guilt at seeing unused yarns sitting in baskets, reminding me that I'd brought them back from Paris and New York and not done a thing with them. The turquoise alpaca yarn was bought with another project in mind, and the angora . . . well, I have long had a thing about angora and bought it because I couldn't resist.

I'd found the spotty cushion pattern in *Home* by Debbie Bliss and decided that I could use up some of my guilt-inducing yarns that way. I took five shades of

pink angora and placed the colors in rows as I went along. I put fluffy stripes on the back and then realized that this was also the perfect showcase for some pretty buttons I'd found in Amsterdam.

We happened to have a huge jar of jelly beans in the house at the time I was knitting, and I noticed just how many pinks there were in there. I immediately recognized the similarity in shape and color between the spots and the jelly beans, and so the series began.

Jelly Bean Cushion II

Jelly Bean Cushion II (pictured opposite, top right) was a second using-up exercise, but this time I went to the jelly bean jar first to check the colors and was amazed to find so many shades of green in there. Purple and lime is a favorite combination; it may seem a touch acid to some, but I love it. And anyway, I wasn't out to make a tasteful piece, I was out to knit with color and it worked. This is a startlingly juicy match, with the greens almost vibrating on the purple and the spots making a clever argyle pattern if you let your eyes move diagonally over the rows. Here was a knitting recipe that clearly worked for me, and I was ready to move on to the next color experiment.

Chocolate Button Cushion

I can't help but see connections between food and textiles, and the next in the series became the Chocolate Button Cushion (pictured opposite, below left, and page 58, left). Giant, creamy milk and white chocolate buttons in four shades of angora on a rich coral background make a mouthwatering combination. I had only two balls of the coral, so I knitted the back in a shade I called bad-tempered camel but that worked well with a few stripes and some vintage Art Deco buttons. This was an exercise in metaphorical and literal taste, and an exploration of the melting, soft qualities of both chocolate and angora.

Healthy, Juicy Jelly Bean Cushion

The Healthy, Juicy Jelly Bean Cushion (pictured opposite, below right, and page 59, right) reversed the basic

colors of the Chocolate Button Cushion but with a citric tang. The cream background makes the vivid, tangerine-orange shades stand out with real zing. The key angora is the wickedly deep, reddish orange from Alchemy, which lifts the whole and makes the more vapid oranges work by contrast.

Paris in Springtime Cushion

Paris in Springtime (pictured opposite, left) is a more organic colorway. This was a departure from food colors as I played with the more natural shades associated with spring. The cushion captures the essence of a short trip I made with Alice to Paris one April when I noticed the limey-chartreuse new leaves, the pale yellow flowers, the dusty, gravelly park paths and the chalky paleness of the buildings all glimmering in the spring sunshine. The spots became seeds and stones and, when seen in the daylight, they even appear to be some sprouting organism full of the energy of the season.

Jam Splatz Cushion

It was back to my beloved Food in Textiles theme with the Jam Splatz Cushion. A sort through my basket of angora revealed a whole group of yarns in jammy colors that would look like dollops of raspberry, blackberry, cherry, strawberry and plum jam spread liberally on a pale cream pastry background like a huge multi-flavored tart. I chose some fabulous buttons from Tender Buttons in New York for their leaf shape and their rich color.

Conker Cushion

The Conker Cushion was knitted at the height of the conker (horse-chestnut) season and was inspired by a conker-collecting expedition along the stately, chestnut-lined Long Walk up to Windsor Castle. Conkers (see page 99, top right) are packaged in prickly, lime-green cases that open to reveal the shiny, deep brown seeds. I took the conker color for the background, used rich autumnal oranges and reds to represent the huge, fiery leaves of the trees, and placed an occasional lime spot for conker shells.

English Drawing Room Cushion

The next in the series is the English Drawing Room Cushion, which was inspired by a painting and a photo of an English writer's room with curtains featuring wonderful rich purple flowers on a deep gold background. Both images demonstrated the loveliness of a combination that struck me as assured and sophisticated and very English. My angora stash yielded sufficient shades of hyacinth, lilac and plum and this time I decided to buy the right background color specifically for the cushion.

Rose Cushion

By the time I arrived at my Rose Cushion (pictured below right), I realized that I was starting to plan the cushions, rather than working with leftovers, and that the jelly bean jar had long been left behind. This one was inspired by some rose buttons found in Paris. As

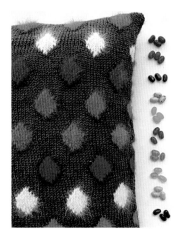

soon as I'd bought them I rushed over to Le Bon Marché department store for the matching fluff and background yarn. The green is the deep green of rose leaves and the "jelly beans" are various shades of roses in bloom.

The cushion also takes me back to the time I had to dress up as an "English Rose" for a Children of All Nations production at my kindergarten. I was devastated at having to wear a frilly white frock when all my friends were in bright, exotic costumes. The only compensation was that my dress had a wide sash with a huge, floppy, red satin rose at the front. That fabric flower was so beautiful that I longed to cut it off and take it home, but nice English roses don't do that sort of thing. So I made this cushion, which I can keep without getting into trouble with my teachers.

Uses and abuses

It's uncanny that the JB Series has proven to be the perfect vehicle for a knitter whose initials are JB. It has provided me with a brilliant medium for playing with color and form on a manageable scale, and the series will continue. Readers of yarnstorm have asked me what I do with all these cushions. Well, as with all our quilts, we use them. We sit on them, put them under heads, feet and bottoms, scatter them on chairs and sofas and sometimes pile them high for effect. They may not last forever this way, but neither does any domestic arrangement, and I prefer to enjoy them all while I can.

Cozy combination

I have been programmed since my early years to recognize yellow and pink as the Battenberg Combination. Store-bought Battenberg cake—a yellow and pink sponge cake, layered with apricot jam and wrapped in a sheet of marzipan—was one of my greatest childhood domestic pleasures. I ate it in a very specific, set order, so I have fond memories of peeling off the marzipan and saving it until I'd eaten the yellow and then the pink squares of cake.

A couple of years ago, however, I had a Battenberg epiphany, a sudden understanding of the true nature of the confection, when I tasted a homemade Battenberg cake for the first time. Everything became clear: there is factory-made Battenberg (small, pale, regular and quite pleasant) and there is *real* Battenberg: large, vibrant, irregular and a very different epicurean experience. Real Battenberg has style and presence, and this cake gave me a new yellow and pink frame of reference.

Soon after, I bought some warm pink and golden yellow yarn in New York because I was once again drawn to the combination. It was inevitable that its

destiny was to be a Battenberg tea cozy. Just like the real Battenberg cake I'd encountered, its proportions are generous to a fault, and it needs a large, eight-cup, Brown Betty teapot to do it justice.

The cozy took a while to make because it is knitted in garter stitch (knit every row), and the strands are crossed at the back like a woven English willow fence to give maximum pot insulation. I then added pom-pom bobbles, because I remember bobbled tea cozies from the days of store-bought Battenberg and then, because this is a super-stylish version, I also beaded it. As I attached the ninety-six gold beads, I felt like one of those mothers in the 1960s who (allegedly) sewed every single sequin on to their daughter's ballroom dancing frocks.

All this knitting gave me time to conduct a deep and meaningful mental survey of Battenberg cakes, and I decided that I would have to bake one to go with the tea cozy. I searched high and low, but couldn't find a good recipe that promised to match the epiphanic cake. In the end, I decided to devise my own.

The Brocket Battenberg Cake

Home-made Battenberg cake is a wonderful combination of soft, slightly almondy cake set out in the characteristic checkerboard arrangement; lightly tangy apricot jam, which acts as a glue to keep the cake and wrapping together; and a generous outside layer of pale gold marzipan.

This is my version, and it's a very large one. I am pathologically unable to make anything of average size (the tea cozy was meant to be for a six-cup pot), and my heart sank when I came across a couple of recipes for a teeny-tiny cake that would never feed a family of Brockets. So here we have it, a homemade, family-size Battenberg cake.

Brocket Battenberg Cake

Makes 1 large cake

Ingredients
1 cup soft unsalted butter
1 cup superfine sugar
4 large eggs
few drops almond extract (optional)
1½ cups self-rising flour
10½ teaspoons ground almonds
½ teaspoon baking powder
pink or red food coloring
apricot jam
approximately 1 pound golden marzipan
confectioner's sugar, for dusting

Preheat the oven to 325°F.

Grease 2 loaf pans, measuring approximately 8" long x 4½" wide x 2½" deep.

First make a basic cake batter. In a large bowl, cream together the butter and sugar, then beat in the eggs one after another. Add the almond extract, if using (I don't because the children don't like it). Sift in the flour, ground almonds and baking powder and fold in gently.

Spoon half the mixture into one loaf pan and level the surface with the back of a spoon. Now add the food coloring to the remainder of the batter until it turns a good pink color. Spoon into the second pan and level. Bake both pans for 30–40 minutes until a skewer comes out clean (start checking after 25 minutes). Leave to cool, then turn out onto a wire rack.

You now need to make four strips of cake. Using a sharp knife, cut each sponge loaf in half and trim so that each side and edge is straight and the four pieces are more or less equal.

Warm the apricot jam so that it is easy to brush on to the cake. Roll out the marzipan on a surface dusted with confectioner's sugar. It needs to be long enough and wide enough to be wrapped around the cake.

Glue the four pieces of sponge by brushing the connecting sides of the strips with the apricot jam and pressing them together. You should now have a long, rectangular cake with yellow and pink squares in a checkerboard pattern. Brush the outside with jam and carefully wrap the marzipan around, leaving the join to go underneath. Trim the two ends so that the cake squares show to full effect.

Knit matching tea cozy and make pot of tea.

Terribly, terribly English

Unlike the art establishment, I think paintings of domestic subjects deserve much greater recognition. I have always been drawn to depictions of ordinary life and am grateful that many artists have had the confidence and prescience to value the quotidian because they do posterity a great service. I would much rather look at a domestic interior or activity or scenes of village and town life than any number of battle scenes and stately portraits. I find it fascinating to imagine how it was to live in a certain time and place surrounded by period artifacts of little or no lasting value apart from what they tell us about real people's lives.

Although I am always seduced by the vibrant, intense, color-filled swirls, strokes, splodges, dots and patterns in paintings by Henri Matisse and Howard Hodgkin, I also have a very soft spot for much gentler, domestic works by a number of terribly, terribly English artists. The pale, grey watery light of English winters may sometimes make me long for heat and sun and brightness, but I am beginning to realize that there is something special in the washed-out tones of England when the leaves have fallen and the days are short.

Eric Ravilious

I have admired the work of Eric Ravilious (1903 – 42) for years. His beautifully observed details of 1930s England in organic, weathered, neutral colors are gentle, evocative and affectionate. By the very act of observing familiar domestic scenes and the objects of daily life, he elevates them to the extraordinary, while evoking a pure and gentle essence of Englishness. Ravilious's watercolors of Main Street shops, simple interiors, greenhouses, garden tools, village lanes and open countryside may look dated, but you only have to visit Sussex and Wiltshire to see that the England of Ravilious is still there, and still beautiful.

There are no jarring elements in Eric Ravilious's art, but a complete understanding and mastery of his relatively limited palette. The tones he chooses are those of faded cottons, tweedy yarns and the soft blues, greys and greens of landscapes (and naval and military uniforms). He almost rations his colors in the same way that other luxuries were rationed in the war years, and yet there is never a feeling of somberness.

In *Train Landscape* (1939), pictured opposite, the hills and fields and the magnificent Westbury Horse (which was carved as we know it on the limestone hillside in 1778) are framed by the three windows of the third-class carriage. Ravilious is a master of surface texture: the grain of the wood, the pile of the diamond-patterned upholstery, the leather of the window strap, the metal of the grate and door lock and the thick, insulating cord are all comfortable, worn and solidly durable. The rolling landscape and the mix of carefully farmed and fenced pasture and wilder, higher ground are dwarfed by the train, and the focus is on the interior. This painting has a companion picture in *The Westbury Horse* (1939), which inverts the view so that the huge horse and hills dominate the scene and the puffing train is reduced to a small, model-scale version winding its way through the valley.

The tones he chooses are those of faded cottons, tweedy yarns and the soft
blues, greys and greens of landscapes (and naval and military uniforms).

The tiny areas of lilac, pink, yellow and green stand out against the whites and greys, and the artist manages to convey depth, movement and a lyricism that is quite delightful.

These paintings emphasize the variability of point of view and give the feeling that this is an England on the cusp of change. The very same palette is applied to the marvelous film *A Matter of Life and Death* (1946), and the muted, watercolor tones work in the same way as Ravilious's do to produce an elegiac yet uplifting vision of wartime domestic English life.

There are many lessons in tonal value and control of color in Ravilious's watercolors, and if I did decide to make a softly colored quilt or to crochet gentle waves of color or to knit a traditional Fair Isle pattern, I would know exactly where to turn for inspiration.

A little light art theft

Sometimes, when I visit a gallery or exhibition, I like to imagine which painting I would most like to take home. There are plenty of works of art that I admire but couldn't have on my walls. The Pre-Raphaelites would be too intense, the Impressionists too lush and Stanley Spencer too disturbing.

If I had to pick one artist whose work I would happily steal, it would be an agonizing choice between Howard Hodgkin, Eric Ravilious and Winifred Nicholson. All English, all twentieth century, all colorists and all with a very recognizable but unique style.

If pushed to decide, though, I would admit to coveting a Winifred Nicholson (1893 – 1981). In fact, I was quite overwhelmed by a desire to possess one of her paintings when I saw them in an exhibition at Kettle's Yard in Cambridge. But choosing just one of her paintings to take to my desert island would be incredibly difficult. I am bewitched by all her flower paintings with their luminescent coolness and their celebration of simple domestic settings. Her use of color is extraordinary and her canvases glow and radiate even though she employs masses of grey and white. She captures the physical properties of light and color in a bold yet delicate manner and has the ability to control and place color perfectly. There is never any detail out of place in these stripped-down still lifes, and the eye is free to focus on the genius of the color.

Cyclamen and Primula (1922 – 3), pictured opposite, is a coolly beautiful example of her art. This is an informal arrangement by a window through which a dramatic but unspecified landscape can be glimpsed. She hasn't even bothered to remove the translucent white wrapping paper from the pots, and this somehow makes them look even more special, as if they are wrapped in silk hoods. The tiny areas of lilac, pink, yellow and green stand out against the whites and greys, and the artist manages to convey depth, movement and a lyricism that is quite delightful.

Winifred Nicholson is also very interesting, not only because she was once married to Ben Nicholson, who left her for Barbara Hepworth, but also because she developed a complex theory of color and created her own color table based on the rainbow. What is really unusual is that it is made up solely of words and without any colors.

So the blue column starts with shadow, mist, sea grey, air force blue, fell blue, turquoise, then azure, and runs on with baby-ribbon blue, sky, forget-me-not, larkspur, lapis-lazuli and finally zenith. It is also striking that the table is couched in terms of everyday objects, plants, trees, cabbages, hay, prune, willow, tomato, heliotrope, brass, faded oak leaf—with the exception of the alarming dragon's blood. Here is a female artist, a mother and wife, too, who created pure poetry of color with reference to the very ordinary and the very English.

I personally don't refer to any theories of color, preferring to make up my own as I go along. But, every so often, I take down my book about Winifred Nicholson* to read the color chart and look at her paintings, and I find myself inspired by her skills with words and color. She reminds me that white and grey backgrounds and light are beautiful and that space does not always have to be filled, and I realize I apply these precepts to my photography and hand- and machine-embroidery in particular.

This is my own, far less criminal, version of light art theft. What would you steal and from whom?

* *Winifred Nicholson,* Jon Blackwood (Cambridge: Kettle's Yard, 2001)

The dark side

I may declare my love of bright color on a daily basis in my house, quilts, baking and knitting, but there are times when *dark* is interesting in the domestic arts. Like dark chocolate, it adds a spicy, bitter contrast to a richer, sweeter diet. I am drawn to the drama of deep colors with evocative names like jet, pewter, coffee, raven, midnight, mahogany and pitch. I am fascinated by the way pools of these colors absorb all the colors in light and, in doing so, draw you into their depths.

I went over to the dark side with these Touch of Goth socks. I wouldn't normally knit with this type of colorway, and the skein of sock yarn from Fleece Artist had been in my TBK (To Be Knitted) pile for a good year before I finally got around to winding it into a ball. As soon as circularity was achieved it looked like a strange and distant planet lurking on the dark side of the moon. I love the way the midnight-dark background is shot through with flashes of lime and cerise, lilac and teal. Just as the night sky is never truly black, so this dark universe is broken up by little comets and meteor showers of color.

However, there is a downside of knitting with such a challenging shade. And this is that it's not that easy to see what you are doing with it when the sun has gone down. Particularly if you choose a little fusion of your favorite pastimes.

While I was knitting my Touch of Goth socks, I happened to come across The Chocolate Block, a cult wine from South Africa, in our local supermarket. It seemed a perfect, and apt, partner for my knitting. It's a deep, dark ruby color and has a wonderfully complex and rich palate. Of course, with a name like that, it called for a little simultaneous chocolate tasting, and Green & Black's seventy percent dark chocolate came up with the goods. To complete a night of darkness, I watched a black-and-white film. Not any old black-and-white film, though. Oh, no. This was *Brief Encounter* with its smoky train station scenes and play on light and dark.

Many tears, slurps of wine, squares of chocolate, and knitted cables later, I was thoroughly immersed in my dark universe. It was only in the cold and unforgiving light of the following day that I saw that my cables had suffered from the suppressed passion of the film and dark pleasures of the wine and chocolate. To say they were erratic would be an understatement of Celia Johnson proportions.

Still, my Touch of Goth socks are perfect for wearing after midnight and in a pair of black boots where they can hide their cabled secrets.

I am drawn to the drama of deep colors with evocative names like jet, pewter, coffee, raven, midnight, mahogany and pitch. I am fascinated by the way pools of these colors absorb all the colors in light and, in doing so, draw you into their depths.

Texture

Keeping in touch

It is so easy to lose touch. We live in a digital era and, increasingly, spend our days in a cocoon of space, dealing with the virtual, not the tangible: on telephones, in front of computers and televisions, in cars, trains and planes. It is quite possible to pass whole days without making contact with any natural surfaces and textures. We can exist in a bubble of emptiness and not even recognize that we are suffering sensory deprivation.

The problem is made worse by the current perception that many domestic activities are unpleasant. We no longer want to scrub with hard bristle brushes, instead we wipe with smooth, fresh-scented cleaning fluids and soft cloths. We buy nonstick pans to avoid using grating, metallic pads. We buy machine-washable everything and rarely plunge our hands in hot, soapy water. We tumble-dry clothes instead of dealing with wet washing in sun, wind and rain. We buy premade meals and keep our sharp knives and grainy chopping boards for display purposes only.

I don't necessarily want a wholesale return to scrubbing floors and polishing doorsteps, harsh powders and immovable waxes, but I do enjoy and prize texture. It keeps us in touch, literally, with life. If we stop feeling our way through life, stop handling materials, we become passive and dependent on the ready-made and textureless. In doing so, we give up an element of independence, control, skill and autonomy. If we can no longer bake a loaf of bread, test a cake for doneness, plant a bulb, knit a simple garment, sew a quilt, we are quite helpless.

The gentle arts are a perfect vehicle for the (re)discovery of texture. This chapter explores the pleasures and delights of the various textures of domesticity. And perhaps by considering the literal we shall also be better able to understand and appreciate the metaphorical texture of our lives

Yarnstorm

I didn't call my blog yarnstorm by accident. Ever since I was taught how to do basic knit-a-row-purl-a-row knitting, I have been entranced by the texture of yarn. Fluffy yarn, smooth yarn, metallic yarn, scratchy yarn, slubby yarn, hairy yarn, furry yarn, natural yarn, synthetic yarn, all yarn is worth exploring.

Earning its keep

I am a great believer in knitting with the best you can afford, but that doesn't mean I automatically buy the most expensive yarns available. I choose yarns that not only meet the pattern specifications and express my color ideas, but are also a real pleasure to knit with. I am going to spend a good deal of time handling a yarn, so it has to repay that investment. Cheap yarn may seem a good idea at the point of purchase, but when it splits, reveals countless knots, knits unevenly and has a rough or downright unpleasant texture, you will regret the decision. And ten or twenty balls of unused yarn can weigh very heavily on your conscience *and* take up a lot of space at the back of your closet when you try to hide them from yourself.

With this basic principle in mind, I give you my favorite yarns, each with their own very definite and delightful texture.

Cashmere: fantasy stuff

When I was twelve, I borrowed a novel from my best friend. It was a 1950s American high-school story, and I think it was suitably easy reading. I can't remember anything of the plot, but I can still see in the middle of the first paragraph the words "cashmere sweater." I had no idea what cashmere was, so I asked my mother. She told me about its indescribable softness and exorbitant price and thus, unknowingly, whetted my appetite for this extravagantly luxurious fiber.

I didn't actually touch cashmere until I was much older but, when I did, I was instantly reminded of my fantasy of being that teenager in that novel wearing that sweater. Cashmere has come down in price dramatically in recent years but, while a cashmere sweater may be relatively affordable now, cashmere knitting yarn is still very expensive. So, when I do

splurge on a few skeins of cashmere, I use them to knit items that allow me to appreciate the texture of this fabulously baby-bottom-soft yarn all the time I am wearing or using them.

The long, thick, undulating Clapotis Scarf pictured opposite, top right, is knitted with four 1¾ oz skeins of unbelievably soft and cozy Mont Blanc cashmere from Axelle de Sauveterre (see Resources, page 282). It is long enough to be wound around my neck and over my ears like a fluffy cloud of warmth and coziness. Even as I knitted, I could see the aura of downy fibers that envelops the yarn in a cocoon of softness and makes it appear gently out of focus in photographs. I wasn't at all surprised to find that the colorway was called Briar Rose as there is an insubstantial, fairy-tale quality to cashmere, as if it could only be captured and spun by yarn fairies with the lightest of touches.

I thought of the scarf as a portable hot water bottle, which led, inevitably, to the real thing (see opposite, top left). There is nothing as cozy as a hot water bottle except, perhaps, a hot water bottle attired in a hand-knitted cashmere cover. While I knitted it, I fantasized about cocoa parties, even though I've never been to one, and I imagined all the other heavenly, soft, warm, domestic textures that could be enjoyed there: smooth hot cocoa, brushed cotton pajamas, fluffy slippers, feathery pillows and woolen blankets.

All that pleasure from a few skeins of yarn. A bargain, really.

Angora: fluffy stuff

I think of angora as a childish version of the more sophisticated, grown-up cashmere. Its exaggerated, manic fluffiness makes me smile every time I touch it. It is as though it's a caricature of itself: nothing could possibly be *that* fluffy. But it is.

Angora used to be much more popular in England than it is today, but it never went away in France, where Anny Blatt still produces the best, widely available angora yarn I know. In the United States, you can get angora from small producers like Lorna's Laces, Alchemy and Joseph Galler.

I am very fond of angora and keep my fluff balls in a wide, shallow basket into which I can plunge my

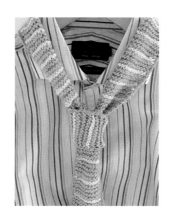

I choose yarns that not only meet
the pattern specifications and
express my color ideas, but are also
a real pleasure to knit with. I am
going to spend a good deal of time
handling a yarn, so it has to repay
that investment.

hands whenever I need a fix of fluffiness. I buy single balls of every color I find and use it as a treat when I need to be cheered up by its intrinsic silliness. The very best yarns are one hundred percent angora, which ensures the fluffy fibers stay upright and waft gently as you knit. Cheaper blends with nylon are just not the same because the fluff factor is reduced and the yarns flatten more easily.

I tend to use angora as a highlight yarn. When I think of angora garments, I think of little ballet-style wraparound cardigans, which are very sweet, but best in pink or white on pretty young girls. So I prefer to use less traditional colors and mix them with other yarns. Angora's fluffiness is heightened when it's next to smooth wool or silk, and I defy anyone not to rub their fingers on even the tiniest patch or stripe of angora.

Angora knits up quickly and easily on size 6 needles and it's a textural treat to handle. The only minor problem is that it can shed some fibers, which may leave you looking like a fluff ball. But a very soft and huggable fluff ball.

Wool: classic stuff

I began knitting seriously at the end of the 1970s, just in time to feel the full force of acrylic. I was seduced by the brilliant colors of the yarns made by French companies like Phildar and Pingouin, which knocked the traditional any-color-as-long-as-it's-not-tasteful English yarns (deservedly) into the shade. But what I didn't realize is that although acrylic is cheap, bright and washable, it's just not nice.

Knitting with one hundred percent acrylic can make your hands sweat, and this makes the yarn squeaky and hard to handle. It has a distinctive crunchy feel and it's a nightmare to break. It also melts in tumble dryers, as I discovered when, one evening in 1980, I pulled my prized hand-knit picture sweater out of a dryer and found that the arms were four feet long. Just as the yarn cooled and stayed that way, so did my love affair with acrylic.

I can still recall the subsequent delight of discovering the then-revolutionary yarns produced by Rowan, which was established in 1978. They were revolutionary because they took pure wool and made it beautiful, with beautiful yarns in beautiful colors that were beautiful to handle. It changed my whole perspective on knitting and color. No longer did I have to wrestle with synthetics and solid primary colors; I could now experiment with texture and nuanced shades.

For me, wool is the touchstone yarn. It's traditional, it's natural, it's classic, but it's also whatever you want it to be. There are wonderful tweedy, heathery yarns in the organic colors of the Scottish landscape with nubbly, slubby surfaces. There are elegant, sophisticated merino yarns in every shade you can imagine, cleverly spun to give lofty warmth and softness. Then there are hand-painted, strong, firm sock yarns, which knit into tight, insulating stitches. Or you can choose a basic, mid-weight, bread-and-butter DK wool, which wraps up heads, bodies, feet, hands, teapots and cushions in its warmth. Wool is what knitting is all about.

Linen: cool stuff

I've worn woven linen garments for years; their coolness, drape and washability more than compensate for the inevitable creases. Fortunately, linen is no longer regarded solely as a utilitarian fiber and is now imbued with a real sophistication. But I have only recently discovered linen knitting yarn.

I was looking for something light, durable, washable and natural to knit an apron (another story—see Practical, pages 120–1). It had to have plenty of yards to the skein so that it would hang well and not be dragged down by its own weight (for this reason cotton would be too heavy and wool too bulky). The idea of linen suddenly occurred to me as I thought of woven versus knitted fabrics. A few Google searches later, I had located some lovely Euroflax linen, spun in Belgium and shipped from the US (see Resources, page 282).

Knitting with linen yarn is a little like knitting with smooth string. There is none of the give or elasticity that makes knitting with wool so easy. All the time you have linen in your hands, you are aware of the tensile strength of the long, elegant fibers that twist into a continuous, smooth and crisp yarn. And the results are stunning, giving a cool, lightly open stitch and a fabulous surface texture that wears wonderfully and softens and improves with washing.

Silk: sybaritic stuff

In high school I once had to write an essay in Russian about my future. I pictured myself somewhere warm and sunny, lounging in a Hockney-esque swimming pool, sipping a cocktail. Well, a girl can dream. My teacher's comment, in Russian, was "What a sybarite." I made a dash for the dictionary to see whether this was a compliment and then laughed nervously. It was only

many years and plenty of silk, chocolate and wine later that I realized how perceptive my teacher had been.

Knitting with silk is as much about the process as the end result. It is texture for the sake of texture. Silk slips on and off the needles with incredible ease, and its strength, surface smoothness and plumpness make it wonderful to have in your hands. It's not easy to find one hundred percent silk yarns, and when you do, they come in tiny little lustrous, jewel-like skeins. Just unravelling them and winding the silk into a ball is an exotic, tactile experience.

If you do find some, keep it for small, luxury projects. The silk tie in Hockney swimming-pool blue and creamy white (pictured on page 73, below center) was knitted for Simon as a homage to my essay. It may not see much wear, but it certainly kept one Russian-speaking sybarite happy with her needles for a weekend.

Mohair: hairy stuff

Mohair, like big hair, had its heyday in the 1980s. It was favored by punks who wore baggy, hairy, black-and-blue striped sweaters, and by fashion victims in massive, ribbed cardigans made even bigger with shoulder pads. Ah, those were the days, when the words "mohair" and "subtlety" never met in the same sentence.

But mohair has changed, and so has its image. It is no longer regarded as a novelty or bad boys' choice, but as a seriously desirable luxury. Mohair's natural fuzziness comes into its own when paired with silk. The silk forms a strong, smooth core for the long, soft fibers and means that the yarn doesn't have to be bulky as well as hairy. The result is a luxuriant but whimsical yarn with amazing color possibilities. Mohair/silk looks as fabulous in jelly shades as it does in more subtle and natural colors. It can be knitted on its own in single or double strands or together with a second, smoother yarn such as pure wool. It gives anything from a fluffy, open, candy floss surface to a simple softening effect. And because it is so ethereally light, a little goes a long, long way.

Knitting with mohair is like handling a very supple, furry caterpillar. It almost tickles your fingers and makes you laugh. Mohair has come a long way since Sid Vicious.

In England, there are few baked treats that generate as much discussion of desirable texture as the humble flapjack. Since they are not expected to be the beauties of the baking parade, their texture, like their inner goodness, counts for much more than their looks.

I think flapjacks should be chewy and pliable, dense but not dry. They are, and should remain, a vehicle for oats and syrup, and the texture should reflect this basic truth. I don't hold with brittle, unyielding flapjacks, nor am I keen on fancy additions such as ginger, raisins, dried cherries or a covering of chocolate. Simon is something of a professional Flapjack Connoisseur, so I've had plenty of time to test my recipe over the years. Flapjacks are also great for children—no mess, no wrappers, excellent in lunch boxes or after school, and you can kid yourself that it's really the oats that count.

The fact that golden syrup is a key ingredient in much domestic baking may vex you if you live outside the UK. There is no substitute, no matter what other books and Google might say, and it is not the same as corn syrup or maple syrup. But the good news is that Lyle's Golden Syrup is more widely available than you may think, so please don't give up here.

If you do manage to find some, the cans make excellent containers for pens, pencils, crochet hooks, cable needles and stitch holders (see Inspiration, page 17, bottom right). The packaging is wonderfully old-fashioned and, on aesthetic grounds alone, I will not countenance the purchase of the recently introduced squeezy plastic bottles.

Chewy Flapjacks

Makes 12–16

INGREDIENTS
¾ cup unsalted butter
¾ cup brown sugar
1 rounded tablespoon golden syrup
1 cup and 2 teaspoons rolled oats

Preheat the oven to 300°F.

Lightly grease an 8"-square baking pan.

Place the butter, sugar and syrup in a large saucepan and heat gently until the butter melts, stirring with a wooden spoon to combine the ingredients. Remove from the heat, stir in the oats until well coated with the mix and tip into the baking pan. Gently press into place and smooth the surface with the back of a metal spoon.

The baking part is crucial. If you overcook them, flapjacks go crunchy. If you bake them in a coolish oven and check before the end of baking, you can achieve the right balance of chewiness and cookedness. So I bake mine for 40 to 45 minutes but check after 35 minutes to make sure they aren't browning too quickly. I take the pan out just as the edges are brown and the surface has turned golden.

Place the pan on a wire cooling rack. Cut into squares after about 10 minutes, but leave to cool completely before removing from the pan, otherwise you'll have collapsed flapjacks everywhere.

Offer to all Flapjack Connoisseurs, amateur or professional.

A world at our fingertips

I'm not a vain person, but I do like my hands. In fact, I am very proud of them. I like the way they knead dough, create stitches, hold yarn, thread needles, sort beads and buttons and deal with fiddly sewing-machine parts. Sometimes I watch them as if they don't quite belong to me and am secretly delighted when they seem to know what to do. They may not be able to play the piano, make lace or spin sugar, but most of the time, they do what I need them to do.

Hands are so vital to creativity that I can't understand why we value the more useless parts of our anatomy more highly. We have two huge black-and-white photographs by Tessa Traeger in the living room; one shows a pair of gnarled, tough, work-worn, soil-covered male hands gently cradling a freshly dug bulb of garlic, while the other features a pair of plump, smooth, clean, female hands holding a huge, circular loaf of bread on an aproned lap. I see these as my daily reminders of the beauty and brilliant design of the human hand.

Our hands play a huge role in active domesticity. We employ them to carry out harsh activities, such as scrubbing, scouring, washing, and we expose them to abrasive textures, corrosive cleaning chemicals, extremes of hot and cold. Yet these same hands are also our entrée into the kinder world of the gentle arts.

The gentle arts exploit the often overlooked, under-used cleverness and dexterity of our hands. They require close work and constant manipulation of materials. They demand precision and delicacy. They need a firm touch and a degree of confidence. In return, the gentle arts repay our hands' effort with innumerable tactile experiences, pleasures and memories. They allow us to indulge in wonderfully sensual, comforting and exciting textures. Softness, gentleness, warmth, coolness, strength and fragility are all at our fingertips when we knit and stitch and quilt and bake.

The art of the stitch

With his strange, quirky, exaggerated style, his eccentricity and his range of subjects, Stanley Spencer (1891 – 1959) is one of my very favorite artists. It took me a while to understand his appeal, but I realize that it lies in the fact that his vision is totally and unashamedly rooted in the domestic. No detail, no matter how humble or prosaic, is overlooked. There is no hierarchy, just an absorbing matter-of-factness about the objects of everyday life.

Even though he is famous for his huge, religious paintings, the wonderful war memorial at Burghclere, a monumental series on Glasgow shipbuilders and many potboiler landscapes, the fact remains that domestic detail permeates the whole of Spencer's oeuvre. Resurrection paintings are set in his home village of Cookham, wounded soldiers eat huge mounds of jam and bread and sleep under billowing sheets, the shipbuilders wear hand-knitted sweaters, and the potboilers are of the rolling hills of Berkshire, front and back gardens, greenhouses, bedding plants and climbing plants. Spencer underpins even his strangest and most unsettling works with a sense of ordinariness, and a reverence for unexceptional people and places.

Spencer also has a masterly way with texture. He uses a limited palette that concentrates on organic greens and blues and, especially, browns. It's as though he sees the world through sepia-tinted glasses but ones that are fitted with microscope lenses. He may use a muted palette, but he has a wonderfully heightened visual sensitivity to surfaces.

Hilda Welcomed (1953)

I know of no other artist who exploits the textures and colors of clothing and textiles the way Spencer does. His paintings are full of plump, bosomy women dressed in an amazing array of fabrics: spotted, striped, checked, floral, wavy, geometric, knitted, woven, furry, lacy. I am fascinated by the way he seems to make no distinction between upholstery and clothes, the way his well-padded, cozy women are virtually indistinguishable from the soft cushions and chairs and beds that also welcome and embrace. Just look at the surface textures of the knitted garments in *Hilda Welcomed*—the swirls, the bobbles, the entrelac, the Fair Isle, the ribbing and the rows. It's like an illustration for a book of knitting techniques and speaks of an artist living happily in the midst of women knitting for comfort and to create human upholstery.

The Woolshop (1939)

Spencer was in love with women and their bodies all his life. While other painters depict women in sumptuous, sexy or sophisticated clothes and position them high on a pedestal, Spencer obviously loved ordinary women who were not beauties and who wore hand-made, tweedy, durable, serviceable and, dare I say it, sensible garments and pursued the gentle arts of knitting and sewing, cooking and homemaking.

He was clearly in his element in a yarn shop, noticing how a customer hugs the yarn to her body, how it becomes almost a part of her clothing and her hair, so close is her communion with its softness. Every detail of the skeins, some with slubby details, others made up of wonderfully plump strands, can be discerned, and there is an underlying intimacy in this shop scene that evokes a very personal pleasure in touching and feeling.

Gardening (1945)

Gardening (pictured below) is a triumph of surface and textural detail. It doesn't matter that we can't see the faces of the two gardeners, for this is a painting that makes the viewer think about seeing and touching and noticing how things look and feel, such as the weave of a tweed jacket, the construction of a straw hat and basket, the texture of the clay soil, the ribbed stockings, the sturdy leather boots. It suggests a balance between humans and the natural world with a pleasure in being a part of the garden and taking on something of its earthiness. I am also very taken with the bright flowers on the woman's skirt—she'll be growing those for real when the summer comes.

Portrait of Eric Williams, MC (1954)

Virtually no other artist paints knitting and knitted stitches with the clarity and complexity that characterizes Spencer's approach. There are many socks and garments in the history of art, but the vast majority are highly simplified or stylized. When Spencer paints knitting, he does so with the same inclusiveness and faithfulness to surface reality that he applies equally to human flesh, brick walls or rusting iron girders.

Not only is he technically gifted, but his insistence on depicting the minutiae of a war hero's thick sweater adds layers of meaning to what could be a run-of-the-mill portrait. Spencer often paints his sitters in domestic settings, which makes them appear modern, approachable and ultimately ordinary, despite their fame or celebrated achievements. In this portrait, Eric Williams is depicted, without any loss of dignity, as a comfortable homebody in a hand-knitted sweater, whose hobby is making model yachts, and not an idealized, remote, military leader.

Portrait of Mr. and Mrs. Baggett (1956–7)

Mr. and Mrs. Baggett were the local businessman and his wife. Spencer paints them in the unpretentious setting of their own home, he on the telephone, and she knitting. It would seem to me that the imagery of this painting points to the fact that they are growing old together, that he is still the one in contact with the outside, masculine world of business, but will soon fall into the shadow of a new, more energetic generation of business. It is Mrs. Baggett with her meticulously observed knitting—every detail of the stockinette stitch, the ball of wool, the needles, the position of her hands and the hands themselves is startlingly clear—who is the one in charge. She makes direct eye contact, is engaged in actively creating something useful and comforting, and appears very much the pivot of their private home life.

If you are looking for a celebration of the domestic stitch in art, Stanley Spencer offers an exceptional vision of unexceptional domesticity. It is fitting that you can see many of his paintings in a small, converted chapel in his home village of Cookham, which has changed very little since he died. There is a lovely walk that takes in the church, the river, his house and many other places he painted. I go there to be reminded that the texture of domesticity is as valuable as that of the more exalted, external world of grand affairs, and often a great deal more interesting.

Edenic embroidery

I find I have to revise my expectations when it comes to embroidery. I am used to having bread that rises, knitting that grows, quilts that spread and tulips that expand. But the time-to-output ratio with stitching is very different.

Admittedly, I am not a particularly speedy wielder of the needle, but I am always surprised by how much time embroidery consumes. This is compounded by my choice of favorite stitches. I love stem stitch, blanket stitch, French knots and lazy daisies, all of which are either filling or fiddly. I also have a particular passion for satin stitch and can never resist running my finger over the smooth ridges it forms.

The close nature of embroidery and the demands it makes on your concentration force you to consider its texture. Decorative stitches are a manipulation of a surface that is changing under your hands as you add more stitches, more expression, more detail. It's instructive to consider that embroidery can even be explored and enjoyed with the eyes closed, so intricate and dense are its textures.

Despite memories of miserable needlework lessons and wonky chain stitch, I enjoy a little light hand-embroidery from time to time—usually in the summer when it is too hot to knit or quilt or bake. I generally choose garden subjects such as flowers and vegetables on an ultra-plain white or cream linen background. Indeed, craft and reality merge seamlessly, as there is nothing more gently satisfying than sitting in the garden on a summer's evening with a glass of wine, an embroidery hoop and a basket of brightly colored embroidery silks. Add to that the sound of Wimbledon tennis in the background, the scratching of hens under the table, the pinging of children on the trampoline, and I am pretty close to domestic heaven.

I don't design my own embroideries and prefer to follow simple instructions (see Resources, pages 280–1, for suggestions), and I enjoy smallish pieces that can be held in a medium-size hoop. One of the great pleasures of starting a piece of embroidery is the stretching of the fabric in the hoop to produce a stretched, drum-like surface through which a sharp needle can pass cleanly and then make a lovely echo with the thread. There is something deeply satisfying in the preparation of a taut tambourine of cloth and

the threading of a needle that makes a stitcher feel terribly accomplished before she has even begun.

Art Deco flowers

Simple, stylized, Art Deco flowers like the ones pictured opposite, top, give just enough scope for the selection of a few favorite stitches and colors. The satin stitch is, well, satiny and forms a silky contrast to the tiny bobbles of the French knots. The ladder-style ridges of the blanket stitch are like a mini-washboard, and your fingertips bounce up and down the rungs. Stem stitch works like a felt-tip marker, outlining and framing petals and leaves with an unbroken color.

Cottage garden piece

The little cottage garden pictured opposite, center, is from an earlier summer of embroidery. We had just moved to our house after six years abroad in various rented places, and I was happy to be planting my own vegetable garden in the ground instead of in pots. The frenzy of growing chard and zinnias, French beans and marigolds, inspired me to create a stitched version that, in the end, was far neater and more productive than the real thing. I spent many sunny evenings creating miniature cabbages with tightly furled bullion knots, cauliflower heads with creamy French knots, smooth satin-stitch radishes and wavy rhubarb leaves with buttonhole stitch. I even added a nasturtium-lined path like the one I'd seen in Monet's garden in Giverny. This little embroidered kitchen garden still acts as a reminder of the texture of that first summer back in England and the happy consciousness of domestic order being restored after years of moving house.

Compare and contrast

Sometimes the most interesting domestic textures are those that contain a contrast. Think of the pleasure of winding a soft, warm wool yarn around a cool, steely knitting needle, or running your finger over the tiny bumps of beads on a velvet handbag or the creamy richness of a crème brulée interior after you have splintered the glasslike toffee surface.

Baking and cooking, stitching and knitting allow the domestic artist to experiment with surface texture all the time. Indeed, there are whole books devoted to stitched surfaces and clever baking combinations— but I don't read them. And I think that's because so many of them don't know when to stop. They end up with layer upon layer, detail upon detail, ingredient upon ingredient, until the reader/maker is over-whelmed and confused.

Simplicity is one of my guiding precepts when it comes to contrasting textures. Let each one show off, but let them also work together to create a wonderful whole.

Which brings me to Lemon Meringue Pie.

Easy-Peasy-Lemon-Squeezy Meringue Pie

I hate overcolored, sticky, cornstarchy Lemon Meringue Pies on a base of grey pastry that has the consistency and taste of recycled cardboard. I dislike the way the gelatinous, gluey lemon layer acquires a life of its own and separates and slides away from its next-door neighbors. I think any layered confection should be greater than the sum of its parts; Lemon Meringue Pie should meld into a glorious combination of grainy, salty base, creamy, acid middle and billowy, sugary meringue.

I spent my teenage years making Lemon Meringue Pie from a packet. It was usually a case of add water and one egg yolk to make the tiniest, day-glo pie you have ever seen, which set like a dream and tasted of absolutely nothing. So I am thrilled with this recipe that gives both texture and taste, and wish I'd been able to use it in the days when I looked for any excuse (or, indeed, no excuse) to spoon condensed milk straight from the can. It may not be the stuff of fancy pastry shops, but it's the kind of Lemon Meringue Pie people really want to eat.

INGREDIENTS
9 ounces graham crackers
½ cup unsalted butter
4 large eggs
14 ounce-can condensed milk
juice of 4 to 5 lemons
8 tablespoons superfine sugar

Preheat the oven to 350°F.

Grease a 8" springform pan. Bash the crackers into fine crumbs. (I place them in a sealable plastic bag, put the bag on a hard surface or the kitchen floor and use a wooden rolling pin to break them up. Children will fight to do this.) Melt the butter in a saucepan, add the graham cracker crumbs and mix well until thoroughly coated. Press the mixture into the base of the pan, using the palms or the backs of hands to make an even surface. Put in the refrigerator to chill while you prepare the lemons and meringue.

Separate the eggs—yolks in one bowl, whites in another. In a third bowl combine the condensed milk with the lemon juice and whisk until smooth. It is essential that you mix the condensed milk and juice *before* adding the eggs; otherwise, horrible things happen. Add the yolks and whisk again to combine. Set aside.

Beat the egg whites until soft peaks form. Gradually add the sugar until the mixture is firm and glossy.

Now assemble the pie. Pour the lemon mixture onto the cracker base and then gently scoop the meringue on top. A spatula is useful for this, as it helps to spread the meringue without pressing down too hard.

Bake for 30 to 40 minutes until the meringue has a golden surface. Leave to cool before releasing from the pan. This pie should be eaten when completely cold and, although it's excellent on the day of making, it will still be good the following day. It is particularly delicious eaten directly from the refrigerator as you straighten up the pie edges (our excuse for fridge-picking).

A special relationship

We should recognize beauty in all its forms, and there is beauty everywhere in domesticity. It's just that we don't always see it. But one of the great benefits of practicing the gentle arts is the opportunity to allow the mind to wander while the hands are occupied with chopping and mixing, knitting, quilting and stitching. Do you think the heroines of Jane Austen's novels were simply counting stitches while they worked? Oh, no, they took these chances to plot love affairs, consider suitors and plan their next moves.

While we may not all have such a vivid agenda while we knit or sew or cook, I find that it's possible at these moments to make connections between surfaces and colors never previously noticed, to see what I like to call "Special Relationships."

I love red onions with their matte, wine-stained color and smooth, papery surface that peels off to reveal a glossy, carmine interior. When I see them on the chopping board, they make me think of the richly colored Manos yarn from Uruguay pictured above, center right. The match is perfect, with even the striations of the onion mirrored in the yarn. And look at the way the textures hold the colors, even though one is firm and layered and the other bulky and soft.

As I prepare Granny Smith apples for an apple tart, I see the same hue of light acid green that drew me to an Artworks silk and mohair yarn (see above, far right). The light bounces off the smooth, waxy skin of the apple in the same way it is reflected off the lustrous silk of the yarn, while the fluffy mohair makes you want to pick up the ball of yarn and cradle it in your palm, just as you do with an apple. And I can't help but notice that the soft fiber has a dimple—just like the fruit.

A long, unwound skein of hand-painted Fleece Artist sock yarn could have taken its inspiration from plums and passion fruits (see above, far left and center left). At one end there is a pale, bluish bloom that matches the surface of a ripe, purple plum perfectly. At the other there are wonderful hints of the pinks and browns and gold of passion fruits, and both fruit and yarn have a crinkly, dry texture.

Red grapefruits, with their lightly pitted, warm pink, coral and gold skins, are the organic version of the Koigu yarn pictured opposite, which even has the same little dark flecks. They look equally delicious and delectable in a fruit bowl.

If we can see them, these connections and layers of texture, surface interest and color enrich our visual and tactile lives with simple touches of beauty. Special Relationships are as important to us as they are to the political world. And a lot more reassuring.

Patterns

Patterning domesticity

As I get older, I find I discern and observe more and more patterns. I don't mean knitting, crochet, sewing and fabric patterns, although these are an integral part of the gentle arts. No, what I mean are the patterns that aren't always obvious, the patterns that are over-laid by, or hidden within, the general chaos of busy domestic life. They are patterns that we take for granted and too often fail to see, patterns that underpin our visual lives but are seldom recognized.

Domesticity requires a measure of patterning and order, structure and routine, for it to function smoothly. Unless we are happy to live in squalor, we accept that we must do certain things to maintain a pleasant domestic environment: clean, cook, wash, tidy, vacuum, shop, decorate, renew and so on. We can choose to fight the tyranny, as we might see it, or we can learn to manage it. I have found that the only way to prevent an accumulation of resentment is to break down the overwhelming barrage of must-dos into regular patterns of activity. So I accept that there are internal house rhythms and have created daily, weekly, seasonal domestic patterns that are now (almost) second nature.

I think we have to impose these overt patterns on our lives in order to support our less predictable, more impulsive and covert creative activities. We need them to form the foundation, the rock, of our existence, and yet they need not all be life-sapping, mind-numbing or dreary. Indeed, stopping to notice humdrum patterns and rhythms and allowing them to enter our thinking can in fact lead to wonderfully creative, imaginative processes that expand our apparently circumscribed, domestic existences.

The patterns of daily, domestic life can be found mirrored in the gentle arts. All require repeated physical actions and an acceptance that doing things yourself is not always quick and easy. But they also have huge potential for satisfaction, self-expression and freedom. This chapter explores the ideas of patterns in domesticity. Patterns for making, patterns within patterns and, ultimately, patterns for living.

When it's hip to be square

Sometimes a pattern seeps into my subconscious and I find myself working with it in different media without even thinking. (Apropos of which, I think it is high time we classed cake-and-icing as a medium of creative expression just like other three-dimensional materials such as wood, stone, marble, clay and metal.)

When I was starting this Blue Breeze Quilt, I cut out a pile of squares from a range of blue fabrics, some of which have touches of yellowy or limey green. Tom, my Quilting Apprentice, saw the squares and made some very deprecatory remarks about my latest choices and tastes. He was skeptical, to say the least, and unconvinced that they would work. So we decided to see who was right.

Instead of agonizing about placement, we kept to a simple pattern of nonrepeating squares and placed them almost unthinkingly on the floor, both of us putting squares down as quickly as we do when playing a game of Slapjack! Then we stood up and stood back, and Tom admitted the result wasn't bad for a first play session.

Patterns with squares appeal enormously. Squares are neat and tidy, each one has exactly the same restrictions of size, angles and space, and yet they have huge potential for the exploration of pattern. They can be used as a formal template with a rigid, unvarying repeat, like a chessboard, which makes your eyes move metronomically, to a set beat, from square

to square. Or you can scatter them more informally and invite your eyes to dart over the surface looking for links and rhythms as they try to work out the underlying composition.

Squares work equally well when they are based on a two-color pattern or when there are masses of little squares full of riotous color. They can contain many tiny details, or frame a single flower. The joy of squares, the one I see in the start of this quilt, is that their simplicity and formality can be exploited to bring together seemingly disparate and chaotic patterns into a pleasing whole.

I think I'll pursue this quilt despite the reservations of my QA, who was, in any case, far more interested in the square dance of cupcakes I baked on the same day. He hovered, as he always does, when I made the icing with lemon juice, waiting for the lovely moment of bowl-licking. It was only after I'd put the cupcakes out in a square formation on the wire rack, and later on a matching cake stand, that I realized I was mimicking not only the square pattern of the quilt, but also the quilt colors. I didn't deliberately choose the sky blue and pale green, they simply presented themselves to me as I picked out jelly beans and food coloring.

I like the coolness and freshness of these colors, and the way the squares work to form an informal blue breeze. In fact, I'm beginning to think that squares may not be so square after all.

Gestation

When I was little I was fascinated by the gestation periods of different animals and surprised at how wildly the patterns varied from species to species. I could easily understand why a mouse might emerge, ready to face the world of cheese and moldings, after a mere 21 days, but I couldn't quite see what a baby elephant could possibly be doing for 650 days inside its mother. And when it was born after all that time, it still couldn't even speak or read.

I am still bewildered by gestation patterns, but these days I tend to think of them in the context of my own creative projects. Why, for example, does it take me nearly 365 days from the idea, the conception, of a pair of cabled socks to actually start knitting them? And then why can the secondary gestation period of a sock, i.e., the time required on the needles to bring it into fully formed being, take anything from two days to two months, so that I'm like a kangaroo with a joey in her pouch but never knowing when it will be able to hop off on its own?

The longest textile gestation period I have ever endured was that of my first quilt. I bought my first quilting book, *Glorious Patchwork* by Kaffe Fassett and Liza Prior Lucy, in 1999, but didn't get around to making a quilt until 2004. That's five years, which beats the whale (500 days) and the rhinoceros (450 days) hands down. Since then I've managed to reduce my quilt gestation periods to anything from 185 days (baboon) to 110 days (chinchilla).

The reason for these unpredictable patterns is that I like to turn ideas over in my mind before starting something new. When I was thinking of my first ripple blanket, I thought about crochet, bought a book about crochet, tried to teach myself crochet, cried over my inability to crochet, went to a crochet workshop, bought a crochet pattern book, thought a little more about crochet, and then finally went and bought some yarn. Even then, at the book, hook and yarn stage of the gestation pattern, I could have stalled while I did a little further planning, but this time I made a deal with myself that it would take no longer than 28 days (muskrat) and that it would be on time (like Phoebe after 280 days).

It is all too easy to announce, if only to myself, the impending arrival of a creation, only to let it gestate well beyond its due date. So I try to set realistic targets that won't interfere with the normal patterns of domestic life (much as I would like to spend all day making wavy crochet blankets or knitting spotty cushions, it's not going to happen) and thus get things done. Every creative project has its own organic rhythms and patterns that are not clear until you begin to tackle them. It's something the mother mouse and the mother elephant accept with equanimity and so, therefore, should I.

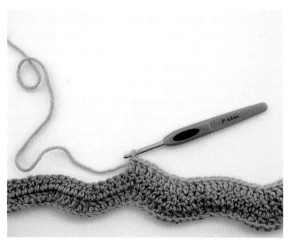

Simple stitches

The simplicity of basic sewing stitches is deceptive. Even with running stitch or cross-stitch one can create all sorts of effects and textures just by using a variety of regular patterns and plenty of colors.

When I say I like cross-stitch, I really mean that I like it when someone else has done it. When I was in my late twenties, I had a major operation to improve my slim chances of having children. This entailed an extended period on a sickbed like Elizabeth Barrett Browning, but without the poetry (and opium) to keep me occupied. I decided that a modest cross-stitch project was required, and I found what I thought was the perfect fusion of pattern and form—a vegetable sampler.

Well, I cannot tell you how great the gap was between my desire to complete this and my ability to do so. I have never been so infuriated by squares and holes in my life. I would look at the pattern one second, transfer my eyes to the fabric the next and, hey presto, the placement would vanish, and I could not for the life of me remember where the next stitch went. I struggled for a while with the cabbages, peas and radishes, and very pretty they were, but as soon as I was on my feet again, they all went in the drawer. I attribute my subsequent fertility to this unfinished pattern, as I never wanted to go back into the hospital to complete it.

In keeping with my passive approach to cross-stitch, I showed Phoebe how to stitch simple patterns when she was younger, and she made this fabulous sampler of running stitches. She chose sweet colors of cotton embroidery thread and happily joined the dots. This stitching is like structured doodling and is a lovely way for her to explore her creativity in simple textiles. While I recline on my chaise-longue and read exquisitely patterned sonnets.

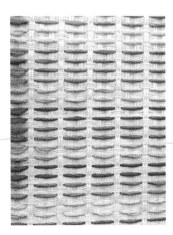

Odes to domesticity

Poems are patterns that fit into pockets of the mind. A poem can be carried around for years like loose change, scarcely noticed until the day you chance upon it again when you need or want to see the world a little differently.

I have accumulated all sorts of poems and poets over the years. I have my own personal "rattle bag," to borrow the title of a classic anthology by Seamus Heaney and Ted Hughes. Elizabeth Barrett Browning and Lord Byron are jumbled up with W. H. Auden and Rupert Brooke. There are poems by Elizabeth Bishop, Christina Rossetti, Walt Whitman and Frances Cornford. I have a magpie eye for pieces of silver by W. B. Yeats, Philip Larkin and Edward Thomas, and in my deeper pockets I store gold nuggets by Shakespeare, Donne and Milton.

If I see a poem I like, I pick it up and pocket it. It doesn't have to be grand or epic or serious or improving, but it does need to contain a flash of illumination, wisdom, humor or a spellbinding image. In fact, the more I look over my store of poems, the more I see that it is the poetry of the ordinary and the domestic that stays in my mind.

I admire the economy of poetry, the way that patterns and rhythms can be exploited to create ripples of meaning that go far beyond the confines of the structure. I like the way devices such as alliteration, assonance and rhyme can support and enhance meaning. I enjoy the closed forms of poetry with specific designs and patterns, and I also love exploring free verse that is deceptively open and yet contains some sort of organic structure.

Domesticity, ordinary life and simple pleasures are perfectly at home in poetry, and I think all domestic artists should have a little pocket in their aprons where they can keep their favorite poems. The poems that cheer you up and make you laugh, the poems that make you cry while you are laughing, the ones that help you to see the beauty in the ephemeral, the ones that make you look differently at socks (Pablo Neruda), cherry trees (A. E. Housman), dappled things (Gerard Manley Hopkins), sowing seeds (Robert Frost) and cold plums (William Carlos Williams). If you have time to pocket only one, make it Pablo Neruda's "Ode to Things" in which he praises "every little thing," like buttons, knives, scissors, cups, hats and thimbles that "bear the trace of someone's fingers." Better still, read this poem and more in *Odes to Common Things* (1994) and revel in the poetry of the tomato, the gillyflower, the onion, the chair and the table.

There should be another pocket for poems that show us just how much pleasure and happiness can be found in the metaphorical patterns, rhythms and repetitions of daily life. In "The Orange," Wendy Cope writes about "peace and contentment" that can accompany "ordinary things," and takes this enjoyment of the undramatic further in "Being Boring," a wonderfully funny celebration of domestic stability in which she declares "I've just one ambition in life: I aspire / To go on and on being boring."

Poems on domestic themes reflect and enhance patterns of ordinary life and should be seen as valuable currency. I am quite sure most people could shake the pockets of their minds and find that some favorite poems fall out. As with small coins, they could all add up to something when you sit down and count them.

Binary systems

I have a thing about Fair Isle knitting. For me, it's the ultimate, the apex, the apogee of color knitting. It is the reason I learned to knit; I longed to use heaps of colors to create clever patterns on traditional tam o'shanters, pullovers, gloves and cardigans.

Not long after I mastered Fair Isle, I knitted a vest for my boyfriend's twenty-first birthday. I used heathery colors and a classic pattern, and knitted with love and devotion. I even insisted on knitting it when I was hospitalized in France, and acquired a reputation with the nurses who checked the progress of what *l'Anglaise* was doing with all those charts and balls of yarn more frequently than her medical condition.

Of course, there is a sad coda to my Fair Isle story. Soon after his birthday the boyfriend went off with a drama student in a big, black mohair number and I never saw my creation again. I then left for a miserable year of teacher training and buried my sorrow in creating a pink, fluffy, cabled, Patricia Roberts sweater which, needless to say, I never wore.

But my love for Fair Isle never left me, although it has dimmed from time to time. I knitted some tiny Fair Isle cardigans and sweaters for the children, and then almost forgot about it. My passion was rekindled when I started knitting a Fair Isle vest last year, and found I was quite happy to go back to knitting old-fashioned patterns rather than seeking out contemporary variations.

The thing about Fair Isle is that traditional is best. You simply cannot improve on the stunning patterns set out by the many generations of earlier knitters. All the original patterns, the ones I like best, are based on an OXO pattern—two basic lozenge shapes on either side of a cross—on background bands of color. Then there are peeries, borders, fillers and seeding in between the main bands. In all of this there is only one golden rule: that no more than two colors can ever be used in a row. Amazingly, these restrictions give rise to the most incredible range of creative and clever interpretations.

I also think that natural colors are the best. In fact, the most effective colors are those that come from the Scottish islands themselves: sea and sky blues, heathery pinks and purples, rowanberry oranges, lichen yellows, cloud greys, peaty browns, leaf russets and reds, wildflower lilacs and maroons, autumnal yellows and ambers. It's incredible when you see examples of excellent, skilled Fair Isle work with their brilliantly modulated gradations of colors and the way in which the symmetrical patterns stand out.

I am of the generation that was taught the binary system ad nauseam in math class at school. I hated all its zeros and ones, but now realize this is the essence of the Fair Isle OXO and the two-color rule. It also amuses me that printed Fair Isle patterns look like early computer programs—these being the very reason we were taught the maddening binary system. Obviously, educationalists thought we were all heading for a brave, new world of room-sized, card-fed computers. They didn't think some of us would be traveling backwards to an earlier, happier, binary system.

Men at patchwork

Down by the river near where we live there is a large patchwork of flat, windswept land that is covered with intricate patterns of rows and strips and squares and rectangles. The blocks are all different colors—reds, purples, whites, yellows, oranges—and the borders and background are many shades of green. There are deep brown lines that crisscross and intersect the whole and, occasionally, a person moves around the neat fabric like a needle, drawing it all together.

I go to look at the local allotments in the spring and summer, but find they are at their most glorious in late August and September, when there are wonderful shows of beans and sunflowers, tomatoes and dahlias, all beautifully laid out to form a magnificent quilt of fruit, vegetables and flowers. As I wander around, I fantasize about the perfect kitchen garden and dream of colorful, witty and delicious combinations and patterns. But, for the moment, I am content to look and dream until I have the time to do it properly.

The allotment culture intrigues me. Although there are exceptions to the rule, I see that the majority of allotment-holders (and kitchen gardeners and prize vegetable-growers) are men, that allotments are still a quintessentially male environment and that, as such, there is something quite unique within them.

I know that many women love their vegetable plots and patches and share in the maintenance of allotments, but I am fascinated by the masculine approach to this type of structured, planned gardening. These sometimes gruff, sometimes taciturn, sometimes burly men create the most wonderful living patchworks full of color and texture, humor and surprise. In fact, as you can see in David Inshaw's *Allotments* (1987–8), pictured opposite, they tend their territory with a devotion to fine detail that matches that of women's patchwork and quilting.

In early autumn you can see the full patchwork effect of the testosterone-fueled planning, measuring, sowing, planting and growing. The nurture of a giant, organic quilt seems to me to be suffused with a tenderness and thoughtfulness similar to that of the patchworker, who is simply using different materials, and working indoors. It's in autumn that the spaces are filled, the colors emerge, the master plan is on full show and the garden quilt is finally arranged.

Just as a quilter takes her basic layout with squares, strips, diamonds, hexagons and triangles, so too the allotment-holder works on his rectangular space and, over the course of a season, colors in the blocks and sections with patterns and metaphorical stitches.

The ultimate masculine patchwork for me is at Villandry in France. When we visited the garden there years ago, I was amazed, amused and inspired by its intricacy and the imaginative use of cabbages. It was the first time I had appreciated the visual artistry of vegetable growing, the juxtapositions of shapes and colors and cultivars that I had only ever considered in isolation, and the sheer vivacity that could be contained within a rigid structure. I want to go back, this time with quilter's eyes, for new ideas and inspiration.

But, instead of waiting for this to happen, I decided to put my memories of Villandry into a quilt.

Just as a quilter takes her basic layout with squares, strips, diamonds, hexagons and triangles, so too the allotment-holder works on his rectangular space and, over the course of a season, colors in the blocks and sections with patterns and metaphorical stitches.

Villandry Quilt

I feel I am something of a quilting outsider. I wanted to make quilts for years, but something held me back, and now I can see that it was a fear of not doing it correctly. I could understand that quilts were simply fabrics cut up and stitched together in beautiful arrangements, but beyond that I also saw rules and methods and how-tos and all sorts of trip wires. Quilting was a minefield as far as I could see, and I was terrified of stepping on an unexploded bomb of mitered corners and seam allowances and insertions and foundation piecing. But then I encountered the Kaffe Phenomenon. The Man at Patchwork for real.

Kaffe Fassett is a human whirlwind. He creates his own vortex wherever he goes, and you can't help but be sucked in by his energy and vision, charm and humor. I first heard him speak when I skipped work one afternoon in the late 1980s to attend his talk about knitting and color at the Institute of Contemporary Art in London. It was the most productive hour of truancy in my life, and I learned more in those sixty minutes than I ever would in sixty lectures on the color wheel.

Fast forward ten years, and I still hadn't made a quilt, but I discovered with joy that Kaffe was now shaking up the patchwork branch of the gentle arts with his messages of color, fun, experimentation and, importantly, his refrain of "just do it," in beautiful, technicolor books written with the clever, talented and witty Liza Prior Lucy. The books became the catalysts for my first hesitant steps on the quilting minefield, and to my amazement all is now reassuringly, happily, quiet and productive on the patchwork front.

Not long ago I went to a workshop run by Kaffe and Liza at the Festival of Quilts in Birmingham. At the same event, I heard him talk about what inspires him. When he spoke about the way he sees the world, he explained that he is constantly aware of a "ballet of color" taking place before his eyes. He notices all kinds of combinations, both fleeting and static, but it was the idea of movement in color that caught my attention.

It all makes sense when you see his quilts, in which he captures those evanescent moments in fabric. Instead of having a scene that moves before your eyes, it's your eyes that dance over the immobile quilt and, if you look carefully, you can see that the colors and patterns are performing *pliés, jetés, pas de deux* and *pirouettes.*

It is exactly this that is happening in allotments and kitchen gardens. The beanpoles could be ballet dancers, their arms and legs curving away from them in shoots and tendrils with frilly tutus of leaves and flowers, their fingers like pods, outstretched and elegant. The cabbages are the footlights and the sunflowers the spotlights, the rows of dahlias the *corps de ballet* and the little marigolds the sweet, round-faced young dancers. I wondered whether it would ever be possible to pin these movements down in a quilt—and the Villandry Quilt is the result of these musings.

The quilt design we began at the workshop is called Potpourri. It's an amazing piece of floral flamboyance and works very simply using just three different size squares. You take fabrics of a similar tone to create a huge display that should merge and move the eye without any breaks or obvious lines. It's built up in three columns but, because the squares are so cleverly placed, it appears far more complex than it really is, and you don't notice the joins.

So I cut up squares and played with the flowers while Kaffe and Liza moved around offering encouragement and advice. And then came the best part. I have to tell you that this wonderfully whimsical but completely appropriate border was Kaffe's suggestion. Until then my quilt had been a bower of flowers, a cottage garden extravaganza, a blooming profusion. But Kaffe held up a strip of turnips next to my layout and, abracadabra, the whole quilt was transformed. The memory of Villandry with its exultation of humble root vegetables, leapt into my mind, and we agreed that was exactly what the quilt should be called.

Once the top was made, I decided to make the reverse side with the strips of leftover rows of vegetables (pretty peas, carrots, tomatoes and sprouts) and use it with wider pieces of a wild flower-basket design. Thus, I have my ornamental Villandry quilt on one side and a simple, domestic allotment on the other. I can't think of anything more tasteful for a permanent interpretation of horticultural patchwork inspired by real and metaphorical men at work.

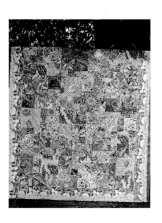

Round in circles

I sometimes find myself going round in circles. One week comes around after the next with another revolution of days. I make circular cookies for the children to recycle into energy and good humor when they come home on a Friday. I sew buttons onto school shirts. I peel apples for a tart. I wind yarns into soft balls. I peer into cups of tea and pry open cans of golden syrup.

And I am hypnotized by knitting socks. Once a sock has been cast on to five double-pointed needles, I adore the mindlessness of going round and round like a hamster in a wheel. I use self-striping yarns, which are cleverly and mathematically calculated to form even circles of color without any effort on my part. (The socks in the photo below, modeled by a muddy-kneed, post-rugby-match Tom, are knitted with Regia Canadian color #4733.) Much of the fun comes from seeing new stripe after new stripe begin, so that after a while this simple knitting becomes a stack of brightly colored hula hoops.

The only way to knit a sock in the round is to keep coming back to your starting point. But, almost imperceptibly, progress is made. It's a pattern, yes, but it's not really a circle, it's a spiral and all the stitches and rows, like days and weeks, are linked to form an unbroken chain. We can think we are getting nowhere with the cyclical nature of domesticity, and yet all the time, as with sock-knitting, we are moving on to a new stitch or a new day and then, suddenly, a whole new row or color or, as in Tom's case, a new shoe size.

To see the world in a sock is probably more than is strictly necessary, but it shows what your mind can do when you observe patterns. Plus, and this is the big bonus, you can watch Cary Grant while your hands knit philosophy.

Circular Recycling; or, Back-from-School Cookies

This is a recipe I've been using since university without any modifications.

Oaty Vanilla Cookies

Makes about 14

INGREDIENTS
½ cup soft unsalted butter
⅓ cup superfine sugar
1 teaspoon vanilla extract
1 teaspoon golden syrup
1 tablespoon boiling water
¼ cup rolled oats
½ cup self-rising flour
½ teaspoon baking powder

Preheat the oven to 375°F.

Line a large baking sheet with parchment paper.

Cream the butter and sugar together until pale. Add the liquid ingredients and mix, then add the dry ingredients and combine to form a dough. Do not overwork. Quickly shape the sticky dough into balls, place well apart on the baking sheet and flatten slightly with your fingers.

Bake for 10–12 minutes until pale gold and delicious-smelling. If you bake them slightly longer, the biscuits will be dark and crispy rather than chewy. We like ours chewy.

For best results, serve as soon as they have cooled.

Twinkletoes

Phoebe has been taking ballet lessons since she was three. That's a lot of repetition and rehearsal. She's been through years of curtseying, scarf-waving and general twirling and swirling. Over time, with all the positions and movements now mastered, she has become an accomplished, graceful and smiley dancer. She has poise and confidence, so that not only can she dress up in a girly dream of an outfit, she can do the right stuff when wearing it.

When I asked her to model the socks I knitted for her (in Regia Canadian color #4732) she automatically followed the pattern of first to fifth position with her feet. Just as I cast on, knit, turn a heel, knit, shape and cast off, so she goes through the necessary motions with ballet. She imbues her patterns with movement and energy and exuberance. It always makes me think I should do the same with the socks I knit for her. So, for Phoebe Twinkletoes, I always choose bright, vibrant yarns in extrovert, lively colors that dance on my needles and dance on her feet.

The sock-Knitter

I go through patterns of sock-knitting. I knit the odd one, literally, then maybe a pair, and then, metaphorically, I go barefoot for a while until I come back to pick up my double-pointed needles once again. Every time I cast on a sock, I never know where it is going to take me. There may be a metaphor in creating something for the feet that in turn inspires all kinds of mind wanderings, or it may be that the Zen "beginner's mind" works perfectly with socks so that I am just there, observing and seeing what occurs. For every time I do knit socks, some new pattern of thought emerges.

Sometimes knitting allows you to observe not only your hands, but also yourself. Knitting is sedentary and quiet, but sock-knitting is even more reined-in and controlled. Knitting socks brings your hands close together and your elbows to your sides while only your fingers move in flicking, spidery actions that appear incomprehensible to the uninitiated.

But there is a pattern to all sock-knitters when they are observed. The sock-knitter presents a compact figure; her head is bent, her wrists are raised to create a lovely angle at the elbow, her eyes look down as she focuses on the tiny stitches and the memorized pattern. She is a wonderful subject for painters who can exploit her profile and the beautiful curves of the slightly tilted head and the rounded shoulders.

I like to think I knit with the self-containment and absorption of Grace Cossington Smith's sister who was the sitter in the iconic Australian painting *The Sock Knitter* (1915), pictured above. I admire her upright position and her concentration (she could be knitting on a train or in a waiting room) and the way the painting captures her isolation, physical and mental, as she knits socks for soldiers.

But, in reality, I am more of a Daisy-style sock-knitter, in a comfortable armchair, near a deep windowsill and with a faraway look. Edgar Holloway was a key figure in the revival of etching in the 1920s and 1930s, and the soft, blurred lines of his picture *Daisy Knitting* (1943), shown below, seem to suggest that although Daisy is physically present, she cannot be captured fully as her mind is freed by the gentle, meditative rhythms of her knitting.

James Jebusa Shannon (1862–1923) is not a well-known painter, but then I often find more of interest in a second-rate artist happy to capture simple domestic scenes than more highly regarded painters who strive to impress with grander subjects. Thus, for me, *The Purple Stocking*, pictured opposite, is quite charming. The control of the palette with its beautiful lilacs and plums and purples, the touch of gold and the pink of the cheeks, all make a beautiful, luminous composition. The girl looks so fresh and young, yet calm and confident with her knitting. It must be no coincidence that she appears to have a halo around her head. The modern domestic angel knits socks, it says, and not in dreary drudgery, but with a spirit of bohemian beauty and independence. Now, that's a thought I am happy to knit into my next sock pattern.

The "diurnal round"

In winter we go ice-skating on an outdoor rink. I can only skate in a smooth oval, and wonder why I like it so much when it's hardly as though I can do any fancy twirls and twizzles. I realize that I thoroughly enjoy the repeated, gentle pushing and gliding that propels me forward, even though I can barely feel the wind through my hair. I think that's why I like the part in *The Prelude* when Wordsworth describes his boyhood ice-skating. It helped me to understand that we can choose to be a part of, or apart from, this kind of repetition, because no matter what we do, the world will still keep on spinning. This is described beautifully by Wordsworth; although he stays with the crowd at first, "All shod with steel/We hissed along the polished ice," he later goes off on his own and then stops short and realizes that "yet still the solitary cliffs/Wheeled by me—even as if the earth had rolled/With visible motion her diurnal round!"*

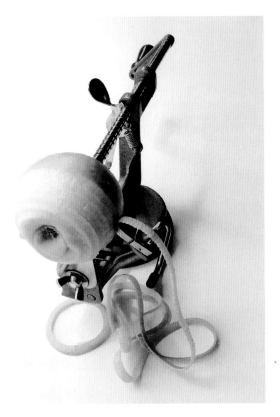

The world of domesticity is a microcosm with its own, inescapable "diurnal round," and a great part of the gentle art of domesticity is an acceptance and then a valuing of repetition. Although I admit that I'll never be thrilled with many aspects of repetitive housework, I have discovered some more pleasurable domestic patterns that, like the hypnotic ice-skating, I am more than happy to repeat.

Every project or creation has its own mode of repetition sandwiched in between the excitement of starting and the delight in finishing. This is the part that offers an often therapeutic and blissful zoning-out during which your mind can wander with your hands "till all [is] tranquil as a dreamless sleep." The mental comfort that comes with leaving "the tumultuous throng" occurs with the repetitive patterns of activities such as crochet, knitting, quilting, kneading dough, icing cakes, planting bulbs, sowing seeds.

Although I love the rush of enthusiasm at the beginning of something new, there is a lot to be said for gentle routine. It's a little like getting back to normal after the highs of the holidays. You know the routine has to be followed or nothing will be accomplished, and so, gradually, you begin to enjoy the regularity of cables, the movement up and down the needles with simple stockinette stitch, the simplicity of the line after line of running stitch when quilting, the measuring and cutting of fabric pieces for patchwork.

Soon enough, all the tasks will be finished with a touch of euphoria. And I think that's another reason why I do manage to finish most of the things I start: I love the repetition of the joy of completion.

* All the quotes are from Book I (lines 425–62) of *The Prelude* (1850) by William Wordsworth.

Sunshine After the Rain Quilt

Generally, I prefer to make simple, basic quilts that allow me to exploit color and fabric. But every so often I step outside my usual pattern of thinking and make a quilt using a very traditional design. There is something immensely gratifying in working with a template that has been interpreted so many times, and in so many ways, by generations of women.

Ever since quilts first attracted my attention about ten years ago I have been fascinated by log cabin quilts. I love the games you can play with the blocks and the endless permutations of pattern. I also like the fact that each block represents a home built out of logs and with a fire or hearth at its center (traditionally, the center square is red). Thus a log cabin quilt makes up a whole community of cabins or homes in a pleasing fusion of creativity and domesticity.

When I start making a quilt, I usually begin with a lead fabric. This is a love-at-first-sight fabric, one I know I have to use as the basis for a whole quilt. From that starting point, and over a period of time, I build up a range of fabrics that I think will work well with it. In this case, it was a fabric called Daisy Bouquet in putty by Denyse Schmidt. It's a yellow and white floral on a grey background, and I decided to enhance the effect by making one half of each block grey and one half yellow. I wanted to keep to tradition and have a hearth and chose a brilliant, fiery orange for the central squares.

As I collected the fabrics, I thought of the yellow and grey as the sunshine and rain and then included a few patches of sky blue breaking through the clouds. In England, we have to live with a constant pattern of sunshine and rain year-round, and while I was sewing, the weather complemented the quilt. It was dull, grey and cloudy while I machine-sewed, and bright and sunny while I hand-quilted.

Initially I had no plan for putting the blocks together; I simply made forty-nine different versions in a mini production line. But when Tom and I placed the blocks, we saw that rays of yellow sunshine alternating with grey diagonals of slanting rain looked just right. Tom was the one who moved individual blocks until it all clicked. This is his favorite quilt, and I'm sure it's because of all the geometrics, patterns and optical illusions.

Just as night comes after day and sunshine after rain, so a log cabin comes to every quilter. You can't argue with cosmic patterns.

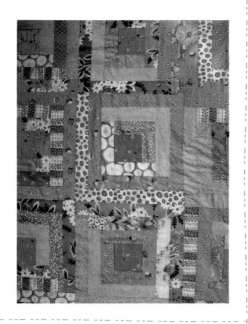

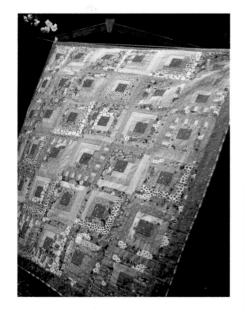

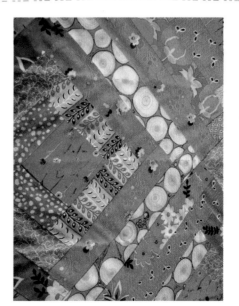

Practical

Life skills

The gentle art of domesticity is the felicitous application of practical skills to the spaces in which we live. It requires a desire to make instead of consume, a triumph of activity over passivity and a return to using our hands and imaginations rather than a reliance on screens and technology. It's part of that wonderful, traditional, often undervalued skill of making our own entertainment—something we are wont to consign erroneously to the dim and distant past of radio, board games, jigsaw puzzles and, dread word, hobbies.

Just as many aspects of domesticity are often derided as old-fashioned, quaint or downright useless, so the skills and practicalities associated with it have fallen out of fashion. Despite the efforts of many contemporary knitters, quilters, stitchers, crocheters, crafters and bakers, the fact remains that the gentle arts are frequently regarded as mildly eccentric, touch-ingly nostalgic and outmoded. Why on earth would anyone prefer to hand-stitch a quilt when you can buy a perfectly good one in a shop? Why knit a pair of socks when they are so easy and cheap to buy these days? Why bake a cake when the store shelves are groaning with ready-made treats?

The answer lies in the not-so-revolutionary idea of seizing the means of production. It's as simple and as complex as that. A modicum of practicality in the domestic space empowers us to make our own choices about what we create and eat, rather than handing over control of our homemaking to profit-making companies. It may sound surprisingly radical, and it is. Embedded in the gentle arts is a slyly subversive streak that encourages free thought, individuality, creative self-expression, imaginative thought processes and not a little self-determinism. All this, and a great deal of pleasure, too.

Kit and caboodle

I do like a nice bit of kit; owning good materials, tools and equipment is one of the pleasures of the gentle arts. But, unlike with some interests, it is not absolutely essential to have a full workbench or palette or toolbox in order to knit and stitch and bake. I sometimes feel that there is huge marketing pressure to buy every single tailor-made item for a certain craft, when in fact a make-do approach can be far more economical, satisfying and, let's face it, creative.

A domestic artist can build up a collection of kit and caboodle over time. There is no rush, and plenty of time to savor each little addition. A spool of cotton here, a handful of old buttons there, a vial of glass beads when you stumble upon the right color. I see that the caboodles I have accumulated organically over the years are much more pleasing and idiosyncratic than any bulk-bought collection.

I enjoy choosing the right color yarn or embroidery or quilting thread as I need it, and this approach necessitates regular trips to haberdasheries, yarn stores, fabric emporia and other suppliers in order to build up a good range. But it's hardly a chore, and I am always glad of an excuse to buy a packet of needles or yard of vibrant fabric. Shopping is enlivened when you have a personal, creative, colorful shopping list underpinning the more everyday, mundane lists, and you can take it with you wherever you travel.

Beauty and the beholder

No matter how modest it is, any domestic kit can possess a beauty that bears no relation to its worth. When I was young, I owned a little box full of "treasure" I had collected. I would take the contents out and turn them over in my hands, like Scrooge with his coins. Strings of sequins and squares of felt from Stockport market, old buttons and badges, scraps of shiny fabrics and broken strings of glass beads, all spoke of glamorous creative possibilities, and I would not have traded those colors and textures for any amount of expensive materials or equipment.

These days I am still enthralled when I open a drawer of beads or threads or embroidery silks, search in a cupboard of fabrics and embroidered cloths or

I first came across these seductively beautiful metal creations in New York. These are the contemporary versions of elaborate, complex, Victorian brass or ceramic molds for cakes and jellies, which are not only practical but lovely *and* entertaining *and* make you feel you are a twenty-first-century Escoffier.

rummage in a yarn basket. I love the chance combinations of colors, the variety and choice and the feeling of sheer wealth. It doesn't matter that these items are not precious, rare or created by famous designers. The sheer ordinariness and anonymity of a practical domestic kit is what gives it charm. And, of course, it has huge potential to be transformed into something stamped with your individual personality and skill.

Color me beautiful

Although I like to grow my collections willy-nilly, I make one exception. When it comes to food coloring, I like to go the whole hog.

I started coloring food when I was young and cochineal was still available. All my creations were somewhere on the scale of pale pink to blood red and, much as I liked using the juice of crushed insects, I did feel a little limited. Later, I graduated to blue rock buns at university, made with mini bottles of thin and insipid liquid food coloring from the supermarket, but still felt something was missing.

And then, a few years ago, I saw the true, deep, rich colors that thick, artificial, additive-laden paste could achieve and, like a true addict, I couldn't stop myself moving on to the hard stuff. I bought a few pots and experimented with the likes of bitter lemon and licorice and chestnut. Finally, I went mad and bought a case full of paste.

It is from Squires (see Resources, page 277), and it is my domestic version of the office worker's briefcase. (I may not commute, but I do long to sit on an early morning train, open up my sugarcraft kit and read a cake-making magazine while all around are working on their laptops and scanning the *Financial Times*.) The joy is that it makes me feel I am an artist at last. There are twenty-four dinky pots in neat rows, like a paintbox with names such as daffodil, gentian,

blackberry, thrift, bluebell, fuchsia and berberis. My heart leaps and my imagination fires every time I click open the case; cakes and scones are transformed into edible canvases, and I become a Matisse of the kitchen. Very occasionally, more is more.

Not-so-plain Jane

I am a Plain Jane at heart, and I choose good quality, practical baking equipment that does the job and lasts well. One of the fundamental tenets of my philosophy is that it is worth paying a little extra for something really excellent that is not only pleasing to use but is also capable of standing the test of time. Experience has taught me that it's better to invest in one really solid piece of bakeware than any number of flimsier, cheaper pieces. As a result, I don't have a huge *batterie de cuisine*, but what I do have is solid, washable and even, sometimes, utterly captivating.

Occasionally, though, I deviate from my usual plainness. Although I have simple, solid, round cake pans, square cake pans, muffin pans and brownie pans, I also own what can only be described as sculptural, high-art cake baking equipment. I first came across these seductively beautiful metal creations in New York. These are the contemporary versions of elaborate, complex, Victorian brass or ceramic molds for cakes and jellies, which are not only practical but lovely and entertaining and make you feel you are a twenty-first-century Escoffier. With them you can enter an enchanted kingdom of baked roses, sunflowers, violets, castles, stars and gingerbread houses where everything is edible and wicked witches don't exist. Perfect for Hansels and Gretels and Plain Janes everywhere.

See Resources, page 277, for details of where to buy artistic food coloring and fabulous cake pans.

Apropos aprons

There is a schism in my apronly soul. I have two apron modes, which each reflect the duality of my personality, my yin and yang, the dichotomy of my life.

On the outside, I am a sensible, practical, feminist apron-wearer. This person wears long, straight, full-frontal aprons with ties that wrap around to meet at the front, made from sturdy linens and cottons. They have a pocket for useful tools and also act as portable hand towels. They wash and dry easily, and hang on door handles, ready for baking and gardening action. This rather puritanical domestic artist's only concession to flamboyance is to look like a walking herbaceous border, as she favors rather loud and vintage floral fabrics.

On the inside, there is an ironic, postmodern, but "really, I just want to be in a 1950s film looking like Doris Day" apron-wearer desperate to get out. This person dreams of wearing frilly, frothy, gathered, pleated, shaped aprons with huge bows at the back, made from impractical, pure white cottons or delicate, floral French fabrics. They have tiny, heart-shaped pockets to hold a hankie or a lipstick, and mucky hands never go near them. They require hand-washing, starching and ironing and are kept in tissue paper in lavender-scented drawers. They are worn when she is handing out plates of iced treats, and their wearer never fails to coordinate her apron colors with her baking.

The former apron person is the one who was educated to work outside the home, and her practical aprons are her compromise, her statement that she now *works* inside the home. The second apron person is the antithesis, the one who actually doesn't want to work at all and who would much prefer to be a feminine icon and enjoy herself all day long watching domestic films (see Inspiration, pages 38–41) and planning her cakes.

It's fair to say that the pragmatic apron-wearer with the work ethic is the one whose strings are tied more firmly round my waist. But both my apron personalities agree that an apron is a wonderful thing and that this simple, modified piece of fabric with its marriage of form and function possesses all sorts of creative possibilities. And there is absolutely no rule that dictates that just because an apron is practical it must be soul-sappingly dreary.

The linen project

Although I've sewn several fabric aprons, I would not call myself a seamstress. But I *am* a knitter, and I thought it would be an interesting challenge to knit an apron. Funnily enough, there aren't many patterns available for knitted aprons, so I had to make up my own design and create the pattern for it. In the end, it was a simple matter of practical thought, and the application of rows and numbers to lengths and shapings. Nine evenings later, a little basic math, three skeins of natural linen yarn and one of red and, *voilà*, I had my first knitted apron.

I knitted it in stockinette stitch with a seed stitch border to stop the edges from curling, and the ties and neck straps are in plain stockinette stitch. I knitted the red spots with a Fair Isle technique—carrying the yarn behind the stitches—and like the way they came out looking like little hearts. And the great thing about a knitted apron is that there is no sewing up afterwards. Which means you can get on with modeling it.

Simon came back from work en route to Paris just as I was taking the photographs. As we stood together for a shot, we saw our contrasting inside/outside outfits or "uniforms." Simon has his business uniform of a jacket, shirt and trousers, and I have my working uniform of an apron. But this is one that drapes beautifully, flatters the hips, and it wouldn't look bad on my frillier alter ego.

Reading round the edges

Simon grew up as one of four boisterous boys. My late mother-in-law, Allison, told me how she would tune out the noises and crashes and fights, and read a book as she cooked the meals. I have never managed to do this (I am more easily distracted), but I am impressed by her devotion to reading while coping with industrial quantities of spaghetti bolognese, twenty-five dirty shirts a week and countless broken windows. Unsurprisingly, a wooden spoon was her weapon of choice when the boys disturbed her reading once too often.

Taking my cue from Allison, I firmly believe that it is possible for domestic artists to cultivate a practical approach to reading good writing. When I had three children under three, I read far too many magazines because I could only manage pretty pictures and short pieces in the breaks between feeds, diaper changes, walks and washing. But I soon lost interest in glamour and perfect interiors when I realized that I *could* read well-written prose in the form of short stories.

One short story writer who is a wife and mother talks about "writing round the edges" of family life and I think that this type of literature is perfect for *reading* round the edges of domesticity. Short stories that have been written in between dusting,

bed-making, answering the door and homemaking are also wonderful for reading in one sitting while you wait for the cookies to brown, while children play, while the bread rises and, if you are as accomplished as Mrs. Brocket Senior, while you are stirring the gravy.

Short stories tend to deal with the subject of ordinary life rather than drama and action. They are often wonderfully domestic in nature—a conversation over the breakfast marmalade, a move to a new house, a special dress or a ghastly dinner party. And because they are essentially domestic, some of the very best are written by women. Writers such as Isak Dinesen, Katherine Mansfield, Alice Munro, Helen Simpson, Mollie Panter-Downes, Dorothy Whipple and Elizabeth Taylor all write elegant, subtle, thought-provoking short stories about everything from boarding houses to cakes.

We can take a leaf out of the books and stories of the eminently practical Elizabeth Gaskell, who wrote amidst the bustle and demands of a large, busy family and who said in a letter to a friend that it is healthy for all women to "have the hidden refuge of Art to shelter themselves in when too much pressed upon by daily Lilliputian arrows of peddling care." Or, indeed, four rowdy boys.

Small skills, big effects

I think it's perhaps because I am pretty much a self-taught amateur in all branches of the gentle domestic arts that I would rather try to make something and get it wrong than not try at all. I ignore most quilting rules but still manage to make quilts that please me; I didn't know how to do mattress stitch for decades but still created dozens of knitted garments; I have only just mastered crochet but not the skillful sort; and my basil grows despite my nontraditional approach.

What this means is that even if, like me, you possess no more than basic skills, there is still a huge amount you can do in the way of creative self-expression. In fact, there is a lot to be said for "outsider" art and craft, the sort of thing that is made by ordinary people with ordinary skills. It has a directness, sincerity and individuality often missing in more sophisticated, refined, knowing art.

It bothers me, though, that many people are easily defeated when it comes to applying practical domestic skills. There really is no secret to running stitch or cake baking or bulb planting. We all have the ability to do these things, it's just that some people don't believe they can. They have lost the gentle art of self-reliance, and lack of practice erodes this further.

I think we need to reconsider small, practical skills, the kinds of skills taught in primary schools, and give them back their worth. Just because we see children doing clever, expressive, creative activities with color, materials, scissors, paint and glitter, doesn't mean that these are childish skills. They are exactly the skills we need to retain as adults in order to enhance our domestic environments and improve our quality of life.

Think of those things every child loves to do: growing a plant in water, watching seeds germinate, playing with thick color and sticking things together. Now, why can't the adult versions be growing fragrant, colorful hyacinths in glass vases, cultivating a jungle of sweet basil in pots on a sunny windowsill and stitching together layers of fabrics and soft wadding to create a unique quilt? These are the skills that generate more emails asking "How?" than any other when I show the results on my blog, yarnstorm.

So, how do I do it? Simple. Really.

Just add water

Hyacinths are a cinch to grow in winter. The key is to buy prepared bulbs specifically for growing indoors or to prepare ordinary garden bulbs yourself by storing them in a paper bag in the refrigerator for four to six weeks. Once ready, all you need to do is place each bulb, root side down, barely touching the water line in the vase (as shown above) and then top off the water when you see the level dropping, especially when the roots are establishing themselves, and keep the bulbs in a bright, warm place. You can buy vases made for this purpose or you can use jam jars. Throw away the bulbs after flowering as they will be exhausted.

My favorite indoor hyacinths are Jan Bos (deep pink), L'Innocence (ivory white) and Delft Blue (soft blue). See Resources, page 279, for recommended bulb suppliers.

Basil rules

I grow basil indoors for several reasons. Firstly, it's warmer because the windows give a greenhouse effect, and secondly, the basil will be protected from whiteflies and other nasties that alight on the sweet, juicy leaves when grown outdoors.

I use 8"-diameter plastic pots with drainage holes (terra-cotta pots are far more aesthetically pleasing but absorb too much moisture) set on matching pot saucers. Put a layer about 1" deep of drainage material in the bottom (gravel, a few stones, a broken and smashed teacup), then top off with multipurpose potting soil. Water the soil thoroughly (until water comes out of the bottom) and then scatter your basil seeds—I use ordinary, sweet basil—quite thickly but evenly over the surface. Cover the seeds with the thinnest layer of soil you can manage. Now cover the pot with plastic wrap and leave it in a warm, sunny place. The seeds will start to germinate within forty-eight hours—as soon as you see activity, take off the plastic wrap.

Most gardeners would "prick out" the seedlings once they are established (i.e., take each one out and replant with space in between) but I find that there is no need. As long as you keep the pot well-watered, always watering *from the base,* and turn it around every so often to allow all the shoots to catch the light evenly, you should soon have a thick, dense growth of leaves that can be cut as and when you need them to go on pizza and pasta, in salads and pesto.

Discard when the leaves are yellowing or when the whiteflies finally scent their prey.

Quick and easy quilting

It's not difficult to make a simple quilt. I machine-sew the pieces together and then hand-quilt. All you need to be able to do is sew a straight line with a machine, and make a relatively straight line in running stitch with a needle and thread.

This silk quilt was my very first attempt at patchwork. I'd seen a photo in a magazine of something similar and had finally realized that I didn't need a degree in quilting to make one. I cut out large squares of silk with a planned, finished size of 12" by 12", so I cut them with a ½" seam allowance all the way around. I used 7 colors and laid out all the squares on the floor before sewing so that I could see if there were any clashes or mismatches. When I'd finished piecing the top and ironed it to press out the seams, I bought some cotton fabric and joined two lengths to make the back. Then I made a quilt sandwich by placing the back (right side facing down), then the batting or quilt filling and then the top (right side up), one on top of the other. I smoothed it all out on the floor, pinned it, trimmed the edges and quilted it.

I sewed large running stitches with DMC cotton embroidery thread on the inside of every other square. The seams were my guidelines and I quilted on my lap (no frame, no hoop). When it was done I made sure all the edges were neat and added a double-thickness binding (machine-sew on right side, fold over and hand-sew the edge to the back).

And that, in essence, is how to make a quilt. You may want more detailed guidance, in which case I suggest you take a look at the book recommendations in Resources, pages 282 – 3.

Just give it a try

Although many may dismiss small, practical skills as outmoded and irrelevant, the mastering and enjoyment of simple, creative acts undoubtedly fuels a sense of fulfilment and well-being in adults. We need to rediscover and cultivate a childish enthusiasm and willingness to try, and attempt to conquer our doubts about our abilities. A misshapen cookie, an uneven row of stitching, a floppy hyacinth and an uneven pot of basil are still better than the bland, neat and regular store-bought versions that look and taste like everyone else's.

Just give it a try.

When the bread bug bites

I know how tempted you are to skip this section about bread. You are already thinking, "Oh, please, not another person telling me how amazingly simple it is to bake fresh bread every day, how perfectly manageable dough can be, how its preparation can be fitted into every busy person's schedule, and how it's all just a matter of clever personal organization," blah, blah, blah. Because I, too, have skipped many a bread chapter in a baking book knowing I would come away feeling only too aware of my own alleged laziness and organizational shortcomings.

However, I adore making bread. I find it one of the most satisfying, therapeutic, enjoyable and primeval activities in life. But I don't do it all the time. I don't impose a homemade bread discipline on myself and I don't feel guilty if I plan to make it and then find I can't. As a result, when I do make bread it's on my own terms, and with great pleasure.

There is something quite magical about baking bread. Once you have mastered a method that suits you, it's like riding a bicycle. You carry the knowledge, the skill, around with you, even when you are not able to bake. It is like a practical talisman or a lucky charm that, when applied to flour, yeast, salt and water, will turn them into a wonderful substance that comforts, sustains and nourishes both the maker and those with whom the bread is broken.

Bread is one of life's great offerings; its symbolic worth is enshrined in the traditional bread and salt welcome of Slavic countries. Even though I had experienced the ceremony many times as a visitor, it took me a long time to realize that it could apply at home. I've baked bread for the family for years, but it is only recently that I have come to understand just how much guests appreciate fresh, homemade bread when they eat with us. I really, mistakenly, thought that bread was too humble an offering. Now I think it is one of the finest.

The Breakfast Table
SETSUKO (1989)

The painting pictured opposite illustrates my thoughts about bread perfectly. The simplicity of the still life of bread, tea and flowers is overlaid with freshness and reverence and creates a trinity of food and drink and newly gathered flowers that would make an enticing start to a day. I particularly like the way the bread is placed in a symbolic basket, a cot or cradle almost, and is given a snowy white cover that looks like a fine, crocheted lace christening shawl. It's as if the artist is asking the viewer to stop and consider the significance of the simplest domestic details and rituals, so many of which center on bread.

Practical magic

When the bread bug bites, it's best to succumb only when you know you have enough time to enjoy the process. Bread should not be rushed and, anyway, the pleasure lies in taking your time, applying an almost meditative approach and letting your mind wander beyond the kitchen window while your arms and hands knead and fold and shape. You need to be responsive to the dough, but you can't bully it.

It's very easy to keep the ingredients for bread in your cupboards, ready for when you have a bread-baking moment. Good-quality bread flour, salt and water can always be on standby, but I think it's worth being fussy about the yeast you use. I prefer fresh yeast, which can be bought in the bakery sections of Sainsbury's here in the UK, and in little packets in other countries. But it doesn't keep long, so I have a back-up can of dried yeast in the fridge. The one yeast I won't use is the fast-acting kind with additives. I like to keep my bread as natural as possible (which is quite something coming from the Queen of Food Coloring, I know).

I used to have a sourdough starter, but found that the process was terribly long and I would frequently not start in time for the bread to be ready that day. I still occasionally use a semi-sourdough recipe by making a sponge, but mostly I employ the very simple recipe on page 128–9, which makes a loaf in 3 to 4 hours, from start to finish. It is made entirely by hand, partly because I don't like to delegate kneading to a mixer, and partly because I can tell when the dough is fully kneaded from the texture under my hands. The recipe can also be adapted to make pizza dough and a version of focaccia. It can incorporate different flours or be plain white. It makes 1 good loaf, or 12 rolls, or any number of small dough balls to slather with garlic butter.

Bread should not be rushed and, anyway, the pleasure lies in taking your time, applying an almost meditative approach and letting your mind wander beyond the kitchen window while your arms and hands knead and fold and shape. You need to be responsive to the dough, but you can't bully it.

The Stuff of Life: delicious, doughy, homemade, hand-made bread

INGREDIENTS

2¼ cups bread flour, plus extra for the work
surface
walnut-sized piece of fresh yeast or 2¼ teaspoons
dried yeast
1 teaspoon runny, clear honey
1 cup warm, but not hot, water
3 teaspoons salt (Maldon salt or French *fleur de sel*
are excellent fancy salts)
apron—in case your nose needs to be rubbed
when you knead bread, as mine invariably does

Preheat the oven to 425°F.

Take the phone off the hook. Sticky bread dough is notoriously difficult to clean off surfaces, plus you want to be able to think beautiful thoughts without being disturbed when you are making it.

Measure the flour into a large mixing bowl.

Put the yeast and honey in a small bowl and mix. If using fresh yeast, it will turn liquid all of a sudden, as if by magic. Add the warm water and stir to mix. Add 2 tablespoons of the flour and mix again. Leave for approximately 20 minutes, until there is a frothy, foamy layer on the surface of the liquid, which indicates

that the yeast is alive and well. If there is no bubbling, the yeast is dead and you need to start again with a new batch of yeast.

Stir the salt into the remaining flour, make a well in the center and pour in the liquid. If the mixture seems very dry, add a little more water. Be careful not to add too much or you will have to add disproportionate amounts of flour. With one hand, work the mixture briefly until it comes together, then leave for a minute or so to let the flour absorb the water.

Turn the dough out onto a floured work surface. Again, be careful not to use too much flour as this will stiffen the dough. I like to work with a sticky dough and flour it little and often, but others prefer to handle a firmer, drier dough.

When it comes to kneading, everyone has their own personal style. Manic gym-style thumping, stretching and pummeling do no good; better to adopt a gentle rhythm and pressure. My method is to press down with my palms, roll the bread, fold it and turn it 90 degrees and repeat.

Knead for 5 to 8 minutes (this is quite enough—it does not need to be a strenuous 15-minute workout) until the texture of the dough changes. My way of knowing that it is ready to be left to rise is when I start to feel a touch of what can only be described as sweatiness, and smell the beginning of a wonderfully bready, yeasty aroma.

Form into a ball. Lightly grease the bowl to stop the dough sticking and return the dough to the bowl. Cover with plastic wrap or a damp tea towel and leave in a warmish place until it has doubled in size (this can take as little as an hour or up to 2 hours, depending on the conditions). It is also possible to put the bowl in the fridge to let the dough rise slowly there—in which case allow 4 to 6 hours.

Now you need to punch down the dough. With a floured hand or two (children love doing this part), gently punch the dough with your fist to deflate it. My children usually see the dough as a mortal enemy and give him/her a thorough bashing, but pacifist bakers can be less aggressive.

Knead the dough until smooth, about 2 to 3 minutes, then shape into whatever loaf you are making. If you are making rolls, it is worth weighing the dough and then dividing that by the number of rolls/balls you want to make and weighing each individual piece as you go along. That way they all cook at the same rate.

Place the shaped dough (well apart if making rolls) on a greased baking sheet, cover with greased plastic

wrap and leave to rise again—about an hour for a loaf, 45 minutes for two loaves, 30 minutes for rolls and 20 minutes for small dough balls.

Remove the plastic wrap and bake in the oven until risen and golden. Bake a large loaf for 30 to 40 minutes, two smaller loaves for 25 to 30 minutes, rolls for 15 to 20 minutes and dough balls for around 10 minutes. The best way to make sure bread is done is to take it out of the oven for a moment and tap it on its underside. If there is a hollow sound, it is cooked, if not, continue baking.

Remove and allow to cool if you can. There is no truth in the old wives' tale that hot bread gives you a stomachache. The only stomachache you may get is simply from eating too much.

Variations

For pizza and focaccia, add 2 tablespoons of extra-virgin olive oil to the water at the beginning. Make as above.

To form the pizzas, roll out flat, thin circles of dough. Add the topping after the second rising, just before the pizzas go in the oven.

For focaccia, shape the bread into a large flattened oval just under an inch thick, leave to rise and then, just before you put it in the oven, drizzle extra-virgin olive oil over the top and scatter on a generous amount of sea salt.

You can double the quantities for hungry/greedy bread eaters.

Haberdashery

Haberdashery is one of those words that you listen to yourself saying. It's a word to turn over in your mind when you have heard it, a good-sounding word like a practical, domestic version of cornucopia or gallimaufry, two more words of which I am inordinately fond.

It upsets me that there are so few real haberdashers and haberdasheries these days. A haberdashery is such a wonderful place. You can always find just what you are looking for and maybe a little treat besides. I love the eclectic mix of products in a traditional haberdashery, from snaps to thimbles, shoulder pads to bra fastenings, hooks-and-eyes to darning threads. But what is truly fantastic about a real haberdashery is the way it can transform a shop full of essentially practical items into a treasure trove.

We have a department store near us that, Bill Bryson once wrote, gives a glimpse of what Britain would be like under Communism. I suppose that even the Soviet Union needed buttons and zippers to hold the fabric of society together, and this shop is now the only place locally where you can find what are fast becoming recondite haberdashery goods. The section has recently been relegated to the basement behind a few pillars, as if there is something vaguely embarrassing about its very existence.

This is a terrible shame, as I think haberdasheries should be the pride of the neighborhood, have gloriously old-fashioned fronts with curving plate glass, a wooden fascia with a cursive sign hand-painted in gold and a lovely display of fabric-covered buttons, men's collars, knicker elastic and diaper pins in the window.

Inside, there should be a proper counter, complete with measuring grid and long brass ruler, staffed by properly helpful shop assistants who know where to find "just the thing for Madam," a chair for Madam to sit on while she makes her selection of buttons and ribbons and threads and trimmings, floor-to-ceiling mahogany drawers with glass fronts and neat, copper-plate labels to indicate where to find the best silks to mend your stockings.

The cash register should be mechanical, impressively large and resound with a triumphant ring, and the goods should be presented in neatly folded paper bags printed with the shop name, address and proud proprietor's claims to being the best in town for choice, attention and price.

Instead, alas, we usually have a full-scale capitulation to the ever-increasing plastic anonymity of our modern retail style. Haberdashery sections are to be found in strip-lit modern department stores where the button selections are shrinking to a pathetic anything-as-long-as-it's-black level and service is uncaring and unhelpful. Did you know that in that once-great haberdashery, Liberty of London, you can no longer buy paper sewing patterns? And that Harrods removed its haberdashery completely a few

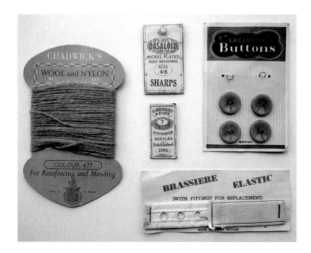

years ago, claiming that no one sews these days? For many of us, true local haberdasheries are a thing of the past to be read about in novels like *Cranford* by Elizabeth Gaskell.

But, thank goodness, philistinism has not yet conquered all the outposts of the humble pin, needle and measuring tape. I am glad to hear there are still a few traditional wood-and-glass gems in the world, to which domestic artists can turn when in need of resolutely practical domestic items. When I wrote a post about haberdasheries on yarnstorm, I received an amazing number of passionate comments sharing my sadness at the demise of a wonderful institution. At the same time, however, it was immensely cheering to be told that, in a few places, haberdasheries are still

respected and indeed thriving. Barcelona, Lisbon, Paris, Portland in Oregon, San Francisco, Los Angeles, New York, Bolzano, Trondheim, Helsinki, Philadelphia, Gothenburg, Leicester, Ramsgate, Lausanne were all mentioned as having outstanding haberdasheries.

Our haberdasheries need us. It's time for a wonderful, global, button-laden Save Our Haberdasheries Campaign.

The vintage haberdashery items in the photos are from my small collection, but the wooden cotton spools and hosiery threads are from a little wooden sewing box that belonged to my mother-in-law. She was a hoarder, but with a sense of value of this type of practical ephemera. I am grateful she left it all intact.

Transformative power

Domesticity is *not* synonymous with housework. In fact, I think there is too much media bossiness about cleanliness and tidiness these days, and nowhere near enough celebration of the joys of homemaking. The buzzwords are control, order, minimalism and discipline, all of which suggest a state which can be achieved and maintained. But I would argue that many of us are far happier in a more fluid state of domesticity with a certain degree of mess and disorder, and a more realistic and welcoming environment that reflects the busyness and creativity of its occupants. We may aspire to a magazine-perfect interior, but, deep down, we know that the price to be paid in mental anguish and impossible effort, not to mention the deterioration of relations within the household, is far too high.

We should, perhaps, take a more practical approach to domesticity. One in which we live and let live, *use* the space instead of attempting to subjugate it to our wills and get on with doing what needs to be done in order to make enough time to enjoy the more pleasurable gentle arts. So it is ironic that by adopting this more relaxed and less demanding approach to domesticity, we create for ourselves huge powers of transformation in which necessary but seemingly dreary and mind-numbing tasks and chores can become part of a wider creative process.

Pretend ironing

Take ironing for example. In my twenties I commuted into London and can still recall the conversation I once overheard on the train between two women discussing the difficulties of ironing the frills on pillowcases. Now, call me a rebel, but I was shocked. Why on earth would anyone iron a pillowcase, let alone one with a frill? And, if you *must* iron them, why not buy ones without frills?

I still dislike ironing and will do a great deal to avoid it. Line-dry, tumble-dry, fold carefully, hang up immediately, bribe Simon. However, my burden has been reduced recently by Tom's enthusiasm for steam ironing; he actually *asks* me if there is any ironing he can do when I am making a quilt. He's not fussy; he happily irons vast lengths of fabric, long seams, fiddly pieces and large blocks.

But it does help that he perceives the iron as a weapon with hidden ammunition of hiss and steam, which transforms him into a James Bond/Bruce Willis of the laundry room. He attacks inanimate objects with jets of steam, loves misting up windows and ambushing imaginary enemies. And who am I to wonder about the deep-seated impulses of a boy ironer when he gets the ironing done?

Taking my cue from Tom, I decided to find an imaginary ironing mode for myself and have decided I am more a Degas ironer. I find that having a mental picture of one of his laundresses slaving in a damp, steamy laundry with traditional hot irons makes me count the blessings of a floral ironing board cover, a modern electric iron and BBC Radio 4 in the background. Or, alternatively, I like to consider the potential of the clothing and textiles I am ironing to fit into a future quilt/to be felted/to be cut up and used in a fabric picture. Many a striped shirt or cotton summer skirt has had its fate decided well before it has worn out.

The application of this transformative approach can be varied as much as you like. Who's to say that you are not really ironing on a Caribbean island dressed only in a grass skirt and floral garland? Or pressing your best frock for an evening of charm and wit with Cary Grant? Or smoothing out the creases in Gregory Peck's linen suits while he chats to you about civil liberties and then takes his turn with the iron?

We may do minimal ironing here, but we do it with maximum imaginative effect.

On the line

I have a solid, Northern English respect for clotheslines. Where I come from, clotheslines crisscross gardens and thread their way around yards and back alleys, like enormous spiderwebs that hold whole communities together. They are supported by sturdy props and, very occasionally, ornamented with a clothespin bag.

Then I moved south, closer to London. At our wedding, my brother declared in his speech that I had now joined the sophisticated Surrey "Gin and Jag" set and that it was only a matter of time before I owned a rotary clothesline. How wrong he was.

One of the very first things I do when I move house—even temporarily—is set up a linear clothesline and find the clothespins. One summer holiday I was so bereft when I discovered a line was prohibited that Tom made me a beautifully woven drying rack with wooden sticks and string.

To paraphrase John Keats, a clothesline is a thing of beauty and its loveliness increases when we see it not simply as a means to drying clothes, but also as a sort of garden installation, one which adds color and pattern and movement to a static background. There is a deep satisfaction in recalling the physics lessons in which we learned about the movement of molecules and why washing that is pinned evenly on a single line and in the sun and wind dries faster than bunched-up clothes on an overcrowded rotary line. There is pleasure in using colored clothespins or traditional dolly clothespins or cushioned clothespins (whatever strikes your fancy) and creating arrangements and sequences, pairs or contrasts. I haven't quite reached the stage where I ruthlessly coordinate my colors on the line, but I know it's only a matter of time.

Clotheslines, with their deeply domestic and practical nature, yet fleetingly beautiful arrangements and movements, inspire my machine embroideries. I have never owned a pink and black lacy bra, but that doesn't stop me imagining what one might look like on the line. Photos of clotheslines draw my eye, and flapping, bouncing, jovial arrangements glimpsed from a train gladden my heart.

I love the painting *Town Hens* (1995) by Lisa Jensen, pictured above, which reminds me of my own clothesline setting. Whenever I hang out washing in my overlooked, suburban garden, the hens cluck around my feet, I feel the breeze or sun on my face and arms, and I am engulfed in a moment of pure contentment. Something is right with the world; the clothes will dry smooth and soft in natural conditions, they will smell far better than if they had been tumble-dried with unnaturally perfumed chemicals, the hens are happy with their worms, the washing dances, the colors play games and, for a brief while, I am part of a much greater event than a simple domestic chore.

Style

Style counsel

Domesticity is an unrivaled opportunity to express our personal style. Fortunately domestic style is a fluid, not a fixed, concept, so it can be developed and explored by anyone with a modicum of interest in applying their imagination and creativity to the spaces in which they live.

Personal, domestic style is also a matter of confidence, of thinking about what you choose and not blindly following media and retail trends. It's a constant process of sifting and choosing and making, of applying criteria or selection and rejection. It's a question of developing your own taste, being open to influences and inspirations and valuing the significance of what is meaningful to you. True style cannot be bought or taught because its essence lies more in how you put things together than the individual features it contains. It's a cliché but true that style works when the whole is greater than the sum of the parts.

My own style follows these precepts about fluidity, choice and abstract qualities. I would say it's colorful, relaxed, comfortable, imperfect and bookish. I concentrate on the detail I can manage rather than trying to impose my style on the whole—a fruitless task. I like to mix vintage and contemporary objects and furniture, and would rather own something with more meaning than value. I revel in textures, colors, light and warmth, and my house is more an expression of me and my family, our interests and activities, than of income or lifestyle. Above all, I like to think my domestic style is a statement of my ultimate aspiration to create a welcoming, lived-in, loved, used and abused space for living.

Philosophies

One of the joys of having children is watching them develop their own personal style. The fact that they all came out of the same peapod does not automatically mean they are as alike as peas.

Alice is a spontaneous cake decorator who works with what is available to make colorful, candy-laden, mouth-watering results. Phoebe is a self-styled cake designer who plans her creations carefully and shops for the necessary materials. Tom is interested in complete edibility rather than effect, so his cakes are iced lavishly and decorated with chocolate treats such as M&Ms, Smarties and malted milk balls. Speed of consumption is uppermost in his mind, whereas the girls prefer to garner a little admiration before they cut their cakes.

The garden cake pictured opposite is a Phoebe creation. Sugar insects and ladybugs, iced flowers and butter-cream frosting are mixed with plastic Playmobil figures, flowers, vegetables and garden implements. The day she made it was an object lesson in the diversity of the individual philosophies in our family. As I considered what we were all doing, I was struck by our different styles.

Phoebe hasn't read Voltaire yet, but she knows, as does Candide, that we must cultivate our garden.

Tom was studying Buddhism in the hope of finding the path to self-knowledge in the near future.

I was reading *How to be Free* by Tom Hodgkinson and thinking wishfully.

Simon was pondering Zen and the art of bicycle maintenance.

And Alice went out to a concert to see the Pussycat Dolls.

Above all, I like to think my domestic style is a statement of my ultimate aspiration to create a welcoming, lived-in, loved, used and abused space for living.

It's my happy hippy heart you hear*

I'm too young to be a genuine hippy, although I made the most of the tail-end of hippy culture in the 1970s. This was when hippydom had hit the retail shops and I wore floppy hats, cheesecloth smock tops, long skirts, and bell-bottom velvet pants. I was covered in fringes, beads, leather belts and fake flowers. The hippy philosophy, with its abandonment of traditional rules and, in particular, its bohemian dress code, was my first foray into self-discovery and led to many run-ins with teachers at school, where I rebelled against petty school uniform rules.

I suppose I am still an old hippy at heart. For one thing, I think Bob Dylan is magic. I have to shut myself in my study to listen to his brilliant *Theme Time Radio Hour,* and it made me laugh when Phoebe once found me in there happily crocheting along. She reckoned I was hooking in time to the music, but I think I was more spellbound by the rhythms of his speech. Bob tells you all sorts of wonderful details about the lyrics, the writers, the history, the performers and the places. Sometimes he goes into a rambling, poetic riff, and it's an education in style. His delivery, the word pictures, the connections, the very simplicity and ordinariness of his interests, all rework everyday life into something special and memorable.

Bob Dylan, rule-breaking and creative approaches to making, thinking and communicating have all had a lasting appeal. I've moved on sartorially, but can still see elements of hippy style appearing in my domesticity and gentle arts.

It was cold last winter, and I resorted to wearing a pair of knee socks to keep warm. I don't think I've worn long socks since school (mine were brown and over-the-knee when the rules said black and knee-high), but it was freezing so I dug out these lovely Missoni striped socks. You may think I'm mad: I didn't buy these to wear, but for inspiration. They took me back to happy, hippy times and I bought them because I liked the stripe formation and colors, and thought these might look great copied in something knitted or crocheted. But I put them on, was instantly warmer and also delighted with the way they went with my Flower-Power Quilt (see opposite, top).

Scottish dancing

The crocheted ripple blanket pictured opposite, below, is part of my hippy renaissance, too. I'd thought once was enough with ripples (see Color, pages 52–3), but I couldn't resist a second version. This time I wanted less of a fiesta or party feel, and more of a laid-back, natural style. So the second blanket is inspired by the soft, natural colors of the Scottish Highlands.

Not long ago, I took Alice and Phoebe to visit friends who have moved to live near Inverness. The trip made me wonder how my color sensibilities and style would develop if I lived in Scotland, and I spent the weekend marveling at the wonderful scenery and considering the hues and shades, which are so gentle on the eye. I was struck by the muted but lovely colors of the landscape and the ever-changing sky. I amused myself by looking at books about tartan and, for the first time, I realized that the huge number of permutations in tartans all reflected local, natural colors; the reds of the rowan berries, the purples of the heathers, the oranges of the autumnal bracken, the blues of the water, the grey-greens of the fir trees and the emerald greens and yellows of the deciduous trees. The combinations of subtle and organic colors are so clever and varied that you could never become bored with designing tartan.

I recalled my visit when choosing the colors for this Scottish Dancing Blanket and began with a rich orange and a teal blue (the colors of my favorite tartan) and then I chose more shades for wildflowers, berries, skies, trees, earth and lakes. Once again, I was amazed at what can be achieved with simple waves of colors placed semirandomly. Every new stripe alters the dynamics of the whole, and it is pure delight to watch it grow. My hook dances over the ripples and I just go with the flow (man).

Happy hippy style makes me feel expansive and unencumbered by establishment thinking. I may not want to live in a commune or wear flowers in my hair, but the nonconformist, peaceful philosophy has enduring appeal. And if, after all these years, it still works for Bob Dylan, it must be cool.

* You can tell I'm not a true hippy, when my first thought on thinking of "hippy style" is the Andy Williams song "Happy Heart" (1969). It's the right era, though.

Pure style

Great style should appear effortless. There should be no signs of hard work, no joins, no lapses. Great style relies on careful editing, whether your preferred effect is sleek and sophisticated or bright and bohemian. It's what you leave out, as much as what you include, and I think this is why so many of us fail to achieve a single, personal style. True style is ruthless and is based on rejection—and not many people can afford the money, the friends or the family we stand to lose along the way if we cultivate it.

Maintaining a single style is too much like hard work for me, but that does not prevent me from studying and admiring the styles of people who get it totally right. I know it's an illusion and all sustained by tricks and an army of stylists/tailors/cleaners/hairdressers, but it can be most entertaining to look at the kings and queens of style. Katharine Hepburn, Audrey Hepburn and Grace Kelly are all style icons, but my favorite, the one who has pure style, is Cary Grant.

I read *Cary Grant: A Celebration of Style* by Richard Torregrossa (see Resources, page 278) as soon as it came into the house. When I say I read it, I mean I skimmed the words and lingered over the photos; I would never have thought you could enjoy looking at pictures of a fully clothed man so much.

The commentary reveals some minute and revealing details about Cary's wardrobe, though. I liked the story about him ordering shirts from a tailor in Japan: if they weren't just as he wanted them, he would return them 10,000 miles to have the collar-tips extended by one eighth of an inch, or something equally obsessive. I suppose the only thing you can say to this is that he had a style to maintain and the wherewithal to do so. I can think of better things to do with my money, but then my face and appearance are not my fortune.

And Cary's face was fabulous. The book is packed with great photos of him in films, on location and at leisure. It struck me that the majority, and the best, are in black and white, or neutral. It made me think that he must have dressed deliberately this way to look great in monochromatic, contrasting fabrics that never detracted from his face and which framed and outlined his tall, slim body. He is nearly always wearing a black or grey suit or a white tuxedo, a startlingly white shirt (with perfectly judged collars) and a plain tie. (You never see a novelty tie or harlequin socks on the lovely Cary.) All of which go marvelously with his black hair when he was young and his grey hair when older.

It can be no coincidence that the two other books I have about Cary sport black-and-white covers. This man's style is pared down to the absolute basics; no frills, no fuss, best fabrics, best cut, best quality design. He is so beautifully and cleanly delineated, he's almost a cutout. But not quite. There's a man inside whom we can't see fully, and this cleverly hidden self is the most tantalizing quality about Cary Grant.

Pure style in action

Whenever I feel in need of a master class in style, I watch a Cary Grant film. Most of his films (but not all) from *Bringing Up Baby* (1938) and his marabou-trimmed housecoat, to *People Will Talk* (1951) and his devastatingly charming bedside manner, to *His Girl Friday* (1940) and his hilarious ad libs, are entertaining and great to look at. But if I want pure, unfettered style, these are the films I watch.

North by Northwest (1959)

The most beautiful play on grey ever captured on film. Cary wears an immaculate, bespoke, Savile Row grey suit that never creases, marks, rips or droops, whether he's drinking in the Oak Room, being manhandled, running through fields chased by a plane or, most miraculously, when emerging from hiding in a folded train bunk. Everything in the film complements him; the UN buildings, the Mount Rushmore café, Eva Marie Saint's wardrobe. Even the train, the *20th Century Limited* from New York to Chicago, is a study in classy grey metal, upholstery and style. The film is marvelously sleek, tailored and visually sophisticated. Just like its leading man (see opposite, right).

I would never have thought you could enjoy looking at pictures of a fully clothed man so much.

That Touch of Mink (1962)

This is not worth watching for the plot, but it's a great treat for locations (huge, smart office; five-star hotel in Bermuda; private plane; New York landmarks) and its stars are never knowingly underdressed. Cary's sartorial role is to provide a smart but understated counterpoint to some of the best outfits ever worn by Miss Day (see above left). Apparently, Cary went to the showroom of Norman Norell with her to help her choose her fabulous clothes. He obviously wanted to meet his real costars before shooting began.

The Philadelphia Story (1940)

The perfect, sparkling, stylish combination of cast, clothes, pools, houses, terraces and cars, and a brilliant script to keep it all together. Katharine Hepburn's incredible, slender, floaty, Greek Goddess look is stunning and contrasts brilliantly with Cary's sober but relaxed and tweedy wardrobe. His ruler-straight hair parting remains under control throughout the film, unlike James Stewart's boyish locks. The ultimate "cashmere film."

To Catch a Thief (1955)

Cary Grant plays a former jewel thief with a strict moral code and an even stricter dress code, and Grace Kelly, in a wardrobe of shimmering pastel and sparkling gold gowns designed by Edith Head, is out to catch him. Easygoing and only moderately tense, the plot is really no more than a support role to the sustained interplay of light and dark. A tanned, nay, mahogany Grant contrasts with the translucently pale Kelly during their game of chase through the classic sunny, stylish Côte d'Azur locations (the Carlton Hotel in Cannes, a sandy beach and sparkling sea filled with beautiful people, a fabulous hilltop villa). What happens after dark is only hinted at, but of course even the innuendo is very tastefully done. And, far from looking like a local, weather-beaten fisherman, Cary Grant even manages to make a striped French sweater appear the epitome of style.

The Queen of Hearts

Just like the Queen of Hearts, I am fond of tarts. But I find that the chances of making a good batch that someone might actually want to steal are about as likely as me winning a game of cards.

Jam tarts have always appeared to me to be the epitome of cozy domestic style and the stuff of nursery rhymes, stories and teas. They evoke a warm kitchen, good baking smells, wearing aprons and helping mother to roll out pastry. They are the ultimate in making-do—using leftover scraps of pastry and jam at the bottom of jars. They can be yellow, orange, red, purple or gold, they can have lattices, stars or full lids on top. They can be simple circles or prettily fluted, large enough to require several bites or small enough to fit whole in the mouth.

So it amazes me that they are tricky to make well and virtually impossible to make with children who are flummoxed by badly behaved pastry, jam that won't slide off spoons, pastry circles that don't fit the tin and, the final insult, tarts that burn the mouth horribly when the bakers are in too much of a hurry to try their wares.

I think the only solution is to take a queenly approach and bake when the rest of the pack is out. I made these Queen of Hearts tarts all on a winter's day, taking my time. I didn't argue with the pastry and resisted the urge to wear molten jam lipstick. I used a buttery, crumbly pastry, Wilkins & Sons Tiptree Sweet Tip Raspberry Jam and put a little heart on top of each tart.

The result? The King of Hearts and three Knaves came in and stole them. A little less nursery style and a little more regal style paid dividends. For once I played a winning hand.

Queen of Hearts Jam Tarts

Makes 16–18

INGREDIENTS
¾ cup flour
¼ cup confectioner's sugar, plus extra for dusting (optional)
½ cup butter
2 egg yolks or 1 egg yolk plus 2 teaspoons cold water
1 jar of jam (whichever flavor you like—I prefer raspberry)

Preheat the oven to 400°F.

Sift the flour and confectioner's sugar into a bowl. Quickly cut in the butter, then add the egg yolks or egg yolk and water to make the pastry come together (use a little extra water if necessary, but try to be as sparing as possible). Shape into a flattish, hamburger-shaped disc, wrap in a plastic wrap and chill in the refrigerator for at least an hour.

Roll out the pastry on a floured surface. Make sixteen to eighteen 2¼" rounds with a pastry cutter, place the circles in tartlet pans and chill in the refrigerator for a minimum of 30 minutes. Using the leftover pastry, cut out the same number of approximately 1½" hearts with a small heart-shaped cutter, place on a flat baking sheet and chill.

When you are ready to bake the tarts, remove the rounds from the refrigerator and spoon a generous teaspoon of your chosen jam into each one. Don't be stingy, but don't overfill—the jam will bubble and rise during baking. Bake for 12 to 15 minutes, checking toward the end that the tarts are not burning. When the edges are turning gold, remove from the oven and leave to cool on a wire rack.

Now bake the hearts for 5 to 7 minutes until golden. Remove from the oven and allow to cool. If you like the effect, sift confectioner's sugar onto the hearts before you place them on the top of the jam tarts.

When completely cold, offer the tarts, in a queenly manner, to your loyal subjects.

Kitsch

Nothing kills the fun of kitsch more effectively than a serious discussion of the subject. I once read several highbrow books about kitsch and came away thoroughly disillusioned by the critics' inability to appreciate the lighter side of vulgarity. However, I am only too aware that one person's kitsch is another person's tasteless and another's tasteful, so I would never claim the high ground when it comes to sharing my own particular brand of trashy style.

For instance, I think this cake stand is the most marvelous piece of Art Deco tableware. I love the wicked, sugary colors, the design, the curve of the handle, and the lightning zigzags on the layers of glass, which suggest something a little racier than a more sedate floral cake stand.

I think the key to kitsch is a certain knowingness and irony. I am too much of a realist to be straightforward in my enjoyment of cake stands and crinoline lady tablecloths. I know that you know that I know this is all quite amusing and frivolous. But, underneath it all, I am interested in what made these objects tasteful at some point; because I am quite sure that someone really did think that this yellow and pink confection was the height of sophistication either in their own home or in a rather sophisticated tea shop. I hope very much that it was proffered by a waitress or maid with a starched, white, frilly apron and matching frill on her hair.

But what's not to like about a kitsch cake stand? It made me think immediately of fondant or French fancies, which look great but leave me feeling quite ill. These are the little pink and yellow iced confections with cake and cream inside that were definitely the thing to be seen eating in the 1930s, preferably with a matching silk dress. So I went out and bought a box and, indeed, the cakes and stand match beautifully.

When the cake stand was displayed for the first time, it was amusing to see the reactions it drew. Simon, accustomed to my kitsch style after years of indulging it, loved it immediately. Tom and Alice barely noticed it (don't ask me how) and Phoebe thought it was fabulous and began planning matching cupcakes. Tim, who paints our house and never balks at the colors I choose, hated it and reckoned that anything I'd paid for it was too much. And yet he didn't turn his nose up at the fondant fancies and was quite happy to eat them when I'd finished my photography.

There really is no accounting for taste.

Bookish style

We all have different names for the sweater vest. Although I grew up as one of the generation of "tank top" wearers, I'm sticking with "slipover" these days. The pale blue version pictured opposite, left, with a deep V-neck and wide ribbing, is my first ever slipover (I never liked the Bay City Rollers so didn't disgrace myself by wearing an Argyle tank top). The night it was completed, I modeled it immediately and then had to take it off several times while the rest of the family tried it on. It's a style that seems to suit us all. I have to admit that Simon looked a little like a has-been dancer with the Ballet Russe in a warm-up outfit, but it gave the rest of us an air of intellectual bohemi-anism and a suggestion of living either in a boys' boarding school or a large, unheated house.

A slipover is the kind of knitted garmet that cries out for club/committee/school badges. I'm not saying it's nerdy, but it certainly moves in that direction. I have some vintage badges that look self-importantly good when I'm in my librarian mode, and Phoebe's Blue Peter badges coordinate beautifully with the general bluishness and bookishness.

As I wore my new slipover, I considered the whole sleeveless pullover phenomenon. They seem to have

been popular from the 1930s onwards with genera-tions of hobbyists, engineers and university lecturers; the kind of men who have creased, corduroy jackets with patches on the elbows, a pipe in one hand and a crossword in the other. A slipover can suggest all sorts of manly interests that could be hampered by long sleeves—from gardening to model railways, from mending machinery to marking essays with ink pens.

Some of our "national treasures" favor the slipover, with its connotations of shabby Englishness. What else would Stephen Fry, Tony Benn and David Hockney wear? The Bloomsbury set wore slipovers with holes in them (Duncan Grant and Quentin Bell in particular) and the 1930s intellectuals and code-breakers are bound to have worn them, shirt sleeves rolled up, bangs flopping over foreheads, while they debated Communism and cracked the Enigma code.

It's also no coincidence that children's author Enid Blyton made sure that her adventurers were well-dressed for outdoor pursuits in slipovers that their invisible mothers and nannies no doubt whipped up for them while they were busy apprehending villains and foiling both criminal gangs *and* the police. And slipovers are beloved of illustrators to connote out-of-school mischief-makers—I'm sure Richmal Crompton's William had a stack of them stored with his cricket balls, pea-shooters, catapults and jawbreakers.

In all of this research, I couldn't find many women in slipovers although there has since been a full-scale reappraisal of the style and suddenly there are masses of lovely, striped, Fair Isle sleeveless tops for everyone. I am convinced Katharine Hepburn must have worn a smart slipover at some point, but it seems my best

style icon is the Prince of Wales (later King Edward VII), pictured opposite. A Fair Isle slipover *and* an apron must be the pinnacle of bookish domestic style, and that's something I can aspire to quite happily.

Fogey style

My second slipover, pictured above right, was knitted while watching the TV programs to mark the centennial of the birth of John Betjeman, poet and writer, railway enthusiast. I've always had a soft spot for Betjeman since I studied his poetry at school. Much as I admire some of his poems, though, I admire his writing on English architecture even more, and his work on railway stations the most.

This slipover is knitted in charcoal-grey merino wool with a bright pink edge (a little like a school uniform slipover on acid). It seems to me to be the ideal garment to wear while wandering around the old railway stations and churches of England, with a Shell Guide in hand (preferably one edited by John Betjeman himself). I've seen a photo of Betjeman enveloped in the baggiest hand-knitted cardigan ever worn by a Poet Laureate, but I could easily picture him in a version of this slipover, with maybe a mustardy or greenish edge, talking lyrically about bell towers and station cafés.

I understand Betjeman perfectly when he writes and speaks about railways. I love his evocative descriptions of trains, journeys and stations, and his documentaries with black-and-white footage of the old, more expansive railways are wonderfully enthusiastic and poetic. I've long dreamed of living in a former railway station on a pretty, rural line using the waiting room as a study and the booking hall as a living room. I even joined the Victorian Society (cofounded by Betjeman to save marvelous nineteenth-century buildings) so that I could stay at the cutting edge of fogeyism.

There's a lot to be said for fogey slipover style: the faintly shabby and eccentric air it carries makes the wearer look as if he or she has just emerged from some time warp where they were having a very pleasant time. And that is exactly how I feel when I've been exploring the delights of the old railways in my Wellington boots and raincoat, book and maps in hand, with the ghost of John Betjeman at my side.

Stitching by numbers

I was solemnly and carefully stitching an iron-on transfer embroidery design one evening, when Alice made a typically astute comment. She was surprised, she said, at what I was doing. She told me she thought that I usually did more creative things, but here I was, just mechanically filling in someone else's design with stitches. How boring, she thought.

Of course, this made me think about the reasons why I was embroidering by numbers, so to speak, and why I chose to stay on, and within, the lines, and color in the spaces using threads like felt-tip pens, instead of developing my own, individual style of embroidery.

I'd been collecting vintage embroidered tablecloths and framed pictures for a while (I still do). I tend to buy crinoline ladies, cottage gardens and floral displays on white or neutral linen or cotton. The more color, brightness and virtuoso embroidery the better, and I am drawn to pieces that clearly demonstrate a certain stitching confidence and expertise. It's a very specific style, which is too sugary and passé for many, but for me it is the highest expression of the "coloring-in" style of embroidery. Crinoline lady embroidery was despised by "art" embroiderers as dull and lifeless and a waste of good skills, but these dainty designs remind you just how few people can embroider beautifully these days.

Not long before the conversation with Alice, I'd realized I wanted to pick up embroidery again, but wasn't sufficiently sure of my design skills. My modest collection of crinoline ladies made me think about retracing a graphic that many other women used seventy years ago. Originally, I considered making a very twenty-first-century, ironic, psychedelic style crinoline lady with lime-green hair and tattoos, surrounded by plants with blue leaves. She was to be machine-embroidered, sequined and beaded and thoroughly postmodern.

Then I decided this interpretation could wait and that what I really wanted to do was bring my own choice of colors and stitches to a hand-embroidered version. It made me realize just how many variables there are in this sort of filling-in. It doesn't feel creatively hollow or mindless; every chosen stitch requires concentration, every new color can make or break the effect, every space can be filled or left empty.

In fact, stitching by numbers is a wonderful way to reconnect with embroidery. It is a meeting point between popular culture and elite culture that has a style of its own and, although highbrow embroiderers could claim it devalues aesthetic standards, those who enjoy coloring-in know the fun, satisfaction and pleasure it offers. It may lack an original design, but then there are only a few embroiderers like May Morris, Constance Howard or Phoebe Traquair, three of the most influential figures in modern embroidery, per generation. The rest of us have to be grateful for the hand-holding and guidance an iron-on transfer offers.

The Tate Postcard Quilt

Tate Britain is my favorite large gallery in London, with its huge, calm, airy space, quiet research room, Rex Whistler murals in the restaurant and legendary wine list. But the jewel in its crown is the collection of Victorian paintings crammed with detail, narrative, melodrama, color and commentary. Whenever I visit, for whatever reason, I always have a quick check to make sure the classics are there before carrying on.

Sometimes, when I'm not pressed for time, I also like to wander through the twentieth-century rooms with their paintings by Stanley Spencer, Winifred Nicholson and Harold Gilman. I think the definitive word here is "wander." It is so refreshing to visit an art gallery without a specific purpose, simply to spend time in front of a canvas you like and walk past the ones that don't appeal. When I visit an exhibition I feel duty-bound to look at everything so that I can form an opinion, which makes it more of an intellectual exercise.

In fact, I reckon that wasting time in an art gallery can be hugely productive. When I had an hour to kill in the Tate recently, I came away buzzing with ideas for a quilt. I'd bought some fabrics but I couldn't see what to do with them. I don't often choose geometrics and primary colors, but this collection of highly stylized florals and graphics reminded me of bold furnishing fabrics and the wild, original Biba-style of Art Deco meets Art Nouveau meets glamour.

Just wandering through the rooms allowed my mind to relax and my eye was caught by a Terry Frost painting *June, Red and Black* (1965), which immediately made me think of the fabrics in my cupboard, waiting for the Great Idea to strike. When I got to the Tate shop, I riffled through all the postcards and found more fabulous paintings that incorporate red, black and white. At home I arranged the cards into a "postcard quilt" with a mix of styles: Post-Impressionist, New English, Tudor, modern, abstract, and photomontage. I suddenly saw that I could take these various pieces of inspiration and, by fusing certain elements, create something that expressed my own style. My fabrics had initially appeared quite difficult to work with, but these paintings helped me to see them in a more manageable light.

I was now able to appreciate the possibility of playfulness even with such dictatorial color, and I saw that the quilt they were to become need not automatically be a solid, 1970s-style statement. Although I'm not always sure how best to introduce an apparently risky color to alter an effect, the cards demonstrated how it could be achieved. I could see that some leaf- or bottle-green could work brilliantly, that the addition of more circles and dots would enliven the mix and that the repetition of motifs could be emphasized to positive effect.

The result is the Tate Postcard Quilt, made up of fabric "postcards" that measure 3" by 7". When I'd finished the top, I put the postcards on the quilt and was amazed to see how many motifs and shapes and patterns had been replicated in the quilt, and yet it matches no single card. It's my very own Tate-style fusion, and I'm proud of it.

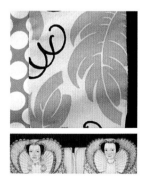

Saintly patrons

Craftspeople and artists have always relied on patrons for support. Invisible purchasers, collectors and sponsors enable financially fragile makers and creators to pursue their work. Matisse needed Gertrude Stein, Christopher Wren needed Queen Anne and Leonardo da Vinci needed Francis I. Some richer souls such as William Morris, Louis Comfort Tiffany and Andrew Lloyd Webber have been patrons as well as creators.

Although, like most people, I can only be a patron on a very small scale, I enjoy the opportunity to practice what I preach in regards to buying directly from makers. I think we should support independent craftspeople whenever possible, and have visited the annual Chelsea Crafts Fair in Central London for many years. Now that it has outgrown Chelsea Town Hall, it has been renamed Origin and has moved to Somerset House. But the concept remains the same. It is still a showcase for new and established craftspeople, and it is still a stylish celebration of the hand-made.

The concept of the "craft fair" is tarnished with a dowdy image of earnest, well-meaning people making dull, plain items mostly from lumpy clay and string. But Origin brings together brilliant, innovative artists making beautiful, desirable, useful pieces in willow, silver, textiles, wood, ceramics and glass. On each of my visits I have bought some small, beautifully crafted work. Even when I have had little or no spare cash, it has always been worth investing in something from a maker whose work I may never come across again. As a result, I have a modest but well-formed collection, and each item within it reminds me of the person who made it.

My purchases may be streamlined, sophisticated and tasteful. Or they may be quirky, obviously hand-made and witty. But each piece is full of character, personal, and carries the metaphorical thumbprint of its maker. I love the large dotted bowl with its Miro-esque pattern, pictured opposite, made by Roop and Al of Ramp (www.rampceramics.co.uk), and I use the cake stand pictured below by Alexandra Mitchell (www.alexandramitchell.co.uk) all the time. It supports a good-size cake, looks quite lovely and is about the same price as a mass-produced version, but I would much rather see my homemade cake on a homemade stand because together they have all the hallmarks of stylish domesticity.

I think that anyone who is interested in the gentle arts should become a patron saint of craftspeople. I guarantee you will be well rewarded, if only in the here and now.

My purchases may be streamlined, sophisticated and tasteful. Or they may be quirky, obviously hand-made and witty. But each piece is full of character, personal, and carries the metaphorical thumbprint of its maker.

Comfort

Comforting thoughts

The gentle arts are all about comfort. They are soothing, relaxing, consoling and caring. They benefit both the maker and those around her with the creation of a comfortable, creative, tactile environment in which individuals can feel secure, at ease, happy—even if it is only a temporary respite from more pressing cares.

Comfort is relative. It doesn't strike me as healthy to inhabit a comfort zone all the time. Better to have tougher, more exacting times that highlight the nature and value of our comforts, than to believe we can remain snug, cozy and protected from the slings and arrows of outrageous fortune forever. I am all the more aware of my own comfort because it has not always been there, and may well not be there in the future, and I find it's better to be realistic than to be wrapped up in a metaphorical, consoling quilt all day long.

For me, comfort is a feeling of well-being, positive thinking and contentment. My sense of comfort does not always have to be tranquil or calm or passive. Sometimes I prefer it to be full of laughs, music, energy and creativity, all of which stems from the fundamental fact that true comfort means being at ease with myself. My personal interpretation of comfort is primarily psychological, and not simply physical; the knowledge that I can have hot baths, cups of tea and warm fires when I want them is as important as the actual manifestations of comfort themselves.

But the gentle art of domesticity allows many combinations of physical and mental comfort, and one often gives rise to, and enhances, the other. And when you make time to knit a tea cozy, bake scones or sew a family quilt, you will be twice comforted; once with the process of making and then again with the comforting end-product.

Coming in from the cold

Isn't it wonderful to arrive home on a cold, wet, dark and windy night to a well-lit, warm, safe, domestic environment? I love the feeling of comfort that comes when you open the door to familiarity, coziness and a cup of hot tea. So can you imagine what it felt like for Captain Scott and his men when they came back to their Antarctic hut after days or weeks exploring one of the world's most amazing yet appalling landscapes?

I am fascinated by Scott's expeditions (1901–04 and 1910–13) and the way the men coped with extremes that tested their mental and physical toughness way beyond the limits most people could endure. I can spend hours looking at Herbert Ponting's stark yet uplifting black-and-white photographs of the ice, and I was amazed when I first saw the delicate, intelligent watercolors by Dr. Edward Wilson of the continent's stunningly colorful auroras. Most of all, I love reading about Scott's Hut (pictured below), the wooden building the men erected on the edge of Antarctica and which held them, their belongings and their discoveries for months on end during the second expedition.

The hut was a literal and metaphorical beacon in a deadly landscape, and it's not hard to be drawn into the photos and descriptions of the warmth and coziness the men created. Here is a perfect example of the male domestic artist, who brings with him photos of home and loved ones, favorite pipes and books, chess sets and playing cards, Christmas presents in a box labeled "festivities," sewing kits to make and repair

sleeping bags, footwear and clothing, baking materials to keep the men supplied with fresh bread and a truly British cheerfulness in the face of unimaginable adversity.

These days, explorers wear scientifically developed synthetic fabrics with myriad properties that combat cold, wind, sweat and bacteria. Scott and his men went out in hand-knitted hats and socks, thick naval sweaters and Burberry outerwear. There is something heartbreaking about their domesticity, and yet it reaffirms the tremendous value of comfort and hominess to day-to-day survival. Scott's diaries are littered with the words "comfort" and "comfortable" when writing about the hut, and he was clearly quite delighted with the domestic space they created. On January 19, 1911, he wrote in his diary, "The hut is becoming the most comfortable dwelling place imaginable . . . a truly seductive home, within the walls of which peace, quiet, and comfort reign supreme."

It's clear that routine, busyness and domestic chores were vital to the men's sense of well-being and mental health. But Scott and his men took it further and created a real sense of comfort that sustained them when they were forced to be in the hut, and welcomed them when they returned. There was no softness in this cramped and makeshift life, which was smelly, drafty and overcrowded, but there is a deep-seated recognition that the gentle art of homemaking can be transported and kept alive even in Antarctica, the antithesis of a comfortable environment.

Here is a perfect example of the male domestic artist, who brings with him photos of home and loved ones, favorite pipes and books, chess sets and playing cards, Christmas presents in a box labeled "festivities," sewing kits to make and repair sleeping bags . . .

Knitting comfort

One of my very favorite knitting paintings is *The Schoolgirl's Hymn* (pictured above left), painted by William Holman Hunt in 1859. Holman Hunt was one of the leading Pre-Raphaelite painters (*the* leading one, if you read his autobiography), and I find many of his paintings overwrought, overblown and over-symbolic. But I adore the simplicity of this picture.

It's very small and shimmers with light and jewel-like colors. It hangs in the Ashmolean Museum in Oxford and is utterly charming. The sincerity and the subject are touching, but I am enthralled by his rendition of the hand-knitted cardigan and scarf. Somehow,

Holman Hunt manages to convey all the comfort of children's clothes, which have love and care knitted into every stitch.

It could have been hands like those pictured above right that made the girl's clothes. They are the hands of any sensible mother or aunt, grandmother or sister, all ready to create comfort for others. They are on the cover of a volume published in 1940 with patterns for comfortable classics such as "A Matron's Jumper," "A Child's Liberty Bodice," "A Warm Knee-cap for Winter." And, of course, "A Schoolgirl's Jumper."

The sacred rock bun

I sometimes think our marriage is built, not on rock, but on rock buns. The rock bun has special status in our house. It is not merely a plain, humble, baked item, but the stuff of intense debate, comparative tastings and emotional investment.

Simon and I discuss the ratio of sultanas (golden raisins) to regular raisins, whether to use undyed or dyed glacé cherries, a fifth or a quarter of grated nutmeg, and what constitutes optimum squidginess. Then, sometimes, all the ingredients come together in a Perfect Baking Moment and we are so busy eating that we forget to analyze why they worked so well.

We have maintained this rock bun discourse all through our married life. It's a perfect metaphor for the way our marriage works. We talk about the day-to-day trivia, the details, the work, the children, but don't really examine too closely the big issues, the reasons why we are comfortable with each other. We find it's far more important to get on with the living and the eating.

Rock buns represent comfort and reliability, and not a little indulgence. The problem is that many people think they should be some kind of penance and like literal rocks—hard, dry and stingy with the sultanas. I disagree. I think a good rock bun, like a good marriage, is a wonderful thing.

Here's my recipe, which will fill your kitchen with warmth and the sweet smell of nutmeg and grated lemon rind. And make others very, very happy.

Fruity Rock Buns

Rock buns are something of a scone crossed with a fruit cake. I don't think they should be crumbly and dry, but fruity, moist, nutmeggy and quite rich. As for fruit, this is our favorite combination, but you can add less, change the proportions or alter the choice. It's also a great recipe to follow with children: lots of basic chopping, measuring, whisking and finger-licking. Tom has become quite adept at cutting the butter into the flour and sugar; I wanted to make sure he could make his own rock bun comfort when he's older and not have to wait to marry someone who could do it for him.

Makes 12

INGREDIENTS

1½ cups plain flour
2 level teaspoons baking powder
¼ teaspoon salt
about ¼ freshly grated nutmeg
¾ cup soft brown sugar
¾ cup unsalted butter (at room temperature)
⅓ cup golden raisins
⅓ cup raisins
⅓ cup glacé cherries (halved)
finely grated rind of 1 unwaxed lemon
1 large egg
1–2 tablespoons milk

Preheat the oven to 375°F.

Line a large baking sheet with parchment paper.

Sift the flour, baking powder, salt and grated nutmeg into a large bowl. Stir in the sugar, then add the butter. Cut in the butter until the mixture resembles fine breadcrumbs and feels sandy. Stir in the fruit and lemon rind.

Whisk the egg and 1 tablespoon of the milk together. Make a well in the center of the dry mixture and add the egg mixture. Mix quickly with a fork. If the mixture is too dry and crumbly, add a little more milk, but be careful not to make it too slack or it will turn into cookies. It should come to a stiffish dough quickly—I think one of the tricks with rock buns is not to handle the ingredients too much.

Using your hands (my preferred method) or two forks, pile the mixture into twelve individual "rocks" on the baking sheet. Bake for 15 to 20 minutes until golden brown and with the tiniest hint of squishiness on top. The buns will continue to cook when you have taken them out of the oven. Leave to cool on a wire rack (although, it has to be said, these are just delicious when still a little warm.)

Prepare tea/juice/gin and tonic, put a rock bun on your plate, make yourself comfortable and enjoy.

Last imperfect

It is quite possible to become inured to the charms of the homemade. We are so conditioned by supermarkets, television, magazines and style pundits to seek perfection in all we buy, from carrots to china, from sweaters to jewelry, that we can lose the ability to see the unique attributes of a hand-made piece. So much of what we now buy is mass-manufactured, streamlined and carefully selected that often no trace of nature or a human hand remains in our homes.

But I think this modern, flaw-free approach to purchasing is cold and sterile. I find a huge amount of reassurance in the hand-made and the homemade, in the rejection of perfection, and I take great comfort in the fact that there are still many domestic artists for whom the "actual doing of things is in itself a joy," as D. H. Lawrence wrote.

For domestic comfort lies in the knowledge that things do not have to be perfect. I don't know how many times I heard the phrase "a good enough mother" when the children were little, and I am still not sure how you would define one, but I *do* know that "a good enough domestic artist" is just fine. Many women in the past had no option but to be good enough because they couldn't afford perfection and had to make do with what they themselves could create.

I have a growing collection of hand-embroidered textiles that date mostly from the 1930s, with crinoline ladies, flowers, cottages and gardens embroidered on tablecloths, tray cloths, tea cozies, aprons, hankies. I am not bothered in the slightest about the monetary value of these textiles, but am passionate about their social and creative value.

In 2002 there was an exhibition in New Zealand of homemade textiles from the 1930s to the 1950s. More than 40,000 visitors came to look at crocheted aprons, embroidered needle-cases, cottage garden tea cozies, patchwork aprons and rag rugs. The scale of interest in what many curators and collectors would deem unworthy, derivative or worthless, gave Rosemary McLeod the impetus to write her book *Thrift to Fantasy: Home Textile Crafts of the 1930s –1950s,* which is full of photos of pieces from the exhibition and her own collection. The text, in which she attempts to understand and explain the place and value of these textiles in the lives of their creators, is also excellent.

These domestic artists created a phenomenal body of work, which brought them comfort, color and pleasure. Although this type of "women's work" comes under fire from many quarters for being symbolic of such terrifying concepts as female submission, repression and patriarchal control, I believe that it offered immense creative satisfaction and gratification to many. The sheer variety of pattern, fabric, stitch, color and skill is breathtaking, and there is humor, whimsy and elegance everywhere you look. This is domestic artistry, with all its imperfections, at its finest.

Textile treasures

I love the French film *Amélie* (see Inspiration, page 40) and its cast of slightly strange but endearing characters. Each one has manic or obsessive tendencies and is a collector: of proverbs, discarded photos, endives, jealousies, copies of a Renoir painting. They accumulate these quirky objects, words and emotions to form quite beautiful, if apparently meaningless, collections.

Watching *Amélie* made me think about my own collecting tendencies. When I was young, I wanted to be a great amasser of undervalued objects, but never wanted to collect valuable items. As a child I had trolls, and then I moved on to dried pasta, sequins and even my own teeth as a teenager. But I have never fulfilled my collecting ambitions, partly because I am afraid of feeling compelled to spend any spare cash on growing a collection purely for the sake of owning objects, and partly because I run out of steam quickly and my magpie instincts are easily distracted by a new whim. I am also loath to keep special things under glass or locked away, and much prefer to *use* any small collections I have.

So vintage textiles are perfect for me. I can whip out a hand-embroidered tablecloth with flowers to match my cupcakes, wrap a hand-made apron around my waist to be transported to the 1950s, place a silk-lined tea cozy on my teapot and hang framed, embroidered pictures of ladies with doves, thatched cottages and hollyhocks where I can see them every day.

I recently bought a number of tablecloths featuring crinoline ladies. I find crinoline ladies completely old-fashioned yet totally seductive. I scour flea markets in small towns when on holiday, friends look out for

I find a huge amount of reassurance in the hand-made and the homemade, in the rejection of perfection, and I take great comfort in the fact that there are still many domestic artists for whom the "actual doing of things is in itself a joy," as D. H. Lawrence wrote.

them, and some I find on eBay. I have a strict budget and I prefer hand-embroidery on natural fabrics. Amazingly, it didn't take me long to make a great little crinoline-lady collection that didn't cost a fortune.

The crinoline lady is a 1930s icon. She was everywhere: on textiles, china, tea cozies and magazine covers. I know she is highly stylized and ridiculously escapist, but I am fascinated by the fact that so many women bought iron-on transfers and, during their breaks from turning the wringer and mopping linoleum floors, sat and embroidered solitary ladies who were, in truth, only good for picking flowers and looking pretty.

Transfers also came free with magazines such as the *Needlewoman* and, once I started collecting, I found several pieces made to the same design. The embroideries shown here are all embroidered on the same basic outline of what has become my favorite design, but all by different needlewomen.

The ladies on cloth 1 (pictured opposite, top left) are in the four corners of the same huge, sturdy linen tablecloth. They are sewn by an accomplished needlewoman who clearly was not afraid of bold color combinations and of setting thickly covered sections next to simple lines, and whose quality of stitching is breathtaking. I particularly like the ribbons in tangerine and deep orange, emerald and cerise, lemon and lilac, which give each lady an engaging personality of her own. The fourth figure is unfinished; I bought the cloth knowing it was not completed because I was so astonished by the unusual, confident colors that seem to belong to a later age.

Cloth 2 (pictured opposite, top right) is on a textured, woven cotton fabric and colored in a very different, more restricted palette of pinks, oranges, blues and purples. The four ladies are almost identical (just the spots on the ribbons vary), and they reveal a creative control and decisiveness on the part of the embroiderer. This cloth is unusual for the way she

created a distinctive hooped, spotted effect with plenty of spaces left open, and the manner in which the ladies appear almost subsumed into their gardens.

Cloth 3 (pictured opposite, center) has four strikingly outlined ladies in lilac who are very much in charge of the flower picking. Their creator has made a different choice of stitches—look at the buttonhole stitches in the hollyhocks and the way these are less dense than the other women's pieces. The focus is on the clearly delineated lady who dominates her garden.

Cloth 4 (pictured opposite, bottom left) is a more delicate piece of work altogether. It's on very fine, light linen and is more traditionally feminine and pretty. The ladies are dressed in pale pink and peaches and sky blue (there are two sets of twins here), and they appear more shy and retiring next to the confident orange and sapphire hollyhocks. They are definitely more Melanie Hamilton than Scarlett O'Hara in *Gone with the Wind*.

Cloth 5 (pictured opposite, bottom right) is spectacular, and these ladies are undoubtedly closely related to Scarlett. They are on a large, high-quality linen cloth and are completely filled in with stitching. The effect is stunningly artistic, and the eye moves over the cloth taking in the exuberant couture dresses and the surrounding flowers skillfully depicted in shades that grow paler with height.

I am fascinated by the way each piece of vintage hand-embroidery I own tells me something about its creator, and there is comfort in handling these textiles, knowing that I am appreciating something that was of great value to its maker. The markedly individual interpretations wrought into these dainty designs are what remain of a generation of domestic embroiderers, and we should certainly not overlook the status of these textiles in a world that was comfortable with the hand-made.

Like all frivolous, apparently meaningless collections, they are truly worth preserving.

Cozy comfort

Tea cozies make me laugh. I think it must be the contrast between their often whimsical and extravagant forms and their very unexciting role in life, namely keeping tea warm. For such a humble symbol of comfort and coziness, the tea cozy gives rise to the most dazzling array of interpretations. Tea cozies can be crocheted, knitted, embroidered or quilted. They can be made from crazy patchwork, tapestry, silk, linen, cotton or felted woolens. They can be cabled, checked, striped, zigzagged, bobbled and have leaves, pompoms or flowers. They can come in the shape of cottages, dolls (complete with head, arms and torso), animals, cakes, Christmas puddings and fruit. All in all, the tea cozy is one of the most versatile vehicles for creative expression available to the domestic artist.

I tend to think of tea-cozy occasions as being the epitome of comfort. I believe tea cozies are not suited to formal events because they are too homely and kitsch. Instead, I like to think of tea cozies being used for the domestic occasions when there is a kettle on the stove or the fire, second-best and much-loved china on the table, a bright, cheerful cloth underneath, a plate of tea cakes ready to be eaten and fresh flowers in a jug. Tea cozies should keep tea hot while drinkers read books and newspapers, exchange gossip, listen to the radio or simply gaze out of the window. There is something unhurried about tea cozies; they demand a little less rush and a little more comfort. Something we could all do with.

Tea and oranges

I have always wanted to make old-fashioned tea cozies, but only knitted my first a little while ago. I found a traditional pattern in *Rowan Classic Home* (book five in the Classic series), which had been updated with modern colors and pearl beads, and this was what I used for my Tea and Oranges cozy (pictured opposite).

When I was seventeen I spent a summer as an au pair, learning French by the beach in the south of France. In return I looked after the two shockingly behaved children of two shockingly behaved parents. But I soaked up the sun, language, garlic, freedom, Racine and Molière, and came home fluent, bronzed and 15 pounds heavier.

As the parents went out most nights, I played their records on my own. One of these was Leonard Cohen's *Greatest Hits* album (1975), and I adored his terrible nasal whine, the sparse sounds and guitar, the amazing lyrics. I played "Suzanne" more than any other, often lifting the record player needle and replacing it so I could hear him sing the phrase "tea and oranges" over and over again. I still play Leonard Cohen when I'm feeling happy, and he transports me to that sunny French summer of topless sunbathing and cheap wine.

So an orange tea cozy was always in the cards. I bought the lovely orange Anny Blatt yarn in Paris and I added peach-colored Gütterman beads to enhance the orange peel effect. Then I needed leaves and I used some leftover, deep green yarns knitted double to make them thicker and sturdier. The leaf pattern is from *Nicky Epstein's Knitted Flowers,* and I made quite a number, ending up with a generous amount of foliage. I think these 1930s style tea cozies need to be less than subtle, anyway. Finally, of course, my orange tea cozy required an orange cake, and Nigel Slater's Marmalade Cake in *The Kitchen Diaries* was just right for afternoon tea, especially when the icing was colored to match.

The Tea and Oranges cozy sits on an old-fashioned, eight-cup, Brown Betty teapot in my kitchen. Teapot, tea cozy, tea, oranges and memories are all comfortably knitted together in one enduring textile.

Quilting comfort

If the coziness of textiles could be measured on a scale of one to ten slices of hot, buttered toast, then I think homemade quilts rate ten slices, plus tea, Marmite, a roaring log fire and BBC Radio 4.

I fell in love with the idea of quilts long before I made my own. I admired the tradition of thrift and recycling old, worn textiles and clothes into a cozy covering that can be snuggled under, thrown over and wrapped around. I was captivated by the incredible range of designs, from the very simplest strips and squares to the most complex hexagons, triangles and interlocking circles. I enjoyed looking carefully at all the colors and fabrics and patterns someone else had selected, the way they had been put together, the choices the quilter had made. And I loved the fact that quilting could be a homey form of creative self-expression to be picked up and put down according to the rhythms of domesticity.

When I started making my quilts I had several objectives in mind. One was to play with fabrics, patterns and colors. The other was to quilt comfort. I've been asked what I do with all my quilts and the answer is: use them. They are on beds, chairs and sofas. We throw them over sick children, cold feet and empty spaces. The children lie on them, Simon uses them as extra pillows, and the hamster is cuddled in his very own Hamster Quilt. And there is no sight lovelier and more gratifying than a child reading a book under a homemade quilt, cozy and oblivious to the world.

Quilts age beautifully, and those made with pure cotton acquire a lovely, worn feel. When I see an old quilt with missing stitches, a few replacement patches and evidence of wear and tear, I think of all the comfort it has offered to those who have enjoyed its warmth and I hope that mine will not stay in a perfect, pristine condition. That would not be a comforting or comfortable prospect.

The Domestic Front Quilt

I am not terribly traditional in my quilt tastes, but the simple and classic American combination of red and white always appeals. My quilt is a very simplified version and is made with rectangles placed to create alternating positive and negative blocks. But, much as I enjoyed playing with the optical effects, I also had great fun with the fabrics. Most of them carry small, domestic motifs such as teapots, hens, lilies-of-the-valley, scarecrows and chrysanthemums. This combination of overarching structure and small, close-up detail is doubly pleasing. I enjoy seeing the overall organization from a distance, and am happy to scrutinize the details of domesticity when I sit with the quilt over my knees.

This has become one of the most-used and best-loved quilts in the house, especially by Tom, who claimed it for himself as soon as it was completed. I named it the Domestic Front not only because of the themed fabrics, but also because I am inclined to think that the home can be something of a battle zone from time to time. Tom, in particular, is always prepared to draw up a plan of attack and apply it until I surrender. He doesn't win all the time, but he did with the quilt. Of course, as soon as a teenage boy lets you know that he likes something you've made, he is already the victor. And you have only to see him under it, tired after a rugby match or a battle of wills, to know that he's not really General Custer.

Verb Quilt, or the Être et Avoir Quilt

Quilting while testing children on French verbs can be very comforting. Unlike verbs, stitches are regular, and quilt patterns are far easier to memorize than conjugations. The occupation of the hands is a great balm to the mind that wants to rage against children not being taught the structure of a language before applying the irregularities—a little like trying to quilt pieces of fabric that haven't been stitched together.

I made this while Tom was learning the present tense of the verbs *être* and *avoir*. Night after night, we sat and repeated the same verbs and the same stitches. At the end of it, he was word-perfect and I had a bright red and turquoise quilt that is warming to both the eye and body. It may have a boy's discomfort with French verbs sewn into it, but every other stitch represents a mother's comfort in a testing time.

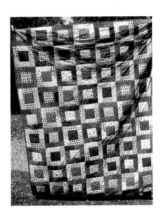

Books and covers

I am not the world's most generous knitter. I rarely knit for anyone else other than the occupants of our house and the house itself. This way, I save myself a great deal of time and guilt. But Nicola Beauman, who runs Persephone Books in London (see Resources, page 277) was so very kind and complimentary about my cashmere hot-water-bottle cover that I was delighted to make her one in dove-grey. And, in fact, this small, soothing piece with its soft yarn and regular cables was a pleasure to knit for someone else.

The knitted cover goes with the book covers perfectly. But there is also a lovely match on a metaphorical level. For I think the Persephone list—mostly neglected fiction and nonfiction by women and for women—contains some of the best hot-water-bottle literature to be found anywhere.

You know what I mean. The kind of book you take to bed with a nice cup of tea and a favorite cookie, or read by the fire snuggled under a quilt. The kind of book that is well written and truly readable. The kind of thoughtful, entertaining book into which you can escape, and from which you return with a new perspective.

The pattern I used for the cover is in *Sarah Dallas Knitting* (another lovely, comforting book, full of mittens and blankets and scarves), but I chose to knit it in Rowan Silk Wool to give an extra dimension of indulgence. Finally, I crocheted a pretty scalloped edge in acknowledgment of the fact that hot-water-bottle literature can offer comfort without necessarily sacrificing style.

Seven comforts

Once upon a time, I was a PhD student. I read the novels of Dickens interspersed with collections of fairy tales. I read deeply serious literary criticism and journals. I worked in hushed, overheated libraries, ate too much candy and used too many page markers. One day, a little bird suggested that maybe I couldn't take this much longer. That maybe I needed fresh air, color, creativity and a lot less printed matter.

Even though the little bird did me a favor, I still think in terms of the themes I was exploring. One of these was the meaning of magic, significant numbers in fairy tales and especially the number seven. As in seven dwarfs, ravens, years, brides, sisters, daughters, brooms, wonders and spells. Even now I find myself counting things and I am not surprised to find I have seven favorite domestic comforts.

Tea

I know it's an English cliché, but there's nothing like a good cup of tea. I was a confirmed coffee drinker until I had Tom and Alice and then I rapidly morphed into the stereotypical mother whose main aim in life is to have a nice cup of tea and take a break. Tea makes a lot of things all right. It makes early mornings bearable, goes well with crosswords, toast and Marmite, and is the perfect accompaniment to books, chocolate cookies, films, knitting, sewing, friends and chat. Tea is the literal undercurrent of my domesticity and, with its immutable timetable, the stuff of comforting routine.

Radio

I am a BBC Radio 4 listener. Radio 4 is a gift to domestic artists, and the online "Listen Again" feature is that gift tied up with ribbons and bows. This option means that you can hear your favorite programs as and when you like, up to seven days after the first transmission. Oh, the sheer pleasure of sewing quilts while listening to the classics being read in beautifully modulated tones, or of knitting while laughing at *The News Quiz* or *Just a Minute,* the joy of weeping to a monologue by Lynne Truss (author of *Eats, Shoots & Leaves*) spoken by the British actor Douglas Hodge while your embroidery hangs in midair as you stop to catch every sound, or of ironing to programs about poetry, books and food. And all in your pajamas, should you wish. Life does not get more comfortable than this.

Unless, of course, you are wearing Birkenstocks.

Birkenstocks

I have never been able to walk in high heels and am amazed that anyone would want to. High heels are supremely uncomfortable, and I belong to that rather quaint school that prefers comfort to fashion. And, by heck, Birkenstocks are comfortable. I now realize why all the doctors and nurses in the German hospital where Tom and Alice were born wore blood-spattered Birkies all day long. Mine may be splashed with

nothing worse than olive oil or juice, but they are my footwear of choice all year round. I have house Birkies, garden Birkies and "going-out" Birkies, and my feet are sublimely comfortable in their lime green, candy pink and gold-topped cork barges. Who gives a hoot about glamour when you can coordinate your nail polish with your shoes?

Cakes

I sometimes find myself in a cake rut. It's soft, warm, spongy and quite pleasant, really, but I could do with expanding my repertoire. I rarely do, though, because there is nothing more comforting than making a favorite cake when the day is cold or miserable or wet or windy, or all four. Cake is comfort on a plate. We all bake cakes here in moments of boredom, stress, listlessness and hunger. The textures, the smells, the ingredients, the motions and rituals all create a sense of ease and well-being. We also like spontaneous, anti–Diet Police creations. Pictured opposite, far right, is Phoebe's Diet Cake, made just after New Year resolutions should have been made but weren't. It demonstrates perfectly the pro-comfort approach we prefer.

Alan Bennett

If I could, I would choose the author and playwright Alan Bennett to be my household god. His shrine, adorned with the combination of red carnations and *Alchemilla mollis* he loves, would be in the linen cupboard, and I would bring him out whenever I needed him. I'd like him to read extracts from his diaries and plays to me, talk to me about the paintings of Eric Ravilious and Stanley Spencer, discuss John

Betjeman, old films, provincial art galleries and northern English places, and make me laugh. Unfortunately, I can only listen to him on the radio, watch his plays and films and read his writings. And wish he was in the cupboard upstairs.

Friends

I love friends and *Friends.* Friends come for tea, cake and gossip; they bring me out of my domestic routine and humor my crinoline lady collection, my home-made creations, and the colors on the wall of my house. I turn to *Friends* when I'm feeling low or under the weather. *Friends* is my comfort blanket, something reliably warm and fuzzy, but with the bonus of laughter. I missed the first few seasons when we lived abroad and have never watched them in order. As a result, Joey's bangs grow and disappear and grow again, Chandler expands and contracts all the time, I can never remember whether Ross and Rachel are married or on a break, and I realize that none of the chronology matters. What is important, though, is the escape into the domestic world of the two apartments where real life barely impinges. And, with two hundred and forty episodes, I am never short of escapism.

And so to . . .

. . . bed. The ultimate in domestic comfort. What more can I say?

Even if I were granted seven wishes, I wouldn't ask for more.

Luxury

The moon and stars

Domesticity has its highs and lows. No matter how creative your approach, there will always be aspects of housekeeping that are less than thrilling. I try to tell myself that a clean bathroom, tidy living room, swept kitchen and a pantry that opens without spilling its contents are worthwhile achievements, but there are times when it just feels like hard, monotonous work.

The remedy is a little luxury every now and again. These days, in the developed world, the concept of luxury is being redefined. It is no longer related to brand and cost, but is seen in more emotive, less tangible terms. It is ironic, of course, that many of the new, sophisticated luxuries are commonplace in underdeveloped countries. Long walks on machines in gyms, organic food flown thousands of miles to a supermarket, outrageously expensive minimalist interiors, detox treatments and untreated textiles are all new versions of Marie Antoinette's *Petit Trianon* shepherdess conceit.

Despite my cynicism, I am pleased to see that luxury is now more likely to be defined in terms of the small pleasures that can enhance your sense of well-being. This has been my philosophy of luxury ever since I went to Bath with a boyfriend who thought it was too extravagant to go to a café while we were in this beautiful, historic city. As a result, I have pursued my "little and often" approach with a vengeance ever since—and I always make sure I visit a café whenever I am in Bath.

It helps to have a state of mind that can turn even the smallest indulgence into a luxury. This means looking positively at your life—considering not what you want to have, but what you can, or already, have. It means deciding for yourself what you class as luxury and not following the media's overblown ideas. Couture dresses, private jets, huge yachts and large gems are very wonderful, I'm sure, but doesn't the fact that only a handful of women in the world can afford them strike you as ridiculous? Far better to treat yourself to a couple of skeins of lovely yarn, afternoon tea and a film, a bright bunch of roses, or a small, but perfectly formed box of chocolates. As Bette Davis says at the end of *Now, Voyager,* "Don't let's ask for the moon—we have the stars."

A little of what you like does you good

"Three hundred small pleasures make people happier than one magnificent one."

DANIEL GILBERT, PROFESSOR OF PSYCHOLOGY, HARVARD UNIVERSITY

Little luxuries are more conducive to sustained well-being and pleasure than big ones. These days, this philosophy of happiness is gaining popularity and, while I don't believe that happiness is an absolute state to which we all have a right, I do agree that a little of what you like does you good.

I would hazard a guess that most relatively contented domestic artists subscribe to this philosophy (both knowingly and unknowingly) and treat themselves regularly in small but significant ways. The gentle arts offer such a wealth of little luxuries that it's not difficult to create a chain of small pleasures that link together to make a necklace of non-precious gems to adorn your life. Pretty buttons, trimmings, ribbons, lovely yarn, half a yard of a beautiful fabric, a good novel or a book of poetry, a few squares of chocolate, a box of French macaroons—all are strung on my personal necklace of luxuries.

On the button

Has anyone else noticed that buttons are like candy for grown-ups? And that button shops, like candy shops, are an endangered species that cry out for our support and protection?

I don't use many buttons, but that doesn't stop me from buying them. After all, I feel it's my moral duty to browse in the boxes and drawers of old-fashioned button shops, looking for the adult equivalent of classic English candy like aniseed balls and soor plums and mojos, so that I can spend my pocket money and emerge with a little paper bag of goodies to take home.

For beautiful vintage buttons, I go to the Button Queen on Marylebone Lane in London, a lane that seems to be held in a gentle time warp where you can still buy a button to match a hand-knitted cardigan and then have a coffee at a Formica table at Paul Rothe & Son. It may not be fancy, but the Button Queen certainly knows his buttons, a rarity these days.

But, apart from this little button enclave, there is so little button-love in England that I have to go to foreign button shops for some button luxury. Buttons are still respected in Paris, New York and Amsterdam, and I have brought home some wonderful buttons from these places. I can spend ages poking around in the boxes, racks and drawers dreaming up excuses to buy buttons, often creating elaborate plans that I know I'll forget as soon as I've left the shop clutching my tiny treasures.

I tend to buy only three or six of any button I like and then keep them until the right moment presents itself. This way, I don't feel too extravagant, and I can bring out my buttons when I need a little cheering up and admire them before putting them away again. Sometimes I even use them—mostly on the Jelly Bean Cushions (see Color, pages 56–9), which are the perfect vehicle for buttons I love but don't particularly want to be seen wearing.

The greatest luxury button shop I have found is Tender Buttons in New York (see Resources, pages 279), which should have "Abandon all hope of not spending a fortune, all ye who enter here" over the doorway. From the witty and thoughtful window display to the frames of rare buttons inside, this is button art at its most enticing. It's the Harrods of button shops, and it has a clientele and prices to match.

Unfortunately, a domestic artist isn't always able to pop to London, Paris or New York to find the perfect button, so she sometimes has to fall back on eBay. I have a set of vintage Bakelite buttons that were my first eBay purchase and an object lesson in the pride and the passion of bidding. I've also bought far less exalted buttons, and there are often some great, mixed lots in which you can find a lovely single button that is just right for a bag or to go on ribbon.

And another delightful aspect of buttons is that, like candy, they photograph beautifully, which means that you don't always have to buy to indulge in button luxury. Although there are some serious collectors' books available, the Japanese book pictured below is excellent because it shows a vast range of buttons from the ordinary to the extraordinary and it also offers lovely ideas for using them. (ISBN 978 4 579 10799 3).

We should support button makers and retailers by consuming them more frequently. And the great thing with buttons, unlike candy, is that after you have indulged in a little button consumption, you don't need to brush your teeth.

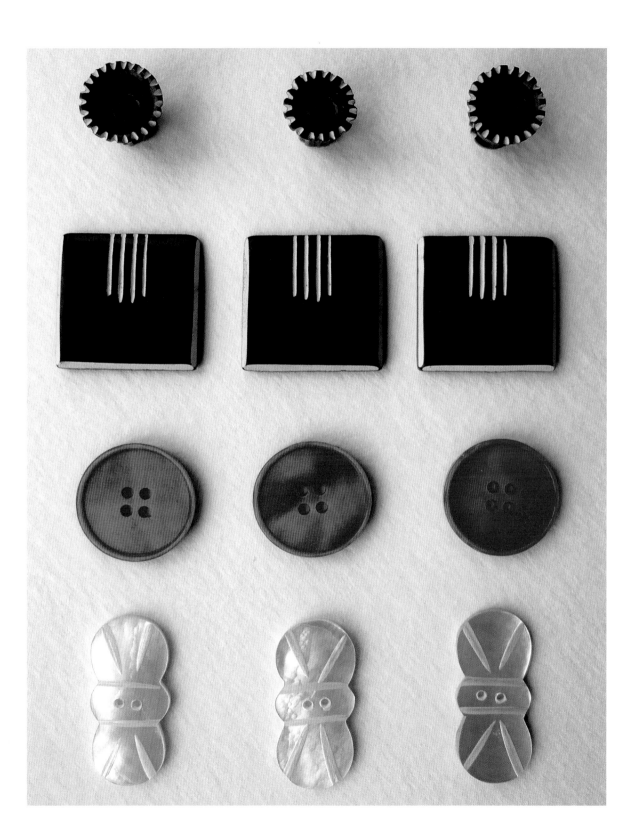

The winning combination

Qualifications for writing this:

BA (Russian and French)
MA (Victorian Art and Literature)
PhD on Charles Dickens—shelved
Master of Wine since 1992
Consumer of chocolate since first birthday
25+ years' knitting experience

I don't consider myself a material girl. I'm not looking for expensive luxuries such as fast cars, designer clothes and glittering jewelry. No, I have long since told anyone who cares to listen that there are four simple luxuries I need to make me happy. Books. Yarn. Chocolate. Wine.

There are, however, a few problems when trying to find the perfect combination of my luxuries. I hereby present the results of my many years of research, trial and error.

1) Chocolate and books

Fabbydoolidoozy, or fabulous, as Katie Morag would say in the lovely illustrated children's book by Mairi Hedderwick. No problems, plus you can use the wrappers as bookmarks and surreptitiously wipe your sticky fingers on the pages. I want to be like Jo in *Little Women,* who dashes off to her attic with apples and a book whenever she can—except that I'd substitute the apple with a chilled Mars Bar.

2) Chocolate and knitting

An almost perfect match. The only difficulty arises when your fingers get chocolaty and, consequently, slow down the knitting. Worse still, if you eat something messy like a Cadbury Flake (as pictured bottom right) while knitting, you can guarantee you will be picking out tiny flakes of melted chocolate from the fibers for a long time afterwards. The solution must be to have a servant unwrap, hold and feed the Flake/Milky Way/Cream Egg to you so that your fingers remain free of clogging chocolate residue.

3) Wine and books

This combination is not a problem if the reading matter is *Hello!* or some other celebrity gossip magazine. But I can vouch for the fact that you will not recognize those eighteen new characters Dickens introduced while you were reading *Our Mutual Friend* under the influence of the grape when you next pick it up. Books do make useful and efficient coasters, though.

4) Wine and knitting

Ah, yes. We like to believe this is possible, but all the available anecdotal and material evidence contradicts it. Dropped stitches, misplaced cables, botched necklines and pattern repeats gone haywire can all be worse than the hangover in the harsh light of the morning after the knitting and drinking spree of the night before. Knit and drink at your peril, unless you are doing free-form knitting.

5) Books and knitting

How I wish I could master the art of simultaneously reading and knitting, but this is the pattern my attempt usually follows: *knit 1 row, read 1 line, purl 1 row, read same line again (twice)*, rep from * to* until you hurl book to other side of room.

6) Chocolate and wine

I don't care what the wine purists say. Chocolate and wine *can* be a marriage made in heaven. Sweet, dark wines such as port and Madeira served chilled with chocolate-based desserts are delicious and rich; red wines from Australia are wonderful with squares of chocolate. I even find that champagne can accommodate the sweetness of chocolate truffles. Trust me, I'm an expert.

The solution

I came to the conclusion a long time ago that the only way to combine my four material passions would be to open a shop selling yarns, books, wine and chocolate. I'm not sure I'd make much profit, but it would be a wonderful way to create the winning combination.

To her son these words conveyed an extra...
if it were settled the expedition[2] were bound
and the wonder to which he had looked forw...
and years it seemed, was, after a night's darkn...
sail, within touch. Since he belonged, even at...
to that great clan which cannot keep this fe...
from that, but must let ... prospects, with
sorrows cloud wh... is actual... at hand, since
even in earliest childhood any ... in the whe...
has the power to crystallise and transfix the
which is gloom or radiance rest... James Ram...
the fl... cutting out pictures ... m the illustr...
of the ... rmy and ... ies,[3] endowed th...
refriger... or as his mother spoke with heaven...
fringed ... th joy. The wheelbarrow, the law...
sound of ... plar trees, leaves whitening befo...
cawing, bro... ms knocking, dresses rustling –
so coloured ... d distinguished in his mind
already his pr... ate code, his secret languag...
appeared the im... ge of stark and uncompromi...
with his high f... head and his fierce blue eye...

Not lost in translation

I like to define a luxury as something that is non-essential but conducive to pleasure and comfort, which puts Japanese craft books high on my list of life's little luxuries. If you also throw in the definition that luxury does not automatically mean excessively expensive, that makes them even more desirable.

If you are new to their magical, eclectic world, Japanese craft books are unlike any craft books you have ever seen. For starters, you can't understand a word. But that, absolutely and utterly, is not the point. It doesn't matter that you can't make head nor tail of the text, or even work out which is the beginning and which is the end of the book. Because Japanese craft books reveal a whole new way of reading.

For someone who spent her formative crafting years reading dull, worthy and appallingly illustrated books full of bossy rules and regulations about the "correct" way to make things, Japanese books are a

revelation. They open up a bright, colorful, witty, inventive, experimental world of domestic creativity. They are packed with fresh and clever ideas, stunning photographs and brilliantly imaginative details. There is a playfulness and exuberance that most conservative craft books never succeed in conveying (if, indeed, they ever set out to do so).

In many ways, the fact that you can't understand the often extensive and professionally laid out instructions is incredibly liberating. Instead of simply following the rules, you find yourself looking, perhaps for the first time, at the way something is made as you try to figure out the structure and the process from the drawings. There are a few measurements and numbers to help you but, for the rest, you are on your own in a brave new world of squiggles and marks.

Other times, of course, it is enough simply to look at the pictures and fantasize about all the possibilities they suggest. My small collection of Japanese books comes out when I need inspiration, ideas, new approaches or a reminder of how many clever craft people there are in the world. Just flipping through the pages of crocheted bags, miniature quilts, appliquéd cushions, beaded fruits, embroidered gardens and couture aprons lifts my spirits, invigorates my mind and makes my fingers itch to be making.

It's easy enough to go to the English pages of amazon.jp and yesasia.com and, as long as you have the ISBNs, very simple (too simple, maybe) to buy the books. When you press "Buy Now" you open the door to a wonderland of Japanese creativity. A huge luxury at a small price. (See Resources, pages 280 and 282).

小間物手口…

キットのアート

ハンドメイドバッ

チャーミングバッグ ch

いつどこかの楽しいシーンを バッグに

トキメク旅心を バッグにつめて

Anano くアのお菓子と小物

モチーフ◎バッグ

きものバッグ bag がほしい

パリから届いたエプ

天然素材が気持ちいい

ニーイ・ンググ・ト

早川恵子のわが家のバッチワーク

Choc-lit

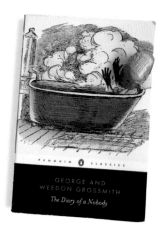

I'm afraid I don't like it when people pronounce chocolate as "chocklit." I thought about this minor lapse of tolerance on my part when I was making thickly chocolately brownies one day. And then it occurred to me that this word could be construed as a reference to a whole category of literature: choc-lit, or books to be read while eating chocolate.

I began to think about the kinds of books that go best with chocolate and surprised myself by rejecting all romantic, weepy, light and easy reads as undeserving. I think that cloying, sweet reads would set my teeth on edge with an overdose of sugariness if I read them with chocolate. (Like the time I saw *Love, Actually* and came out of the theater feeling as if I'd eaten an entire super-size package of marshmallows when I'd eaten nothing, actually.)

For me, domestic novels (see Inspiration, pages 26–9) are chocolate-cookie books, biographies are apple books, thrillers and mysteries are gin and tonic books, illustrated tomes are wine books, poems are best with grapes, and newspapers are perfect with fish and chips. But I find that it is the classics that are best with chocolate. I suspect this is because I have to digest and savor them slowly (they are not always the easiest reads), and need to read them in bite-size chunks and reward myself every so often for my valiant efforts. The works of Dickens are the ultimate choc-lit, as are most nineteenth-century doorstoppers or, indeed, any of the great works of literature.

It is true luxury to have a huge box of chocolates and the time to devote yourself to some of the best domestic classics ever written such as *Dombey and Son, Anna Karenina, The Diary of a Nobody, North and South, Madame Bovary* and *The Mill on the Floss*.

Pass my chocs, glasses and books, please.

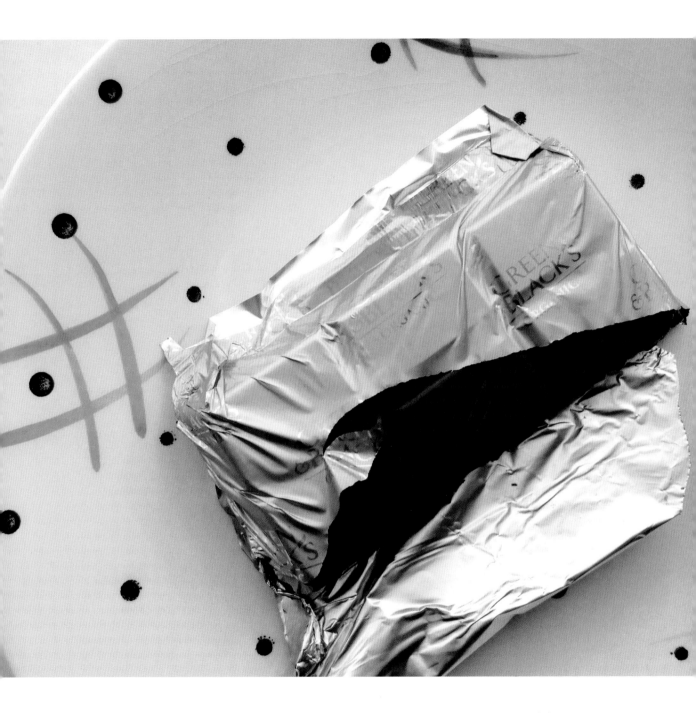

I find that it is the classics that are best with chocolate. I suspect this is because I have to digest and savor them slowly (they are not always the easiest reads), and need to read them in bite-size chunks . . .

Beribboned

Prefixes, as a rule, don't get much attention. But I am very fond of the prefix "be-," which is used to form words with a sense of around, on all sides, thoroughly. I want to be bedecked, bedizened, bejewelled, beplumed, befringed, behatted, and I want to be thoroughly beribboned.

Why are ribbons so lovely? Why is the word so attractive, even without my favorite prefix? "Ribbons" sounds light, fluttery and carefree. It's perhaps no coincidence that it goes with "bows" to make a wonderfully dancing phrase. And there are so many ribbons to like. Maypole ribbons, hair ribbons, hat ribbons, medal ribbons and dress ribbons. I am particularly keen on wide sashes on old-fashioned dresses, satin ribbons on huge boxes of chocolates and richly colored, deeply tactile, velvet ribbons. In fact, I love the idea of ribbons almost as much as I love ribbons themselves.

My favorite ribbon shops are VV Rouleaux in London and M&J Trimming in New York (see Resources, page 283), but I am also besotted with the American designer Laura Foster Nicholson's exquisite ribbons. Laura is a talented weaver and textile artist, and her skills come together in her machine-woven masterpieces. The small scale and witty details are amazing, and it's so pleasing to use them to tie an apron or gift or bunch of flowers. They are like tiny tapestries and are, quite rightly, in several museum collections.

Laura's ribbons are the epitome of my kind of luxury. They are affordable (you don't *have* to buy yards and yards), artistic, whimsical, and every time I touch one, I feel I am holding a valuable and delightful little treat.

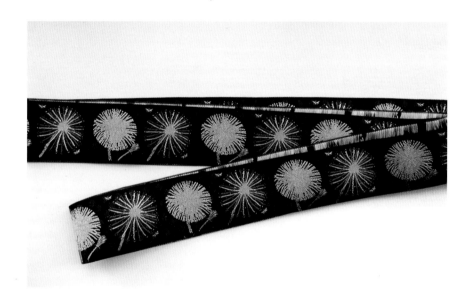

I want to be bedecked, bedizened, bejewelled, beplumed, befringed, behatted, and I want to be thoroughly beribboned.

Chocolate Box Quilt

Although it may sound like the lady doth protest too much, I don't actually eat chocolate *all* the time. I manage a reasonably healthy diet in between my chocolate fixes, but I must confess that chocolate does take up quite a large amount of my thinking time.

I am shocked, though, that the subject of women and chocolate has been hijacked by contemporary cultural commentators. Once upon a time, you could indulge your cravings and not worry about the feminine guilt issues. Now, though, chocolate is part of a wider discourse about taboo foodstuffs, self-image and body shape. The eating of chocolate simply for pleasure and a taste of luxury is overlaid with anxieties about lack of willpower, whether dark is "healthier" than milk, whether someone knows better than you what is good for you. I hate to be stereotyped, and I am not happy to see chocolate and women being categorized in any way—by magazines, marketers or the media. If you like chocolate, eat some.

Or make a chocolate box quilt.

This quilt's genesis lies in a range of fabrics designed by Martha Negley for Rowan. Many of Martha's designs feature food—vegetables, fruits, cupcakes and icing—and of course they appeal to me, the founder and sole member of the Food in Textiles movement. I saw her cakes and ribbons collection just at the time I'd been thinking about a brown and pink quilt. It suddenly occurred to me that it would be quite simple to design

a quilt based on a chocolate box layout, with the chocolate-brown boxes each containing a different selection of chocolates, and each section wrapped up with ribbons.

This is the very first quilt I designed, so it had to be simple. It took me a few tries to work out the optimum size for the "chocolates" and for the width of the boxes and the ribbon sections. And then I had great fun filling the boxes with cherry, rose, raspberry, strawberry and other pink cream fillings. I decided it was worth the effort to "fussy cut" (cut out specific parts of a design on a fabric) the fruits, icing and flowers so that they made pleasing and meaningful arrangements. I made twenty-four boxes of chocolates, pieced them all together and backed them with Martha Negley's amazingly vibrant and happy bows and ribbons fabric to make it look like one enormous, chocolate-box extravaganza.

I love the old theatrical tradition of taking a fancy box of chocolates wrapped with a pink satin ribbon to the ballet. It seems virtually no one does it these days, although I have discovered one chocolatier who still produces a Theatre Box (see Resources, page 278). But I'm confident that my huge chocolate box would see me and a few friends through a performance of *The Sleeping Beauty* ballet; I have happy visions of the box in a box and plenty of contented sighs at the tutus and chocolates. And nary a guilty conscience in sight.

Tea and luxury

Tea at the Ritz. Tea at Claridge's. Tea at the Savoy. These evocative phrases conjure up visions of floaty, silk tea dresses, delicate bone china, fine Darjeeling or Orange Pekoe tea, silver teapots, dainty sandwiches, a grand piano tinkling in the background, a discreet exchange of gossip and, most important, attentive waiters to serve you warm, fresh scones and jam.

Afternoon tea is a lovely institution. Even though it harkens back to the days of ladies ringing bells and being served by maids, it would be a shame to let it fade and be replaced with something horribly modern and calorie-free, like a decaffeinated green tea in a cardboard cup consumed while talking into a hands-free set and accompanied by something minimal and healthy such as a handful of unsalted sunflower seeds.

No, I think we should all be calorie millionaires every so often and enjoy the deep refinement and traditions of afternoon tea. We should plan an hour between two and three o'clock, tell the maid not to admit any callers and bake a batch of fresh scones. Then we should change into something a little more floral and, between three and four o'clock, receive our guests and ply them with scones, clotted cream and jam. Our lives would be enriched immeasurably by the occasional afternoon tea, and the oasis of comfort and calories it provides.

When the children were small and all three were at the same school, it was easy to bake almost every day so that I had something to feed them when they came in, ravenous and tired. As they grow older, change schools and schedules, incorporate independence, rugby practice, paper routes and detours to friends' houses, I find my baking is less predictable. But every so often, when I know everyone will be at home or when we are all on vacation in some wonderfully historical but spartan Landmark Trust property, I bake scones and we have afternoon tea. There is a distinct lack of discreet conversation, translucent cups and cucumber sandwiches, but we make up for the hearty nature of our Brocket Afternoon Tea with plenty of luxury to apply to our scones.

Caviar, jam and scones

If the truth be told, scones are nothing more than a vehicle for cream and jam luxury. But, just as great caviar needs a great blini for transportation to the mouth, so our luxuries deserve an excellent scone.

The key to a great scone is freshness. Scones do not keep—even from morning to afternoon—and should be eaten as soon as possible after emerging from the oven. Like pancakes, they should not sit on a bakery rack, café plates or in plastic packaging. Instead, they should be whipped up—it is possible to have scones ready to eat just thirty minutes after you begin making them—and consumed all in one time-frame.

My scone recipe makes lightly buttery, pale yellow, airy scones as I am not keen on lardily heavy, white, doughy scones. When it comes to the addition of currants, I say never (currants are only for Eccles cakes, another traditional tea-time treat) and would only countenance raisins if I thought my marriage was on the brink and I needed to appease Simon and his raisin passion. I prefer plain scones and lashings of toppings. Would it surprise you if I said I am fussy about my toppings? No, I thought not. Afternoon tea is such a rare luxury that I firmly believe it's worth buying some excellent jam and cream to make it special.

I don't put butter on my scones, but many people do. If I did, it would be Bridel salted butter from Brittany. The cream could be very pleasant, light, white, whipped cream or thick spooning cream, but the queen of scone creams is undoubtedly Cornish clotted cream; thick, golden and sinfully rich.

When it comes to jam, there is now a wonderful selection made by small, quality producers with all sorts of fruits and flavors. But I still favor the traditional English choice—raspberry or strawberry. I choose Wilkin & Sons Tiptree Sweet Tip Raspberry (sweet but tart, deep ruby color, exudes raspberriness) and the children go for Wilkin & Sons Tiptree Little Scarlet Strawberry (sweet and fruity, dotted with whole, tiny strawberries). It amused me to discover that our favorite strawberry jam has become something of a cult item when I read an article entitled "The Hunt for Little Scarlet" in the *Washington Post* (September 15, 2004, available to read online). I now have visions of small tins of Little Scarlet changing hands for thousands of dollars like some sweet caviar. All the more reason to enjoy this affordable luxury while you can.

Luxury Scones

Makes 9

(Double the quantity if you have lots of fragrant ladies or not-so-fragrant teenage boys coming for afternoon tea.)

INGREDIENTS

1 cup organic self-rising flour
pinch of salt
2 teaspoons superfine sugar
handful of raisins (optional)
⅓ cup unsalted butter (not too cold and hard)
1 large egg
2–3 tablespoons milk
clotted cream or ½ cup whipped heavy cream,
    butter and jam, to serve

Preheat the oven to 425°F.

Line a baking sheet with parchment paper.

Sift the flour and salt into a large mixing bowl. Stir in the sugar and raisins, if using. Cut in the butter until the mixture resembles fine breadcrumbs. Beat the egg in a small bowl and mix in 2 tablespoons milk. Make a well in the center of the dry mixture and pour in the egg mixture. Using a fork, and working quickly, bring the ingredients together, adding more milk if necessary to make the dough damp.

Form a ball with the dough and place on a floured work surface. Roll out quickly and gently with a rolling pin (no need to knead) until the dough is approximately 1" thick. Form into a rough square and cut into 9 smaller squares or use a cutter to make round scones. Place well apart on the baking tray and bake for 10 to 15 minutes until the scones are well risen and golden on top.

While the scones are baking, change into your best silk dress, set the table, spoon the cream and jams into glass bowls and make a pot of tea.

Remove the scones from the oven, allow to cool on a wire rack for 5 minutes and eat warm.

Time and space

Every domestic artist knows that there is no such thing as a time-space continuum. If we stay with the mathematical analogy, time and space are, in fact, fractals.

The laws of the domestic universe dictate that all time and space is fragmented, shattered, broken up into small pieces. Rarely does the creative practitioner of the gentle arts find even the beginning of a time-space continuum, let alone inhabit one. Domesticity, by its nature, is made up of many tiny, separate chunks of time and space. Cooking, tidying, transporting, shopping, washing, wiping, husbands, wives, partners, offspring, friends, family, work, commitments and responsibilities, all make claims and demands that mean that it can be very difficult to capture even the smallest particle of time or space for oneself.

For many busy domestic artists, time and space alone is a true luxury. It can be difficult to obtain, but I feel that we all need to create, negotiate or simply permit ourselves this luxury in order to think creatively and enjoy the small details of life.

The luxury of time and space allows the domestic artist to consider, plan, research, read, wander, daydream, imagine, play and make. I find that if I am deprived of time and space, my need for them becomes physical. I am not claiming that I produce masterpieces when I'm alone, just that my creativity and imagination are boosted immeasurably by even short spells of noncontact.

Depending on how much time I have and whether I can get out or not, this is how I like to spend my precious luxury of personal time and space:

* Read a good book in total silence
* Bake a cake, biscuits, rock buns, bread while listening to the radio
* Knit or crochet while watching a great film
* Read the weekend newspapers in bed with tea and toast (this is mostly a fantasy)
* Visit a gallery or see an exhibition and be inspired
* Go to a café and be served by a smiling waiter/ waitress while I read papers and magazines I would never normally buy
* When it's warm and sunny, water the flowers in pots and do a little light dead-heading like a true lady of leisure
* Listen to music while I machine-sew blocks for a quilt
* Take a walk or go for a swim and plan my quilts
* Look at pictures and paintings in books, magazines and children's illustrated books for colors, beauty and ideas
* Read a few great blogs and be energized by other people's creativity
* Play with fabric to find the perfect combination for a future quilt
* Cut out a quilt (the rotary cutter is a lethal weapon and the perfect excuse for plenty of space)
* Sleep
* Go the whole hog and visit London or Paris or New York, where I can combine all my domestic passions and more

I have perfected the nonscientific art of compressing maximum luxury into minimum time. I trained myself to do something creative or enjoyable in the short spaces of time when Tom and Alice were quiet when they were tiny. I learned to expand and contract my plans according to the opportunities and to keep something ready to pick up (knitting, reading) at short notice. With time, I was able to do more and more, but I have never come back to the time-space continuum of my childhood. My life is still a fractal, but one made up of many different, contrasting facets, and one in which even the shortest time-space opportunity is a domestic luxury to be enjoyed to the full.

Sharing

Investing in sharing

The essence of sharing is giving something away: something of yourself, or something you might have wanted or taken for yourself. Unfortunately, though, it appears that sharing is seriously out of fashion at the moment, with many people cultivating separate, parallel, untouching lives as they inhabit their personal pods or universes, cut off from the outside world by phones, hands-free sets, private music and cars.

Despite the fact that domesticity, too, is a deeply unfashionable concept, experience tells me that it is a wonderful means of building and supporting and sustaining relationships. A creative domestic space is one that not only enables individuals to flourish, but also encourages shared lives and experiences. I am always shocked when I read about children taking meals to their bedrooms and watching TV on their own, or when people happily announce that they have got rid of the dining table to make space for an Xbox or plasma screen or something equally large, imposing and impersonal. It is true that the shared meals and the one-or-none TV rule that we have maintained for years requires a degree of effort, but I never doubt the benefits of our shared domestic moments.

The domestic arts are also ideal vehicles for crossing gender and generation borders, and for enhancing life with friends and family. Passing on, sharing and communicating the value of skills such as baking and sewing and creating textiles is the best possible way of keeping them alive. Now that such sharing is no longer an obligation or duty but a pleasurable choice, the gentle arts help us build connections with those around us—younger, older, similar age—and they bring their own, very real rewards.

Useful lessons

When it comes to the gentle arts, I am mostly self-taught since I have absolutely no artistic background or training. As a result, I have had my fair share of frustrations and craft tantrums over the years when attempting to master new skills by looking at books or through trial and error. These days, though, I know better, and when I want to learn a new skill, I find someone to teach me.

It's a shame we can't all have a benevolent soul at our elbow, guiding us gently through knitting and purling, piecing and quilting, double and treble crochet. In the past, this would have been a grand-mother, mother, aunt, sister or neighbor. Some people are still fortunate enough to have someone like this to help them, but many of us have to look further for a creative mentor.

Because the gentle arts are so shockingly under-valued, overlooked and marginalized, a whole network of natural teachers is in danger of being eroded unless we begin to see just how much pleasure and fulfill-ment can be gained from sharing and practicing domestic skills. A few years ago, I would have said that all was lost but, thankfully, there has since been a quiet but significant growth in knitting, quilting, stitching and crochet courses, which can be wonderful granny substitutes.

Six solid hours of beginners' crochet with a patient teacher is far more productive than the same time spent with a book, unable (as I was) to even grasp the basics of holding the yarn and hook correctly. Two days of patchwork and quilting with an energetic, organized tutor and no distractions will convince you that a quilt need not take years, or even a lifetime, to make. One day on a finishing techniques course will improve the look of your knitting forever. And on top of acquiring all of these useful skills, there's the bonus of meeting others who want to perfect their intarsia or log-cabins or ripple blankets.

Even though I pay to attend these courses, the dividends are out of all proportion to the initial invest-ment. It feels good to be part of a chain that links communities and generations, *and* preserves life-enhancing skills, and all without tears.

See Resources, page 276, for suggestions on how to find courses and workshops.

Martianmallows

Marshmallows to share with aliens? No problem. We can make those.

I saw the *The River Cottage Family Cookbook* by Hugh Fearnley-Whittingstall and Fizz Carr recommended on a blog and, never one to ignore a new book, had a look at it, thought it was excellent and bought it. I was impressed by the tone and content; it is suitable for children to use on their own or with adults, and it doesn't patronize or oversimplify or concentrate on sweet stuff only.

Phoebe claimed the book immediately and ran off to find a fresh egg to boil à la Hugh, but it was only a matter of time (counted in seconds) before she discovered the wondrous marshmallow recipe. I'd always thought that marshmallows were made by some kind of industrial chemical reaction and was fascinated to discover that they are actually the product of a domestic chemical reaction. I don't like eating them because of their strange texture, but I was happy to help Phoebe make something we'd always assumed we could only buy.

Phoebe's friend Emily was here on our debut marshmallow-making day. I have found that one of the very best shared activities for visiting friends is a session in the kitchen. Children of all ages can have a great time kneading and rolling and icing and cutting and decorating. Even though it makes a huge mess, it's worth it for the sheer pleasure of watching children's delight in cooking and baking, and I would much rather have creative children in the kitchen than passive ones in front of a screen.

As the guest, Emily was invited to choose the color of the marshmallows and she decided on blue. Then, with the help of four children, I followed the recipe (gelatin, sugar, egg whites, water), and the kitchen was transformed into a culinary laboratory with all sorts of exciting bubblings and frothings.

The result was a complete success—all sticky and coated in dusty icing sugar, with that revolting, authentic foaminess of real marshmallows, and we gave the book an A+ for making a culinary chemistry experiment highly entertaining.

Emily's inspired color choice meant the marshmallows turned out with an extraterrestrial blue glow, and Tom, one of our in-house punsters, christened them "martianmallows."

Marshmallows have since become one of our signature sharing recipes to be used whenever young chemists are visiting. We have made green and lilac versions, and Phoebe came up with the idea of a pink marshmallow heart for Tom and Alice's Valentine's Day birthday. Home really is where the heart is.

Guess who's coming to dinner?

You may not have noticed the earth move, but there has been a seismic shift in knitting publishing in the last few years. Gone are the individual patterns featuring wholesome models such as '50s teen idols Cliff Richard and Roger Moore, gone are the heavy, uninspiring, black-and-white knitting guides, and in their place is a raft of colorful, innovative, imaginative and beautifully written knitting books. Some are modern collections of patterns for socks, classics, home items, but others take a theme and expand it. So we can read about knitting cafés, simple knitting, knitting with color, from nature, with cables, with loops, at the last minute or at the weekend. This shift to a more lateral, and less literal, mode of thinking about knitting has changed my perception of the status and craft of knitting quite radically. (See Resources, page 281, for details of books.)

One book I particularly like is *AlterKnits* by Leigh Radford with its "Imaginative Projects and Creativity Exercises." These encourage the reader to move outside her usual mental knitting zone (comfy chair, plain wool, repetitive pattern, nonthinking approach) and into one where she can begin to see the huge creative possibilities of two sticks and some yarn. My favorite exercise is the "Dream Knitting Party" to which you can invite any three people, and this is just the kind of thing I like to ponder as I knit.

This is my dream knitting party:

I'd be happy to pose for Matisse while I knitted with some fabulous cashmere, laughed at Dorothy Parker's witticisms and listened to Vanessa Bell's accounts of Bloomsbury shenanigans.

Vanessa Bell

I have long been fascinated by the artists and friends who formed the Bloomsbury Group in the early twentieth century. Virginia Woolf, Clive Bell, Roger Fry and Duncan Grant may be more intellectually scintillating or artistically progressive, but it is Vanessa Bell whom I admire the most. She was the linchpin of the Charleston Farmhouse ménage, but she managed to combine children, housekeeping, gardening and interior decoration with her own work as an artist.

Vanessa would be a wonderful guest at the party. I would be happy to watch her elegant hands holding the yarn and needles and knitting. She would imbue her pieces with maternal love and a sense of balance and home. She could show the rest of us how to select just the right color to set off resonances and contrasts, and her experience of textile design with the Omega Workshop (a short-lived but highly influential artist's collective) would teach us a great deal about pattern. Plus, she could make the bread (her granddaughter recalled how she would always remove her rings before kneading the dough) and paint a luminous canvas of our small group of knitters for me to keep.

Dorothy Parker

We would need someone to entertain us while we knitted, as laughter and gossip are surely one of the fundamentals of knitting parties. Dorothy Parker carried her knitting with her in a bag and took it everywhere she went, so she would be more than ready to whip it out and knit while she delivered her bons mots.

When the artist Luis Quintanilla painted her for his series of "Portraits of Authors as How They See Themselves" [sic], he asked Dorothy to tell him how she saw herself. She wrote, "I could only tell him the desperate truth; as a pastel old party, sitting in the corner knitting." She said that he made her into a "non-arithmetical Madame Defarge" (as in *A Tale of Two Cities* by Charles Dickens), and I have the feeling that Dorothy would be knitting barbs into her piece as quickly as Vanessa Bell would be knitting bobbles of love into hers.

Henri Matisse

If I am having the ultimate knitting party, Henri Matisse would have to be there. He would be knitting with balls of hand-painted, colorful silk and cotton yarns and would periodically drape his creations over the shoulders and bosoms of his fellow guests to see the effects of his work.

Matisse grew up surrounded by women and weavers. His sense of color, placement, pattern and composition were all developed by the silk jacquard weavers and embroiderers in his home town of Bohain in the northeast of France. His portraits are full of amazing textiles, and he clothed his models in beautiful fabrics, stitches and folds, as in *Woman in a Purple*

Coat (1937), pictured above. It would be a challenge to teach him to knit and then to see what he would do with color and flat pattern. In return, I would ask him to enlighten us about the artist's creative impulse and show us how to develop our own.

I'd be happy to pose for Matisse while I knitted with some fabulous cashmere, laughed at Dorothy Parker's witticisms and listened to Vanessa Bell's accounts of Bloomsbury shenanigans. We would eat Vanessa's freshly baked bread, drink fruity red wine from the south of France brought by Matisse, and Dorothy would mix lethal, stitch-dropping cocktails.

Who would you invite to your knitting party?

Peas, peace and laughter

Domesticity should be punctuated with a healthy level of giggles, guffaws, snorts, chuckles, cackles, hoots and screams of hilarity, glee, mirth, merriment and amusement. Laughter makes the repetitive nature of so much domesticity bearable; a funny radio program alleviates the boredom of ironing, chasing hens in the yard enlivens lawn-mowing, Alice's Diverted English distracts from washing dishes, a cup of tea and a laugh with a friend is a welcome relief from routine.

This is why I like the painting *Chatterboxes* (1912) by Thomas Kennington so much (pictured below). I won't pretend that these two young women, who are no doubt in service in a grand house, would have had an easy life, but I love the fact that they are enjoying a moment of laughter over a shared domestic duty.

Perhaps it's elevenses, time for a midmorning cup of tea, and there is a large Brown Betty teapot on the table, or perhaps it's midafternoon, and they are just about to shell peas for dinner. Whatever the context, I am struck by the sense of ease and enjoyment that emanates from this beautifully clear, limpid picture. The contrast of the bright white clothes with the dark, perhaps less lighthearted, background emphasizes the evanescent, fleeting nature of life-enhancing, shared, domestic laughter.

Tasks such as shelling peas or stringing green beans can create ideal shared moments. Carl Larsson painted a mother and two children shelling peas, heads down, pea pot on a table, pea pods all around their feet, and the scene contains a wonderful sense of calm and companionship. I sometimes buy fresh peas in their

pods just so that I can sit with the children and chat and laugh while our hands are busy. There is something delightfully old-fashioned and basic about handling smooth, green vegetables and using your fingers to prise out small peas or pull the strings off beans. It's repetitive, calming, peaceful, and the vivid green of the peas against the bright, shiny silver of a colander creates a simple but stunning temporary kitchen still-life, like the one in William Nicholson's painting *The Lustre Bowl with Green Peas* (1911).

Cherry ripe

I also enjoy pitting cherries, but I use a kitchen implement for this task. If you sit outside or with the door open, cherry-pitting is one of the most pleasant summer evening activities I can imagine. But a boy may see things differently, and when Tom offered to help me pit cherries, we ended up laughing at his antics.

I'd found a tray of tiny Kentish morello cherries, the sour variety that makes a wonderful frangipane, crumble or pie and reminds me of our six years in Germany and Belgium, where all sorts of cherries are available in season. I explained how the cherry pitter works, and Tom couldn't wait to get started when he realized that it pushed the pit out of the cherry rather like a bullet emerging from flesh, complete with a spattering of blood-red juice. He was happy to see the bright red juice squirt everywhere until he and the kitchen looked like something out of *Pulp Fiction.* I then moved him and his victims outside to finish the job but was quite taken with the gory but luminous pink effect on the cream bowl.

There wasn't much flesh left after the pits were removed, but there was enough to make a little clafouti, an eggy, milky, French pudding whose blandness is offset by the tart cherries—and which everyone ate directly from the baking dish. Afterwards, I thought how amazing it is that a simple utensil and a bowl of cherries could make a kitchen ring with laughter.

Fairy buns

Although most people call them cupcakes, in our house we like the title fairy buns. I've loved this name ever since I was little and had to kneel on a kitchen stool to help cream the butter and sugar with a huge wooden spoon. I never questioned why we called these small, iced cakes fairy buns, but I did wonder just how large the fairies were who ate them. (To be honest, I've never believed in fairies, but skepticism never prevented anyone from enjoying fairy culture.)

Nowadays, my buns are more burlesque fairy than Tolkien faerie. They are the buxom, brash, baking equivalent of Angela Carter's Fevvers in *Nights at the Circus,* rather than the pale, elfin Shakespearean Cobwebs and Peaseblossoms of *A Midsummer Night's Dream.* It may have something to do with the fact that I'm not of fairy proportions myself, or perhaps I was deprived of glittery wings and pink tutus as a child.

But I do have a baking fairy in Phoebe. She was wholly immersed in fairydom when she was younger, and she made gorgeous lilac fairy buns in gold cases (pictured below), topped with white, pink and cerise sugar roses. My goodness, this girl has taste. It must be a gift from the fairies.

Whichever side of the color fence you sit (and you can change from sophisticated to gaudy as often as you like), fairy buns are a magical way to enter the kingdom of baking. They are quick and easy to make and are a great collaborative activity, bringing old and young and their friends together in the wave of a wand. We've had several birthday parties at which the main event has been cake-decorating. I prebake several dozen fairy buns, put out bowls with various colors of icing and assorted sweets, decorations and toppings, then stand back and watch as eight girls go wild under the spell of color.

This is my classic fairy bun recipe.

Fairy Buns

Makes 12

INGREDIENTS
½ cup unsalted butter (at room temperature)
½ cup superfine sugar
2 large eggs
few drops vanilla extract (optional)
½ cup self-rising flour

Preheat the oven to 400°F.
Line a 12-cup muffin pan with baking liners.
In a large bowl, cream together the butter and sugar until pale and fluffy. Add the eggs and vanilla extract, if using, and beat well to incorporate. Sift in the flour and fold in gently with a large metal spoon (you don't want to knock the air out of the mixture).
Divide the mixture between the cupcake liners. Bake for 15 to 20 minutes until golden and firm on top. Leave to cool slightly on a wire rack before taking the buns out of the pan.

The fairy buns must be *completely* cool before you begin icing; otherwise, the icing will melt and slip off. Not a good look. Sometimes I cut the peaks off the buns so that the tops are flatter and therefore support more icing.
You are now ready to ice your buns.

Fairy bun icing

I have had many emails asking me how I make my icing so bright/thick/glossy/garish/unsubtle/worryingly neon. I can't say there is any secret, unless it's the fact that I can't be bothered with runny, wishy-washy icing that gives only the thinnest veneer of covering. My fairy buns are well and truly iced. The key is to make thick icing using more confectioner's sugar and less liquid than you may ever have contemplated, and then to slather it on generously. After all, we want the fairies to like these buns.

As for the color, do not bother with liquid dyes. They make the icing runnier and give meager colors. Even if it's the palest, pastel shade you are after, paste is the only way to go. Pastes are relatively dry and highly concentrated, and produce wonderful results at any depth. I use pastes made by Squires or Sugarflair (equally good, but Squires has the edge in imaginative color names, such as poinsettia, bulrush, wisteria and cyclamen). A little paste goes a long, long way.

Icing

Makes enough to ice 12 fairy buns

INGREDIENTS
1 – 1¼ cups confectioner's sugar
juice of approximately 2 lemons
  (water is fine but tasteless)
food color paste

I start by sieving 1 cup of confectioner's sugar into a bowl. Add the juice of half a lemon or a small amount of water and an "itchling" of paste (as Alice would say) on the end of a wooden toothpick, which can then be thrown away. (I use this method as I don't like to put a utensil covered with icing back into the paste jar.) Mix well using a sturdy knife. Now add more liquid and/or color until you are happy with the consistency and color. It's important not to add too much liquid early on as it will get sloppy, and by the time you have thickened the mix, you will have enough to ice the entire work surface as well as your buns. Or you will run out of confectioner's sugar. I speak from experience.

You are aiming for a thick, glossy, evenly colored icing that is spreadable but that won't slide off the buns. Apply generously in a swirling movement with a palette knife. You don't need to go right up to the edge as the icing will spread out a little.

Et voilà! All you need to do now is decorate tastefully/outrageously and arrange on a plate. And wait for the fairies to arrive.

Fattypuffs and Thinifers Cake

We have a Jack Sprat situation when it comes to Victoria Sponge Cakes. Tom and Phoebe like more jam and less cream, while the rest of us enjoy lashings of cream as well as oodles of raspberry jam.

In order to have a Victoria Sponge that can be shared happily, I make a Fattypuffs and Thinifers Cake (after the children's book by André Maurois*).

On the Fattypuffs side, we have maximum calorific value with clouds of cream and squishings of jam, and on the Thinifers side, we have a sweet, but relatively lean, spreading of Wilkins & Sons Tiptree Sweet Tip Raspberry Jam and only the lightest hint of cream.

I put a paper doily on top of the cake and sieve confectioner's sugar over to make a pretty lacy pattern.

The result gains the approval of Jack Sprat, his wife and their children. The book's Ministry of Slimming may not be so thrilled, though.

* Patapoufs et Filifers (1941)

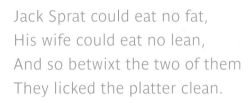

Jack Sprat could eat no fat,
His wife could eat no lean,
And so betwixt the two of them
They licked the platter clean.

NURSERY RHYME

Magic moments

As you read this, you need to be humming "Magic Moments" as sung by Perry Como in 1958. I have execrable taste in music, I know, and am surely a throwback to the 1950s, but whenever we share a family magic moment, this theme tune pops, unbidden, into my head.

Once in a while, everything comes together and all five of us find ourselves in the same room with the same objective in mind—to get comfortable and read. We all lie on the sofas, get cozy under quilts and get out our books. The only sound is that of pages turning. No TV, no music, no Connect 4 arguments, no card games, no homework. I daren't even knit as the clickety-clacking needles would spoil the peace.

Magic moments are one of the highlights of domesticity. There is nothing sweeter than seeing your family (or friends, partners or pets) wrapped up in the quilts you have made and all enjoying the companionable calm and quiet. These special times make me think of the Russian custom of a minute's shared stillness and silence before parting, and remind me that we should cherish our magic moments, for they are soon lost in the never-ending arrivals and departures of life.

Squeezing in Foyles

My knitting isolation came to an end a couple of years ago when I began knitting with a group. Now, whenever I can on Tuesday mornings, I take the train to London, squeeze myself into a space at the wooden table in the café at Foyles bookshop, and knit with a wonderful group of people who have changed my perspective on shared knitting.

Sometimes there is enough elbow room to knit with long needles, and sometimes, when we are all squeezed in with our yarn, patterns, mugs and muffins, we would all be better off knitting socks on short double-pointed needles to minimize the chance of needle-related injuries. But I am quite happy with a little compression, because it reminds me of the value of knitting groups like ours.

I can think of no other way of getting together with like-minded people on such an informal, yet friendly and welcoming basis. You don't have to book, you don't have to reserve your seat. You can arrive and leave as you please, there are no age limits, and you can knit whatever you fancy. You may never see any of your fellow knitters except on Tuesdays, or they may be your best friends all week long. You don't have to wait to be invited, and you don't have to spend half the session discussing and agreeing which project you are all going to undertake. You can be a beginner or an old lag, a whiz at lace or a solid stockinette-stitch knitter.

We welcome new people all the time. Some knitters come just once or twice when visiting London, others come week after week. We have people from all over the world and some from down the road. There is something quite magical about sitting around a table with a group of chatty, engaging, sociable knitters who all seem to have an opinion on everything from movies to opera, restaurants to cafés, books to gossip, film stars to soap stars. After my years of lonesome knitting, I find the group therapy an excellent way of bringing out my knitting and laughing with people who have plenty to say that doesn't involve children and schools, and I will do anything I can to squeeze Foyles into my schedule.

Knitting groups are now springing up everywhere. They are nothing new, no more than a revival of the time-honored tradition of women (and men) meeting to stitch and knit and gossip and share. They are the modern equivalents of quilting bees and wartime sock- or bandage-making groups, and they are still just as valuable in knitting communities together.

There is something quite magical about sitting around a table with a group of chatty, engaging, sociable knitters who all seem to have an opinion on everything from movies to opera, restaurants to cafés, books to gossip, film stars to soap stars.

Birthdays

We don't have many family traditions, as I feel that they could become restrictive and vehicles for guilt (I thank Simon, the least fettered man in the world, for freeing me from the tyranny of Hallmark-card occasions), but birthday cakes are sacrosanct.

When the children were little, they were allowed to choose their cakes from the actress Jane Asher's brilliant cake-decorating books. I made a fairy-tale castle, a Humpty Dumpty, a Sleeping Beauty Barbie, a rocket, several candy shops, a train and a dachshund. I have to admit that I enjoyed making them at the time, as they were much-needed creative challenges, but I am also relieved that the days of making turrets from ice-cream cones and walls from Milky Ways are over.

Thankfully, the tradition has now become a little more manageable. The birthday girl or boy is allowed to choose his or her cake—chocolate, vanilla, lemon, carrot—and the decorations to go on it, because it turns out that the more ingenious a cake, the less edible it is. So the children realize that it's content, and not appearance, that matters (a life lesson worth learning, even if it is from cakes), and now they choose their ingredients carefully.

February 14

Valentine's Day is BIG in our house. It's not that Simon and I are a pair of sentimental romantics, it's just that February 14 is Tom and Alice's birthday, and somehow we have never managed to get that two-of-us thing back when it's quite clearly a two-of-them day.

Tom and Alice were due on 3.9.93. I liked the neatly patterned number and pencilled it into my diary with all the faith and optimism of a first-time mother. On Saturday 2.13.93 Simon gave me the most enormous and beautiful bouquet of tulips in advance of Valentine's Day (when the stores would be closed), and that night we discussed the indications of impending labor without realizing that I had all the tell-tale signs. So when I was rushed into hospital in the early hours of Valentine's Day, I wasn't ready to be parted with my tulips and, in shock, kept asking Simon to bring them with us. Sensibly, he busied himself with more pressing matters.

Today I look at our Valentine's babies with their full heads of hair and even fuller vocabularies and the way in which they are able to cope with life and people and ideas and challenges. Their teenage years seemed an age away when I took home my tiny, sleepless, noisy pair. Now they are a big, noisy pair, but at least they have mastered the art of sleeping.

So Valentine's Day is a day for Tom's chocolate cake covered in chocolate buttons, malt balls and candles that burn with colored flames like a chemistry experiment (pictured opposite, middle row, right), and Alice's colorful candy cake with lollipops, gummy hearts and strawberries (pictured opposite, bottom left).

One day, Simon and I may be able to share Valentine's Day on our own, but it won't be half as much fun. In the meantime, I can enjoy the tulips that Simon buys, unfailingly, every February 14. What a love.

Bonus birthday

Phoebe takes the matter of birthday cakes very seriously indeed. Her solo birthday is one of the benefits of her singleton status, and she is delighted she doesn't have to share it. But she is canny, and she worked out quickly that if she had her party on a different day to her birthday, she could have two birthday cakes. Thus, she still manages to have two cakes like her siblings.

Phoebe spends 364 days of the year planning her cakes and frequently goes to bed with books by Jane Asher and wedding cake designer Peggy Porschen. She likes to have a concept and write lists, sketch designs and generally project manage the whole thing. In recent years I have been the sous-chef following her instructions, but now that she is a fully fledged Cake Designer, she is in charge, and I have been demoted to the task of washing the dishes.

Pictured opposite are two cakes she designed when she was ten. Top right is the Pierre Cardin-style, white chocolate, space-age creation that was her birthday birthday cake. The idea was to create a dark chocolate cake with as much white chocolate as possible, so there are white chocolate buttons inside the cake as well as on top.

And bottom right is the birthday party cake, which Phoebe art-directed. It was inspired by a dream sequence in an episode of *The Simpsons* and by the idea of a candy shop. It was huge, colorful and a hit with her friends, and the hens in the yard loved the leftovers.

I have found that the most significant conversations with children often take place in the car. This may be because there is no eye contact, less likelihood of major parental overreaction, or simply because minds wander when staring out of windows. But it has certainly been true for us.

There is one conversation that has stuck in my mind for years. I was driving the children to school one morning and they were discussing what everyone was going to do that day. "Daddy's going to work. Thomas and Alice are going to school. Phoebe is going to nursery. And Mummy is going to the supermarket."

I was aghast. Is this what those dedicated teachers at my girls' school worked so hard for? To have their pupils get top A-level grades, study at fine universities, gain professional qualifications and break down the sexist barriers in the workplace? Or was it so that my children could think I spent my day in the super-market while the rest of the family was at "work"? Then I laughed and realized that it was up to me to demonstrate clearly to my offspring of both genders that there are many different ways to live your life, and that my chosen path was an alternative, but equally fulfilling, choice.

Untaxed inheritance

My children will not inherit titles, land, wealth or even a great wine cellar, but I do hope that they will inherit a few life-enhancing skills.

I am keen to let my children find their own paths in life. I have no desire to live my life vicariously through them, and am happy to be more of a supportive shadow than a beam of light focusing on their every move. But I do believe in encouraging their creativity through play and activities, and have found that the colors, textures, patterns and possibilities of the gentle arts are wonderful vehicles for the development of self-expression, concentration and imagination.

The Quilting Apprentice

Tom is my Quilting Apprentice. In fact, he is now so accomplished that I am thinking of becoming his agent and selling his services as a quilting consultant.

When I am making a quilt, I lay out cut pieces on the floor and then play with them. It's like a huge textile jigsaw, but one in which each piece has several possible slots and it's up to the jigsaw master to decide where the piece looks best. Maybe it's because it looks like a game, but Tom was immediately attracted to quilting and has helped me through all the quilts I have made. He has developed great color placement skills and can see patterns that are invisible to me until he points them out. He knows what works, and what can ruin an effect. He makes inspired suggestions for borders and backs and even takes the scraps to create his own quilt designs, like the Hamster Quilt.

In return for quilting advice, we talk about rugby and BMX bikes, paper routes and school. As we kneel on the carpet and move fabric like chess pieces, we share skills and snippets of each other's lives. I come away not only with a far superior quilt than the one I would have made on my own, but also knowing more about Tom's interests and hopes and plans. It's a case of share and share alike.

Knitting bee

I have no illusions about my children's desire to knit. Knitting is a skill I am happy to share with them, but there is no point in forcing needles and yarn on an unwilling pair of hands. So I have made the offers and waited, and when they have been accepted I have had to stifle any whoops of delight for fear of startling a shy knitter.

Phoebe was keen to learn before Alice and, after I had shown her the basics, we went to a Rowan Parent and Child knitting weekend at the Rowan mill in Yorkshire. It was an amazing experience to sit for two days in a large room surrounded by young girls (and a couple of boys) and their mothers or helpers, and to see everyone knitting like old pros. If anyone ever had doubts about the value of teaching children to knit, then they should see one of these workshops in full flow. Tables are covered in patterns, yarn, needles, beads, buttons and books. There is a steady flow of chatter and tea and juice, and an overarching sense of purpose, focus and, best of all, enjoyment.

Phoebe adored the whole experience and talked excitedly about her knitting nonstop for 190 miles of the 200-mile journey home. And then she fell asleep.

Never doubt the capacity of knitting to expand a girl's mind.

One small stitch for Alice, one giant cast-on for me

Alice is a more reluctant knitter than Phoebe, so I cannot tell you how much the little piece of hers pictured below right means to me.

When she asked me to teach her to knit, I worked on the principle that if she started with yarn and needles she liked she would be more likely to keep going. So I gave her some bright Colinette Prism and some smooth, chunky, bamboo needles.

Patience has its rewards, and this is one of them. If I had reminded Alice of the joys of knitting on a regular basis, I would have turned her off the idea. Instead, I had to bide my time and hope that positive reinforcement worked. You can take a teenager to yarn, but you can't make her cast on.

It turned out she is far more careful and deliberate with her knitting than I would have predicted, and there are few sights more beautiful than a daughter slowly, but surely, creating stitches. So now all three of us go to the Parent and Child workshops at Rowan and I have double the amount of joy in watching both my daughters working with yarn.

Winding wool

Unlike many knitters, I don't have a ball-winder or swift to turn my loose skeins of yarn into neat, dumpy cylinders. But I do have a pair of hands, and I enjoy the gentle, hypnotic motion of winding a ball of yarn myself.

There is something satisfying about this old-fashioned method, which produces old-fashioned, uneven spheres of yarn. I can still remember having to sit with my hands and arms set rigidly and uncomfortably apart as I held a skein for my Nana, and these days I don't subject my children to this task, as I have a fine pair of knees that do an adequate and less complaining job, although Phoebe's feet look as if they would make good, if unconventional, "posts."

But I do like the connection that ball-winding makes between two people. As Robert Service wrote in his poem "Winding Wool," there are "two active hands and two passive hands," a winder and a holder, a subject and an object, an active and a passive role. Of course, this is a perfect subject for painters and writers: one person held captive and immobile until the other frees them. It can be seen as a way of subjugating children to parental control or simply as a way of bringing two people close to each other and literally bound up together.

I like the way the usual arrangement is reversed in the painting *Winding Wool* (1914) by Harold Harvey (pictured opposite). The girl holding a skein of brilliant red yarn is the focus, the bright wool standing out against her white dress and her neatly braided hair. She is upright, open, clear, organized and like a small statue. The winder, normally the main subject in such paintings, is hidden, shrouded in dark clothes, with her hair tumbling over her shoulders. She is bent and held in, with her hands close to her chest, and she appears to be uncommunicative and introverted. It is an unusual scene with the holder set above the winder, the holder more dominant and in control. It's a beautiful snapshot of a moment in two girls' lives, perhaps a turning point when the older one is becoming secretive and the younger one is still trusting and transparent.

I have also come across paintings of mothers and daughters winding yarn. In some they work happily together as equals, but others from the nineteenth century highlight the controlling aspect of winding yarn with the poor girl having to behave in a proper manner and stand still while her mother educates her

She'd bring me a skein of wool
And beg me to hold out my hands;
So on my pipe I cease to pull
And watch her twine the shining strands
Into a ball so snug and neat,
Perchance a pair of socks to knit
To comfort my unworthy feet,
Or pullover my girth to fit.

As to the winding I would sway,
A poem in my head would sing,
And I would watch in dreamy way
The bright yarn swiftly slendering.
The best I liked were colored strands
I let my pensive pipe grow cool . . .
Two active hands and two passive hands,
So busy winding shining wool.

Alas! Two of those hands are cold,
And in these days of wrath and wrong,
I am so wearyful and old,
I wonder if I've lived too long.
So in my loneliness I sit
And dream of sweet domestic rule . . .
When gentle women used to knit,
And men were happy winding wool.

"WINDING WOOL," ROBERT SERVICE (1874–1958)

to be both prettily becoming and subserviently useful.

Then there are some amusing paintings of yarn winding in which the man holds the skein for the woman in the ultimate act of courtship, while he is still prepared to humor his loved one and help her with a dainty, feminine task. For a moment, the woman has the upper hand while the man is merely an inanimate object; what a shame that it could all change once they are married.

But the best shared yarn winding occurs when the task is imbued with respect and tenderness as in the poem by Robert Service, and the easiest and most painless way is to do it on one's own. I look at the neatly wound, smooth, stumpy tubes that come off the clever winding devices you can buy and compare them with my loopy, less-than-spherical balls, and still I prefer to feel the yarn in my hands as it turns into an object of my making and design. It's like a proper introduction to what is going to be a long-term and, I hope, balanced knitting relationship.

Nature

Natural pleasures

Nature forms a wonderful backdrop to domesticity. It's like an external room with an ever-changing wallpaper, rugs and carpets that alter by the month, and lights that brighten and dim with the hour and the season. It's full of colors, textures, shapes, smells, patterns, designs and sheer cleverness. Nature provides space, pleasure, inspiration, solace and life itself.

I say this knowing that most people's domesticity is surrounded by quite ordinary nature, just as mine is. But, as with so many other simple pleasures of domesticity, those of nature are so often undervalued and taken for granted that it can take a concentrated effort to appreciate them. If we look carefully and with an interested eye, it is possible to notice something new every day, whether it's a branch with new buds, a surprise flower or blossom, or a self-sown seedling.

My days are circumscribed by the school run through a suburban, domestic landscape, and yet I see magnificent magnolias, walls dripping with purple wisteria, mists on the river, daffodils on round-abouts, lime-green robinia trees in spring and deep rust-colored horse-chestnuts in autumn. I have favorite gardens I drive past to see wallflowers, pansies, dahlias, lilies, marigolds, green beans and tomatoes, and even on the noisiest, dullest road, I rejoice when the hawthorn and the cow parsley are proclaiming spring.

Nature can inspire the domestic artist not only with its visual treasures, but also with its sense of energy, its rhythms and its fundamental need for cycles and repetition. Nature is doing outdoors what we are doing indoors and, of course, our creative domesticity can be taken outside, extended and applied to our surroundings. Growing and nurturing plants, using and observing the natural space we have to the full, sharing it with hens, children, friends and family are all pleasures that come with the cultivation of the gentle art of natural domesticity.

Green fingers

When I'm asked whether I enjoy gardening, I have to be honest and say that it's the growing part I like, and not the hard work of digging, mowing, raking and hoeing. I much prefer the business of books, catalogs, bulbs, seeds, trays, pots, trowels and compost. I enjoy the fiddly, fine-motor-skill aspects of gardening—handling the smooth or rough or spiky or knobbly seeds, the sprinkling, planting, potting, pricking out and the general nurturing of little plant lives.

I'm more dreamy than practical, more informal than formal, and just a little wayward. I like pulling leaves off plants—lemon balm, lavender, thyme and basil—to rub and smell, wafting around the garden dead-heading the dahlias and roses and picking the flowers and vegetables I have grown. My secret horticultural ambition is to emulate the writer Vita Sackville-West and create coolly gorgeous white gardens, wear pearls and boots for gardening, and have a team of dedicated but silent under-gardeners to do the hard work.

My less-than-practical approach extends to my choice of reading. I'm not good with sensible books that contain page after page of timetables and calendars telling you when you should be doing everything, because they inevitably make me feel like a failure when I sow my broad beans a week or two late. So I choose poetic, anecdotal or creative gardening books that give me a vivid sense of place, possibility and romance. Old books can be informative, entertaining and full of garden wisdom, while modern volumes offer amazing ways with brilliant flowers, imaginative vegetable plantings and unusual color schemes.

I have a very basic, simple approach to growing plants. I have never been able to justify a greenhouse, as I would only use it for a short period of the year, although I may not always be able to resist the lure of a cozy place crammed with seeds, trusses of tomatoes, cups of tea, packets of cookies and BBC Radio 4. Instead, I germinate seeds wherever I can. In spring, windowsills, floors and tables are covered with trays and plastic wrap (I am very low-tech) and the family has got used to finding chilies and tomatoes and morning glories germinating all over the house. I find it exciting to check my seeds each day, and I am always delighted when I see signs of life. There is something so reassuring and downright clever about tiny seeds that are programmed to turn into huge sunflowers or brilliant snapdragons.

My laissez-faire style of gardening means I welcome self-sown flowers with open arms. I am charmed, not annoyed, by the profligacy of love-in-a-mist, marigolds, verbena, nasturtiums, cosmos and all the other annuals whose seeds are blown around the garden to flourish where they land. Some gardeners resent these gate-crashers because they defy their rules and regulations, but I am always grateful to find seedlings and flowers in unexpected places.

In fact, I think self-sown flowers encapsulate all that is good about an ordinary, domestic garden. It should be a welcoming, hospitable environment with a pleasantly haphazard structure, which runs according to natural laws and is always ready to welcome surprise guests.

Flower power

Flowers are one of the gentle joys of domesticity. I learned long ago that you don't need to have a celebrity budget or spectacular flower beds to appreciate flowers. I once bought five tulips the day before I was due to fly to Moscow for a week. They were an unusual, deep violet color, and I couldn't resist a bunch. For twenty-four hours I took the vase of tulips with me wherever I went—to my room while I packed, to the kitchen while I cooked, to the bathroom while I had a bath and to the living room while I watched TV. Although I had to throw them away before I left for the airport, every detail of their shape and color is still imprinted on my memory. What may have seemed like extravagance was actually an education in flower appreciation.

Much as I would like to have a fabulously well-stocked garden, I take my pleasures as and when I can. I grow some flowers to pick—marigolds, dahlias, tulips, nasturtium, fritillaries, cosmos—but do not have the time to keep the house overflowing with flowers.

We also have some lovely perennials that I can't bear to cut because they are part of my summer evening routine of inspection. One June evening, I went around the garden at dusk and peered into some of the big blooms we have at that time of year. I was stunned and delighted by their colors, forms, shapes, details and sheer weirdness, and I noticed that when you are up close and personal with flowers, they become almost abstract—less a flower, more a quirk of nature.

The large, star-shaped, carmine clematis pictured opposite, top left, has a wonderful, wiggly center that looks as if it has been dipped in a jar of maroon ink.

The pair of arum lilies pictured opposite, top right, glowed in the evening light and looked like a pair of love-hearts—almost, but just not quite, touching.

I love the crumpled petals of the "Black and White" Oriental poppy (*Papaver orientale*—pictured opposite, middle row left), which look like an unironed silk handkerchief (you see, I take my cue from nature when it comes to ironing). The deep, blackberry-color stains look as if they have been freshly applied and have run like ink on blotting paper.

The soft apricot pleats of the David Austin rose (label lost—pictured opposite, middle row right) are just as good as anything that the fashion designer Issey Miyake could design; I am amazed that something so layered and complex can emerge from a single, tight, pale peach bud.

I am enthralled by the drama of the *Papaver orientale* "Cedric Morris" pictured opposite, bottom left. It has pale, dusky-pink frills with a shockingly black center and seed pod. This is one of my very favorite perennials, but I do think it's misnamed. It really deserves a graceful, feminine, balletic name like Marie Taglioni or Fanny Elssler.

The Cambridge-blue bearded iris pictured opposite, bottom right, makes me laugh. I half-expect the caterpillar-like beard to get up and crawl away. Unfortunately, its sturdiness and stillness attract the attention of Tom with his BB gun looking for target practice. This is why we don't have Gertrude Jekyll-style flower beds (but I have to admire his accuracy).

Flowers are not a domestic essential, but even if you can only have five tulips or a single hyacinth or a free branch of lilac, it's worth taking the time to look properly at nature's incredible cleverness.

Looking down on nature

Little children often run along looking down, as if there is some treasure to be found on the ground. This is why they are always running into lamp posts, legs and trees, but they are, of course, quite right.

I find I look up and around most of the time and, because I am tall, I usually get a good view of what's coming. But even though it's a fair way down to the ground, I've discovered that if you make an effort to look down in autumn, you will be startled by the magnificent, colorful leaves and natural debris covering pavements and gardens.

Feeding the hens has made me look down far more, so I see what I have been missing, especially in autumn. When I go out into the garden to give our seriously pampered birds some old croissants or couscous and watch them happily pecking and scratching, I find all sorts of magnificent, rich, burnished colors on a backdrop of deep green box hedging, emerald-green grass and pale, mottled gravel.

One autumn when I was at nursery school, we had to collect leaves and use them to make pictures. I showed my mother what I had made and she was suitably impressed with my "brown" leaves. Until I corrected her and told her that they were in fact *russet*-brown leaves. I suppose I am still the same all these years later—finding wonderful colors in maple and beech leaves that have fallen off our trees, and expanding my color vocabulary by looking down on nature.

Stitching from nature

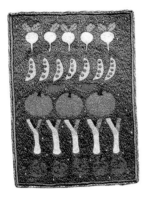

Machine-embroidery has many connotations, not all of them positive. It's often seen as a poor relation to hand-embroidery, less subtle and less skilled. I admit I don't like a great deal of modern machine-embroidery, which manipulates surfaces to the point where they become overloaded and muddled. Instead, the machine-embroidery I like and practice is "free" embroidery, or stitching without the feed-teeth that hold and guide the fabric. At first it's quite terrifying—until you learn to treat the needle as a pen and the fabric as the paper (except that it's the paper that moves while the pen stays in the same place).

Because I am hopeless at drawing, I prefer to make very simple designs that can be sketched with a pencil directly onto the fabric. I have found that natural subjects such as fruits and vegetables are the perfect vehicle for free stitching and, at the same time, they satisfy my deeply ingrained love of garden allotments and my imagination. The neat rows and simple shapes allow me to experiment with color and beads, all the time keeping control of the potential wildness of this method of machine-embroidery.

Fruit salads

I find I repeat some designs in machine-embroidery over and over again, often with slight variations of palette or embellishment or scale. Rows of buns, cakes, ice creams or beach huts and laundry on lines are reworked regularly but, time and again, I come back to my beloved fruit and veg.

I've made several "Fruit Salad" pieces in which I simplify but accentuate the various, lovely shapes and colors of my favorite fruits. Deep amethyst cherries, often depicted as "earrings" (when two stalks are joined together—we can never resist wearing them on our ears), curvy, ripe, golden pears, luscious, coral-pink strawberries, juicy cerise raspberries, Granny Smith – green apples, smooth, orange apricots and bobbled clusters of lilac grapes. Everything, in fact, that you might find in a fruit bowl in the kitchen.

Because I'm just a girl who can't say no to a pretty bead or spangle, I also scatter spots of gold thread on the background and hand-sew a few beads to create highlights or add surface texture to the fruit. This is the point at which I imagine I'm in an haute-couture *atelier,* sewing thousands of crystals onto a fabulous dress. And then I look down and see my fruit salad and I remember that Grace Kelly never wore a fruity frock. She didn't know what she was missing.

Vegetable soups

I think many people find fruits far more glamorous than vegetables. Fruits suggest warmth, sun, bucolic scenes of orchards and apple-picking, exotic aromas, unusual textures and tastes. Vegetables, on the other hand, are often bound up with images of heavy soil, digging, spades, boots and rain. They are often dirty, knobby, encrusted with earth, and rarely are they displayed in bowls in kitchens.

But I am passionate about the look of vegetables. This comes partly from handling them when cooking, but also because I grow them (on a small scale), and

I appreciate anything that survives my gardening techniques. Finding the first, ripe, scarlet chili on a plant or pulling up a sparkling white spring onion or watching an orange pumpkin fill out and expand has made me look more closely at humble vegetables. My heart races whenever I see a productive kitchen garden or colorful market stall, and I get a thrill from vegetables that are lovingly portrayed in photographs and on film; a dewy, early morning field of sprouts or cabbages is quite capable of upstaging the hero or heroine for me. (For excellent films starring vegetables, I recommend *Amélie* and *Brodeuses*—see Inspiration, page 40. You will never look at an endive in the same way again.)

So I thoroughly enjoy stitching vegetable soups. I might make an autumnal piece on a background of warm-brown, loamy earth with little emerald peas in pods, pointy white radishes, curvaceous pumpkins, leeks in layers of green and ripe, juicy tomatoes and a chili or two dotted in between. Or I design an allotment piece with green grass paths and borders and raised beds containing carrots, peas, onions, radishes, tomatoes and heavily beaded cauliflowers. Another soup might be in a controlled, delicate palette of shades of green and white on a pale gold background with silvery highlights on leaves and a grey slug crawling up the side.

I am drawn to any abundance of vegetables, whether they are in the garden, in markets, in soups, and my machine-embroideries are lasting reminders of this natural richness. I never overlook an artichoke or underestimate an eggplant, for vegetables are just as much beauties of nature as fancy flowers and magnificent trees.

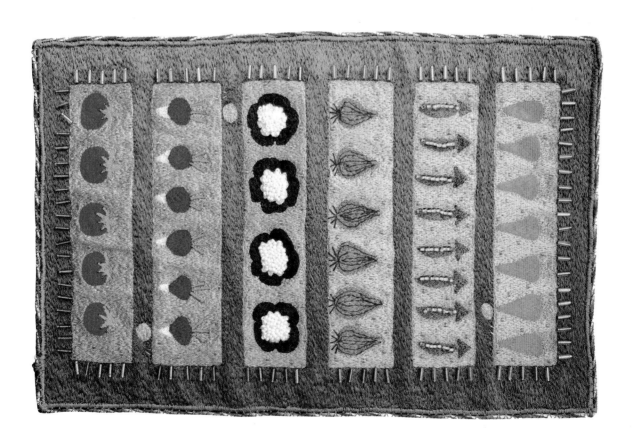

Quince

I am not quite sure how to explain my fascination with quinces. They are not your average fruit, they are rarely seen in markets, you can't eat them raw, and people rarely recognize them when you do grow them. In our garden we have one, solitary quince tree, but the pleasure it gives me is out of all proportion to its crop.

I think it may be the quince's exotic and ancient heritage that appeals. It is called *cydonia* or "honey apple" in Greek, and is believed to be the botanical antecedent of apples and pears. It was a favorite fruit of medieval times (together with the medlar, another recondite fruit I like), and it can still be made into wonderfully old-fashioned pastes and jellies. When the creamy flesh is cooked with sugar and nutmeg and cloves, it is transformed into translucent jelly, like garnet or ruby stained-glass.

The quince tree is plain and unshowy but has large, open, pale pink flowers that are the epitome of spring blossom. The fruits are ready to pick in October, by which time they have acquired a beautiful look and smell. As they mature, their color changes from pale lime green to a deep golden yellow and their fragrance increases. A bowl of quinces can fill a room with their delicate, sweet scent. Their curvaceous, globose shape, small blemishes and fluffy, fuzzy covering combine to give them a simple, natural and unmodified beauty. When you see quinces amassed in a bowl, you can see why Van Gogh, Lucian Freud, Cézanne and Chardin all put them into their paintings.

The word associations also delight me. Peter Quince in *A Midsummer Night's Dream* stands out in a play full of whimsical names, and I always wanted to eat "mince and slices of quince" with a runcible spoon at my wedding like Edward Lear's Owl and Pussycat. But it is Keats's poetry, which I first read at school, that gave me my first "taste" of quince. I have never forgotten the thrill of first meeting the quince in "The Eve of St. Agnes." Keats, the master of the word-picture that appeals to all the senses, captured my imagination forever.

> And still she slept an azure-lidded sleep,
> In blanched linen, smooth and lavender'd,
> While he forth from the closet brought a heap
> Of candied apples, quince, and plum, and gourd;
> With jellies, soother than the creamy curd,
> And lucent syrops, tint with cinnamon;
> Manna and dates, in argosy transferr'd
> From Fez; and spiced dainties, everyone,
> From silken Samarcand to cedar'd Lebanon.

Stanza XXX
"THE EVE OF ST. AGNES" (1820)

Now, each autumn, I have my own Keatsian quince moment. I pick the fruit and admire and smell it for a few days before baking it with sugar and spice and serving it with thick cream. It is my direct link to centuries of gardening, cooking, domesticity and poetry.

As they mature, their color changes from pale lime green to a deep golden yellow and their fragrance increases. A bowl of quinces can fill a room with their delicate, sweet scent.

Jolly hollyhocks

I have always thought of hollyhocks as belonging to a world outside my domestic domain. They belong to traditional cottage gardens, Suffolk lanes, French kitchen gardens and Monet's garden at Giverny. They star in the works of the Dutch flower painters, Van Gogh and Berthe Morisot. They can be found on vintage tablecloths, old teacups and saucers and in the amazing hollyhock tapestries, screens and mosaics created by Kaffe Fassett.

Hollyhocks are a splendid combination of stately and shabby, imposing and shy, magnificent and humble. They flourish in poor soil, in cracks in pavements, at the corners of houses, next to fences and hedges. They are tough and can tolerate winds and drought, but have soft petals like crushed, pleated silk. They can be huge—up to eight feet tall—and yet they feel homey, friendly and charming. They seem to be happiest in jumbled, natural and free-spirited conditions, but I am convinced that they turn shy and introverted when you try to coax them.

I was thrilled, therefore, to discover some hollyhocks in our garden a couple of years ago. For years I had tried seeds from packets or bought plants from nurseries, and finally, in desperation and thinking all hope was gone, I scattered a handful of seeds collected from flowers in a friend's garden. Then I forgot about them until I saw that a few had established themselves in the most unlikely parts of the garden.

It was like having a group of famous people turning up unannounced. I took photos to prove they had been there and set up a bodyguard zone around them so that no one could get within two feet of them (I bellowed at them if they tried).

Fortunately, I feel I am on firmer ground when it comes to embroidered versions. The hollyhock's height, deeply veined leaves, tight buds and flowers in all shades of pink, peach, yellow, ruby and maroon make it a lovely vehicle for different stitches. Hollyhocks are incorporated into many crinoline lady and cottage garden embroideries, where they can be used as a lovely framing device for the ladies and their billowing skirts. Their shape is often exaggerated by the iron-on transfer designers so that the firmly delineated hollyhocks seem to upstage the delicate, pretty lady. The outlines allow embroiderers to experiment with stitches; some fill them in and create deep, densely colored flowers while others use looser, open button-hole stitch to suggest movement and delicacy.

While I was looking for jolly hollyhock color ideas for my own embroidery, I came across some wonderful hollyhock paintings. There are single hollyhocks and double hollyhocks, fleeting, impressionistic hollyhocks and hyper-real, detailed hollyhocks, old paintings and new paintings, small floral still lifes and huge borders full of hollyhocks. Hollyhocks look marvelous grouped together, or as counterpoints to more floppy roses, peonies and twining, curling morning glories. I would happily give wall space to *Hollyhocks* (1889), the painting pictured opposite, by one of my all-time favorite floral artists, Henri Fantin-Latour. He captures all the beauty and personality of hollyhocks.

I shall persevere with hollyhocks, both in the garden and on linen, because they never cease to charm me. They are one of the best flowers of summer and evoke happy holidays at the Suffolk seaside, and who could resist a flower that matches the local Suffolk-pink houses, the pink ice cream *and* the pink milkshakes?

Come tiptoe through the tulips with me

One of the pitfalls of writing a blog like yarnstorm, which is based on my daily domestic life, is the possibility of repetition, particularly when it comes to the seasonal pleasures of nature. But I make no apologies for my annual, personal tulip festival, for I am truly besotted with tulips.

Tulips are far and away my favorite flowers. They appear in April and May when I am in dire need of color, variety and loveliness after the winter. I am deeply impressed by the fact that one, single, curvaceous tulip bulb can produce a flower that may be upright, stately, elegant and refined, or floppy, frilly, frivolous and flamboyant, or small, delicate and natural-looking, or tall, strong and with what could pass for an artist's hand-painted stripes and markings. They are also ridiculously easy and rewarding to grow and require no gardening trickery or sleight of hand.

Growing tulips

I buy my bulbs directly from two exceptional specialists in the UK: Bloms Bulbs and Peter Nyssen. To help myself choose from the long lists of wonderful-sounding tulips, I keep magazine and newspaper articles and photos, more expensive catalogs that have pretty pictures but sky-high prices and copies of my previous orders. Each spring I try to visit a garden with a good tulip collection and I note down the ones I like. Then, when the catalogs arrive in June, I work out my order and choose a mix of old favorites and tempting new tulips.

The bulbs arrive in September in boxes full of neatly labeled brown-paper bags. The sight of the evocative names such as "Ballerina," "Queen of Night," "Blue Parrot" and "Douglas Bader" makes my heart flutter with excitement and anticipation, but we have to wait until November to plant the bulbs because that's the best time. This is when my bulb-planting minion, Simon, heroically digs a series of large, deep trenches about 10" across and 6" deep, and puts in hundreds of bulbs. My contribution is to place the paper bags of bulbs at the ends of rows so he knows what to plant where and make plenty of cups of tea and rock buns to sustain my minion. I also design to put some bulbs in pots.

And what do I do after the bulbs have flowered? Well, I throw away the bulbs that have flowered in pots, since they are exhausted and will not flower properly again. I then take a risk with the tulip trenches and leave the bulbs in the ground for a second season. Sometimes the gamble pays off and we get a good repeat performance, and sometimes the show is pathetic. If you want really stunning blooms, it pays to plant fresh bulbs each November. However, there are some smaller, less designer species tulips that can be left undisturbed for several years, and of these I plant *Tulipa sylvestris*, *Tulipa tarda* and *Tulipa bakeri* "Lilac Wonder."

Happy Day tulips

There is a sunny, spring day that I look forward to during the dark, gloomy days of winter. It's the day I am woken up by a fat bee, trapped between the curtain and window and buzzing madly in frustration. It's the day I can hang out laundry on the line and bring it in dry, and it's the day I can pick the first bunch of home-grown tulips. It's the day I can examine "Zurel" (pictured on page 242, left) with its ivory petals feathered with deep beetroot-juice pink, peer into the center of the flower and see the lemon-yellow base, watch the stems curve and bend in the vase. It's the day that marks the beginning of our domestic tulip season, and it should be marked on the calendar as a Happy Day.

Red tulips

It will come as no surprise when I say that I am fussy about my tulips, and *very* fussy about red tulips. The basic red tulip, with its inevitable partner, the basic yellow tulip, is to be found everywhere; it's the staple of suburban gardens, municipal planting and florists, and yet it's such a boring tulip. So if I am going to choose a red tulip, then it has to be one that is worth growing. Because there are red tulips, and there are *red* tulips.

"Jan Reus" is my *red* tulip of choice. It may seem plain next to some of the more extravagant or decorative tulips I grow, but there is something about its

simple magnificence that makes me plant it year after year. Describing its color reminds me of having to pinpoint the nuances of red wines; this one is a rich, warm, burnished, velvety garnet, like a fine, mature Rhône wine. With its fine shape and slim leaves, it makes a classic and stunning tulip that bears little resemblance to the ubiquitous red tulip.

More recently, I have grown "Uncle Tom" (pictured on page 241, bottom left), which is the double, or peony flower, version of "Jan Reus." I'm not that keen on tulips that look like other flowers, as I am the kind of girl who thinks a tulip should be proud to declare its tulipness (or should that be "tulipity" or "tulipitous-ness?") but the color of "Uncle Tom" could not be ignored. In wine terms, I would say this is a fruity, young, ruby red, perhaps that of a young Valpolicella or Beaujolais. It's much shorter than "Jan Reus," but it makes up in generosity of flower and longevity in the vase for what it lacks in stature. To call it a "double" tulip seems a little on the mean side, for this is at least a "quadruple."

Artists' tulips

I am a carnival queen at heart, but every year I try to tame my brighter instincts and include some subtle tulips in my order. I think the tulip has the archetypal flower shape—it's the kind of flower that children

draw—and it is this simplicity of form that enables the grower and viewer to focus on the colors. So a tulip with more delicate coloring can be just as beguiling as a party-time tulip, because there is little foliage to distract from its charms.

"Ivory Floradale" is one such tasteful tulip (pictured above right). It's a "stunner," as the Pre-Raphaelite painters, who used the word to describe their well-proportioned and beautiful models, might have said. It has huge, egg-shape flowers in a pale, buttery cream color but they gradually change to a richer egg-custard yellow and become flecked with small specks of deep pink. They are very tall, graceful and self-contained, and would look quite perfect in a painting by Dante Gabriel Rossetti.

High-kicking tulips

"Menton" tulips pictured on page 244, left, were *the* discovery of one recent spring. In the catalog, they looked like a variation on an "Apricot Beauty," which is a tulip I like but have always found to be just a little too pale and blushing. So I ordered some and when they came up I could not believe my luck.

These tulips must have been on steroids. I left Tom's hand and wrist in the photo to demonstrate the sheer scale of the blooms. Each flower head was about 4" to 5" high, the stems were thick and strong

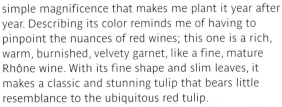

and stood erect in a vase without flopping and bending. They started out with closely furled, pale salmon-pink petals that looked as though they could be guarding something. Well, they were—an amazing color change. As they grew and opened and bloomed, the flowers changed to a warm, sunny, mango shade on the inside and a lovely, rich coral on the outside. With their fine, sturdy, disciplined form and striking colors, they were the high-kicking dancing girls of the tulip patch.

Bendy tulips

Each year I include a couple of varieties of lily-flowered tulips in my bulb order because they are so delightfully expressive. As well as possessing lovely lipstick colors, such as rich orange, sweet pink and deep claret, lily-flowered tulips are also elegant, graceful, and very, very bendy, like Romanian gymnasts. The petals of "Burgundy," which is actually a stunning magenta-purple (pictured on page 241, top left), arch backwards when they open and make me feel that I really should do a few more stretches now and again.

Tiptoe through the tulips

I can't saunter past tulips. I have to stop and tiptoe around them, bend down to examine the underside of the flowers, and then peer into them to get a good, bee's-eye view. If I did saunter past, I'd miss their colorful floral fireworks.

So I do like the day I can paint my toenails for the first time in the year and find a tulip to match the nail polish color. Pictured on page 241, middle row, center, is the lovely "Mariette" a lily-flowered tulip with petals that arch gracefully and are a beautiful satin-pink color. Just perfect for tiptoeing toe tips.

The boots were made for tulips

As with all seasonal goodness, there is always the possibility of an *embarras de richesses,* or an abundance of tulips, which poses a practical problem. Each morning at tulip-time, I pick my bunches while the flowers are closed and before it starts to warm up (this way they last longer inside) and sometimes I leave them in a cool, dark place until I am ready to deal with them. And then the question arises of which container to put them in.

I quickly use up all the vases I own, and the kitchen windowsill begins to resemble a seventeenth-century Dutch still life, the kind that teems and overflows with feathered, flamed and brilliant tulips. One morning, I noticed that the bunch I'd picked and left on our porch, which is stuffed with sneakers, tap shoes, flip-flops and other sundry footwear, matched Phoebe's rainboots to perfection. It occurred to me that the floral boots (pictured on page 243) would make fabulous alternative flower holders for a mix of the deep, dark, double "Black Hero," the elegant coral "Menton," and the extravagant striped "Zurel." It was just as well that Phoebe was also tiptoeing that warm weekend as her rainboots were *hors de service.*

Floréal

It so happens that the tulips' major annual performance in the northern hemisphere coincides with Floréal, which is the eighth month of the French Republican Calendar; it's the month of flowers, and runs from around April 20 to May 20. I think it would be marvelous to reinstate Floréal as an alternative way of mapping the year, and that this "month"

Joy of lilac-time

"Warble me now, for joy of Lilac-time," wrote Walt Whitman in his poem "Warble for Lilac-Time" in *Leaves of Grass* (1900), and I would if I were a poet.

I think of lilac as a supremely domestic plant. Lilacs can be found in ordinary gardens all over suburbia. They are by front gates, back doors, fences and walls. They can be relied on to grow without fuss and to flower on cue every May. They are as predictable as their inevitable springtime companions, laburnum and forsythia.

I grew up with all three in our small, suburban garden. I dislike forsythia precisely because we are expected to be grateful for its bright contribution to the spring garden, whereas I think it's messy and unattractive and, much as I like the climbing form and drooping tendril flowers of the laburnum, I am not keen on its vicious yellowness and poison.

But I fell in love with lilac when I was little, and it remains a touchstone of my domestic nature. We had a lilac bush in the front garden of the house I grew up in, but I never noticed except when it flowered. This is why the unassuming bush is so surprising; it looks like any other bush except when it bursts out with its

richly scented, large panicles or clusters of tiny, waxen flowers in all shades of ivory, mauve, violet, lavender and, of course, lilac.

Strangely enough, we don't grow any lilac in our current garden, as I think it's the kind of plant that should be passed on with a house. I prefer to enjoy our neighbor's lilac bushes, which happily lean over our gate and bend over our fence so that, for one, brief moment of the year, I am drenched in the scent of lilac that floods in through the windows. Sometimes I ask if I can cut some branches so that I can bring them indoors and look at them more closely. The flowers don't last long, but they permit me a lovely lilac-pause.

"Lilac" is such a beautiful word. The sound is simple, fresh and clean, but also perfumey, delicate and decidedly feminine. It makes me wonder why more girls aren't called Lilac; Lilac May or Lilac Rose Petal or Lilac Claire would be lovely names. The lilac I like (see how easy it is to start playing with the word) is the plain and simple *Syringa vulgaris*; I'm not bothered about the double or French lilacs, and white lilac appeals only because of its purity and pale, creamy color. I like my lilac lilac.

Lilac makes a great subject for a frothy flower painting. It is particularly popular with artists in Russia, where lilac is an early, welcome sign of the summer after a long, cold winter. Huge, luxuriant arrangements of lilac sit on tables next to samovars and teacups and create soft, pastel still lifes that are suffused with the sense of spring.

Lilac is such a lovely color, too. It's flattering, lady-like and not too flamboyant and makes the ultimate tea dress or bridesmaid-dress color. Perhaps it detracts from wrinkles and thickening waists and makes an older wearer feel younger and a younger one feel more sophisticated. I have found myself wondering why I don't have any lilac in my wardrobe and whether it's time to invest in a silk and lace tea dress. I would love to wear one with a necklace of amethysts and take tea in a drawing room with matching lilac tea cozy, lilac china and very polite conversation.

I have a little stash of lilac fabrics, beads, yarns, threads and ribbons and enjoy putting lilac with other colors because I think it needs something like the "dark green, heart-shaped leaves" Whitman describes, to set it off. Lilac looks beautiful with sky blue, golden yellow, deep plum and vibrant lime.

These are all colors I used in my predominantly lilac quilt, which was inspired both by my teenage years and the powerfully Proustian effect that lilac has on me. Lilac is irrevocably associated with so many memories that it is perhaps just as well that its beauty and perfume are fleeting, as I could not live with that level of synesthesia all year round. But it's quite something while it lasts, and I can "warble for joy of Lilac-time."

Teenage Quilt

The lilac and green combination that Whitman described is the basis of the Teenage Quilt. When I was thirteen, I was allowed to choose the paint colors for my bedroom and I created a variation on the theme with vivid lime green walls and ceiling, and deep purple radiators and furniture. It was brilliantly uplifting and a great backdrop to James Taylor, Simon & Garfunkel, heartache and homework.

My love for the purple/green combination has never wavered, and that's why I bought several yards of a plummy, leafy Amy Butler fabric with no specific project in mind. Then, thinking about the teenage

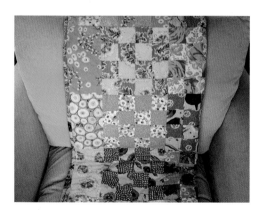

bedroom, which was the scene of my first attempts at a creative domesticity, I realized it would be the perfect starting point for a textile interpretation of a room so firmly entrenched in my color memory.

I picked up fabrics in various places, looked through my cupboard for pieces to use up, and found I had all I needed to make a quilt based on the "Salad Days Table Cover" in *Glorious Patchwork* by Kaffe Fassett and Liza Prior Lucy (see Resources, page 282). I used smaller pieces than Kaffe and Liza, as I like the lightly faded, old-fashioned, genteel look that is created by masses of tiny floral squares. I made forty-nine blocks (each made up of twelve 2" squares) placed in a seven-by-seven arrangement in an alternating lilac/green pattern. It took an age to cut, lay out and piece but gave me plenty of time to think lilac thoughts.

I discovered that I didn't have enough of the Amy Butler fabric for the entire back so used a few of the larger leftovers to make an extra panel. I like this effect; someone once said to me that the back of a quilt should always offer a little surprise, and this does, especially the graphic vegetables. Nor did I have enough of any one fabric to make the binding, so I joined strips of three fabrics to make an informal, pretty edge. I then hand-quilted it with a regular zig-zag pattern—perhaps subconsciously mirroring the ups and downs of my teenage years. . . .

I was pleased that, by the time it was completed, the Teenage Quilt was not imbued with memories of angst and introversion, but with the spirit of the more hopeful teenage spring days when the lilac bloomed outside my bedroom window and I saw and smelled what would become "souvenirs of earliest summer," as Whitman wrote.

You make me feel like a natural woman

Slate, silver, pewter, steel, charcoal, iron. Call them what you will, but sometimes grey-weather weeks are just plain overcast, gloomy, wet, chilly and very . . . grey. Vast, overshadowing greyness makes me focus gratefully on splashes of color as I attempt to banish the clouds, and I can always rely on lemons to do the trick.

Lemons are one of nature's greatest pick-me-ups. They are naturally bright and juicy, smell wonderful and add a much-needed zest to life. Simply rolling a lemon between the palms of my hands, or squeezing one on an old-fashioned glass juicer, or grating the peel with a fine, razor-sharp grater, is a good antidote to gloom. Sometimes, as I grate or squeeze, I like to picture myself sitting in a tiled courtyard in Seville, surrounded by lemon trees in pots, drinking a glass of chilled fino sherry and enjoying spring sunshine.

And sometimes I am more practical and I make a lemon cake.

Despite my passion for food coloring and bright textiles, every so often I like to go au naturel, so to speak. In fact, underneath all the colors and dyes I favor there is usually some very nonartificial and nonsynthetic fiber or food, and an undyed, wholly natural, lemon cake will go a long way to counteract the undyed, wholly natural grey skies.

This is the best recipe I know for a lemon loaf cake with a difference. It is truly lemony, but not tart, and the cake is deliciously damp and soft. I found it in *Baking with Passion* by Dan Lepard and Richard Whittington, and have adapted it over time. It can be eaten by a family of five in a nanosecond. Or the squeeze of a lemon.

Natural Lemon Cake

Makes 1 cake

INGREDIENTS
2 large eggs
½ cup superfine sugar
3 ounces heavy cream
grated zest and juice of 1 unwaxed lemon
½ cup self-rising flour, sifted
1 teaspoon baking powder
4 tablespoons unsalted butter, melted
½ cup confectioner's sugar
2–3 good squeezes of lemon juice (maybe more)

Preheat the oven to 350ºF.

Grease a small loaf pan measuring approximately 8" long x 4½" wide x 2½" deep, and line with parchment paper.

In a large bowl, beat the eggs with the sugar until just mixed. Add the cream and beat well. Then add the zest and juice of the lemon (this must be added *after* the cream) and mix. Gently fold in the sifted flour and baking powder, followed by the melted butter.

Pour the batter into the loaf pan and bake for 35 minutes. (I often place a sheet of aluminium foil over the cake after 20 minutes to prevent the top from browning too much.) Test with a skewer after 30 minutes for doneness. If not fully cooked, return to the oven for 5 to 10 more minutes.

Leave to cool for 10 minutes, then remove from the pan.

When the cake is *completely* cool, make the icing. Sift the confectioner's sugar into a bowl, add sufficient lemon juice to make a thickly spreadable icing and apply to the cake. You can, of course, add some color to the icing, but even I would counsel restraint this time. I sometimes put a line of yellow jelly beans along the top, but no more. This cake is meant to be au naturel, after all.

Eat as soon as possible, before the rain stops.

The dahlias of Brocket Hall

Here at the lesser-known, less spacious, and less notorious Brocket Hall, we like to maintain high standards of color coordination. And this means growing dahlias to match my toenail polish.

One spring we planted dozens of "Arabian Night" tubers, which would not have disgraced the gardens of the well-bred, thoroughly English ladies with names like Lavinia, Laura and Lily in Angela Thirkell's domestic novels, except I suspect they would never have revealed their colorful toes to the gardener or the world. I was delighted that the flowers' deep, velvety reddish-pink was the same shade as that summer's nail polish, a vivacious little number that made my toes look as if they had been dipped in morello cherry juice.

The dahlia is slowly coming back into fashion as a somewhat ironic, kitsch floral statement, but I fell in love with it long before the arbiters of taste declared that it was fine to have huge, neon, frilly, pompom, decorative, spiky and clashing dahlias in smart gardens. I've always liked the dahlia's ridiculousness, showiness and unrivaled range of startling shapes and colors.

I was influenced by visits to France as a teenager, when I saw that the dahlia is regarded as a fine flower for domestic gardens there and is planted in rows with vegetables and flowers, ready to be picked to brighten a *déjeuner* or *dîner*. I can think of no better combination than potatoes and zucchini and dahlias both in the garden and on the table.

When I ate at the Petersham Nurseries' restaurant near Richmond in autumn, there were simple but exquisite vases of dahlias on each table. They had been grown in the kitchen garden alongside the vegetables that appeared on our plates. This is the kind of garden we need at Brocket Hall, with dahlias to match every shade of nail polish I own. All we need to realize my plan is a few cantankerous, but dahlia-loving, gardeners like the generations of Turpins in Mrs. Thirkell's Barsetshire novels.

I was delighted that the flowers' deep, velvety reddish-pink was the same shade as that summer's nail polish, a vivacious little number that made my toes look as if they had been dipped in morello cherry juice.

A "slave to the springtime passion for the earth"

"Putting in the Seed," written in 1916, is a typically lucid and deceptively light poem by Robert Frost (1874–1963) in which he describes his delight in sowing peas and calls himself a "slave to a springtime passion for the earth" that makes him forget to come in for dinner. I can't write poetry, but I do have an inkling of this passion.

There comes a time every spring when my internal clock tells me it's time to buy and sow seeds. I have no idea where this comes from and, since I am hopeless with dates (the only time I am ever aware of them is when I read the sell-by date on milk cartons), can only assume that it's some sort of innate biorhythm. I somehow find myself, like Robert Frost, "a slave to the springtime passion for the earth," with an instinct that compels me to plant all sorts of seeds, both sensible and not so sensible.

I used to buy mail-order from catalogs, but now I prefer to read all the extravagant claims and descriptions on the seed packets, and to compare the different merchants' ridiculously touched-up colors to see who has the brightest carrots, the reddest tomatoes and the greenest of sweet, green basil. The show-off theatricality of seed packets is an art worth enjoying.

I buy my seeds at the shop at the Royal Horticultural Society's garden at Wisley in Surrey. Most garden centers stock only one or two companies' seeds, but the RHS carries a stupendous range of commercial and specialist brands. There are racks and racks full of packets of potentially perfect flowers, vegetables and herbs, and not a single slug, snail, aphid, nematode or marauding hen in sight.

It is quite easy to get carried away by the promises on the packets, and I try to keep to the old, tried-and-tested favorites such as nasturtiums, love-in-a-mist, sunflowers, morning glories, marigolds and cornflowers, with perhaps a few "new and improved" strains and colors. But I am invariably seduced by the vegetables.

Who could resist such alluring red cabbages, gloriously golden zucchini and incandescent beets? Especially when they come from Italy and have romantic names and carry instructions in at least five languages. I took many photos of these "Seeds of Italy" packets and, when I uploaded them on to my computer screen, found that they made a vibrant patchwork of vegetables. They look like a quilt, or a fabric that could be used for a vegetable design, and I would dearly love to plant a kitchen garden like this.

It is perhaps just as well that I usually lose the packets after the seeds have been planted and my passion has abated, for the seeds of my imagination never quite match up to the plants of my reality. But I remain an undaunted slave.

Franchi
SEMENTI
DAL 1783

BIETOLA DA ORTO
TONDA DI CHIOGGIA
Beetroot - Beterrave rouge - Rote rübe - Remolacha de mesa

Franchi
SEMENTI
DAL 1783

Franchi
SEMENTI
DAL 1783

BASILICO
ITALIANO CLASSICO
Basil - Basilico - Basilikum - Albahaca
Manjericão - Bazilika - Базилик

Franchi
SEMENTI
DAL 1783

Franchi
SEMENTI
DAL 1783

BASILICO
ITALIANO CLASSICO
Basil - Basilico - Basilikum - Albahaca
Manjericão - Bazilika - Базилик

Franchi
SEMENTI
DAL 1783

SELEZIONE
SPECIALE

Franchi
SEMENTI
DAL 1783

PEPERONE
PICCANTE DI CAYENNA
Pepper - Piment - Paprika - Pimiento
Pimento - Paprika - Ardei - Paprika

Franchi
SEMENTI
DAL 1783

Franchi
SEMENTI
DAL 1783

SELEZIONE
SPECIALE

Franchi
SEMENTI
DAL 1783

PEPERONE
PICCANTE DI CAYENNA
Pepper - Piment - Paprika - Pimiento
Pimento - Paprika - Ardei - Paprika

Franchi
SEMENTI
DAL 1783

Franchi
SEMENTI
DAL 1783

IBRIDI

ZUCCHINO
GOLD RUSH - IBRIDO F.
Marrow - Courgette - Speisekürbis - Calab
Aboborinha - Bučke - Kaba

Franchi
SEMENTI
DAL 1783

IBRIDI

ZUCCHINO
GOLD RUSH - IBRIDO F.
Marrow - Courgette - Speisekürbis - Calab
Aboborinha - Bučke - Kaba

Franchi
SEMENTI
DAL 1783

Travel

Travels with my template

The idea that one's domesticity is rooted in a single, fixed spot is, I think, erroneous. Domesticity is not confined to the physical and the concrete, as it is also a state of mind or a way of life. I don't see that travel contradicts the domestic. Far from it. Instead, I view travel as an extension of my domesticity, and enjoy finding ways of making travel relevant, enriching and inspirational. Travel broadens the mind, it is said, but the mind needs to be broad in order to make travel meaningful. And so I travel with my domestic template.

Traveling with my domestic template, or agenda, simplifies and focuses my time enormously. Since I know I want to further my interest in the domestic arts while I am away from home, I can eliminate all the energy-sucking tourist activities that leave me cross and tired. Instead I visit shops for yarn, beads, buttons, fabrics, trimmings, ribbons and lovely haberdashery. I look for cake pans, baking ingredients, craft and art books. I seek out the best cafés and bakeries. I choose art and craft galleries where I can discover more about domestic life and imagery and creativity. I look at the colors, flowers, gardens and doors. I wander on foot to see where and how people live, going into local shops, visiting food markets, seeing what the locals, and not the tourists, buy.

Traveling with a template may sound like common sense but it can provide an imaginative and personal way of bringing back more than just a few purchases. It can be applied to large cities, small villages, to breaks that last hours or days or weeks. My template travels everywhere with me and, best of all, it doesn't take up any luggage space.

Embarrassing Knitting

The idea of portable domesticity is very appealing. I don't mean I want to be like a snail with my home in a backpack, but I do like the portability of some creative projects.

As I have said elsewhere, I was a solitary knitter for a long, long time. But I was also very much a domestic knitter: I would only knit at home or in my room. It never occurred to me to knit outside, on trains, on planes, in cafés, at swimming pools or abroad. And I would certainly never have thought of knitting in a movie theater because that would have been too, too embarrassing.

When I finally took my knitting out of the house and into Foyles café where I knit with a group, I heard about "knit flicks." Once a month, on a Saturday morning, a group of knitters heads for the Ritzy Cinema in Brixton, London, and watches a film with the auditorium lights on. The lights are dim, so simple knitting is required, there's always the problem of your ball of yarn rolling away under the seats in front, and weeping at sad films doesn't make things any easier. But it's great fun and, should you turn to look behind, the sight of elbows and needles moving silently and half-lit faces looking up at the screen is quite surreal and amusing, but strangely comforting.

Not long after my first knit flick, I said I'd take Alice and Phoebe to see a 12A film (a rating that meant they needed me to go with them). I reckoned that two hours in a darkened movie theater would be the ideal opportunity to get some plain knitting out of the way. Throw in a few chewy candies and even the most unremittingly awful teen flick can be viewed with some degree of equanimity.

You would be forgiven for thinking that my choice of knitting caused the embarrassment, for who would want to be seen with unremittingly boring stockinette stitch in a shade of Bad-Tempered Camel? But no, the embarrassment came when Alice and Phoebe realized I was going to knit it there and then in the movie theater.

They were horrified. I was going to do *what* and *where*? They decided the only option, short of leaving me to watch the film alone, was to sit as far away from me as possible. They took their popcorn and disappeared into the darkness. So I had a row to myself (no one else wanted to sit next to me, either, it seemed) and could knit and chew to my heart's content. In fact, I managed to complete the whole section without dropping a stitch while critically reviewing the appalling quality of teen films. It was only when the film had ended and they were sure I'd put my knitting away that my two daughters reappeared from the depths of the back row.

Even though there is still a frisson of anxiety whenever I take a bag of knitting out of the house, Alice and Phoebe are less acutely bothered these days. And I now knit happily on trains and planes, on vacation and in cafés. Anywhere, in fact, that I can take my portable, embarrassing knitting.

Time travel

Coconut macaroons are the nursery version of the grown-up almond macaroon. They are big and chunky, filling and satisfying. What they lack in refinement they make up in likability. They are a passport to my childhood, when they were an unglamorous treat and suffered by comparison with the showier, more colorful and more decorated iced treats, fruit tartlets and Genoese pastries. But even then I knew that it was wrong to judge on looks alone.

When I feel in need of a spot of time travel, I make coconut macaroons and am transported back to the days of going to the local bakery, choosing carefully but plainly, walking home with the folded top of a white paper bag scrunched in my hand, and then happily sitting on a back doorstep while I ate my palm-sized macaroon in the sun.

This recipe recreates these treats with their pearl-escent, crispy outer shell and their dense, moist and extremely coconutty center. The results are also an improvement, since the spiky desiccated coconut of yore that stuck in your teeth for hours has been super-seded by the sweeter, softer shredded variety, which gives a much better texture and flavor.

It's interesting just how many fellow time-travelers decide to join me when I make these.

Proper Coconut Macaroons

Makes 8 – 10 old-fashioned-size macaroons

INGREDIENTS
2 large egg whites
¼ teaspoon cream of tartar
⅓ cup superfine sugar
2 tablespoons ground almonds
1 teaspoon vanilla extract
1¼ cup sweetened, shredded coconut
pinch of salt

Preheat the oven to 350°F.
   Line a baking sheet with parchment paper.
   Beat the egg whites with the cream of tartar until they reach the soft peak stage. Add the sugar gradually and beat well between additions until shiny, firm peaks are formed. Fold in the ground almonds, vanilla extract, shredded coconut and salt to make a sticky, but not loose mixture. Using your hands, make 8 to 10 gently rounded balls and place them well apart on the baking sheet.
   Bake for 20 minutes, or until the tops of the maca-roons are discernibly dry and lightly flecked with gold.
   Cool on a wire rack then pack in preparation for time travel.

Parallel lines

I love the old branch lines, which connect small communities like strings of bright Christmas lights. They are so much more interesting than high-speed trains, which move on the railway equivalent of highways.

Parallel lines are dear to my heart. My love affair with railways began many years ago, when I stood on the platform of the station I used when I was growing up, and saw the parallel lines of the tracks stretching away in both directions. That realization of the excitement and the possibilities of train travel has never left me, and I still make detours to look at stations and pore over Ordnance Survey maps to locate existing and defunct lines.

Despite having traveled by train in Europe, India and the former Soviet Union, I have a very domestic notion of the railways. I love the old branch lines, which connect small communities like strings of bright Christmast lights. They are so much more interesting than high-speed trains, which move on the railway equivalent of highways. They take their time, winding through the ends of gardens and alongside allotments, crossing main streets and traversing small bridges over streams. If you cycle on old, disused tracks you can appreciate just how close smaller, domestic lines are to the towns and villages they serve.

The implied sense of movement and discovery in parallel lines appeals to me when creating textiles, too. Quilts made from strips are fantastically easy to make and have a beautiful randomness that is kept in check by the parallel lines of pieces and stitching. My Dorothy in Kansas Quilt follows the basic pattern for the Wallpaper Quilt in *Kaffe Fassett's Quilt Road* book (see Resources, page 282). It is made, very simply, with 3"-wide strips joined together to make longer strips and then pieced in parallel strips. The quilt top is built up like an uneven wall with varying sizes of bricks (the

one rule is that none of the short, horizontal seams match exactly—they should always be offset).

The initial color plan was a soft, gentle mix of duck-egg blue and buttery yellow, but as the idea took hold in my mind and I traveled down those parallel lines in my imagination, I added lilac and purple, dove-grey and dusky pink. Before I knew it, I was in Kansas on one of those wonderful, trans-America trains, staring out of the window at the fields of yellow and gold corn and up at the wide, open, blue skies. I was traveling with Dorothy from *The Wizard of Oz,* so I added a very Dorothy-style fabric for the quilt back, the sort of thing she would have used to make her next dress (after the blue gingham pinafore she wore in the film), and she would most certainly be wearing a pair of matching purple, sequined, sparkly shoes.

Finally, I quilted each long strip with two parallel lines of stitching to help the mind and eye travel up and down the tracks, and to give the impression of being whisked through the prairie under cloudless skies.

The whole exercise proved to me that you can travel on the parallel lines of the imagination just as far as you can on the parallel lines of the railways.

My Monopoly, my London

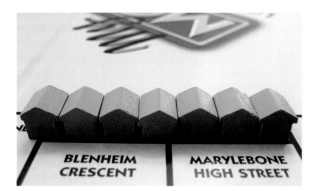

BLENHEIM CRESCENT　　**MARYLEBONE HIGH STREET**

I can't always stop myself from seeing London in terms of the Monopoly board. I played marathon games with friends when I was a teenager, and my objectives were to own all the railway stations, to build a terrace, or row, of houses on the pretty pink properties and *always* to win second prize in the beauty contest.

I still get a thrill when I find myself at the Angel, Islington (nice turquoise) or on Marlborough Street (bright orange) or Whitehall (pink, and no two-up, two-down terraced houses at all in reality), and I have even made detours just so that I can use Marylebone Station. The feeling of being a temporary visitor in London, one who should throw dice or turn over a card before walking up Bond Street or proceeding to Park Lane, has never left me. This is quite ridiculous, really, because I have worked and studied in London, and lived nearby for years.

While I was playing with the children recently, I thought how great it would be to redraw the Monopoly board so that it reflected the London that I travel to nowadays. Rolling her eyes at my mad suggestion, but nevertheless keen to demonstrate her knowledge of esoteric websites, Phoebe told me about the site where you can design your own, tailor-made game.* And so London for the Domestic Artist, my very own Monopoly, was created.

I have kept the railway stations as they are the vital points of entry, but I have changed them to include the ones I use or have used over the years (Paddington, Waterloo, Euston) and the one I think should be kept on the board because it is so atmos-

pheric: Marylebone. Then, as soon as I have stepped off the train, I'm off around the board, clutching the £200 I collected as I passed Go, ready to spend it in my favorite places.

I start off at a café and buy some bread. Instead of the usual places, I have put the best bakeries, Paul and Poilâne, on the boring brown squares. Once fortified, I proceed to a gallery to look at the collections I like best in the National Portrait Gallery, Tate Britain and the National Gallery. Having avoided jail for stealing a painting or two, I am now ready for a good wander.

There are several streets in London, crammed with treats, that are best enjoyed at a leisurely pace. You can't dash up and down Marylebone High Street; you must stroll along gently, looking in at the bookshops, food shops and cafés. On Blenheim Crescent, near the colorful rows of houses of Notting Hill, you need to take your time buying cookbooks and spices and turning corners to discover the joys of Elgin Crescent and Portobello Road. If I played My Monopoly on a Sunday, I would hope to pick up the Chance card, which tells me to advance to Columbia Road, passing Go and collecting another £200, so that I could go wild at the flower market and look at the quirky, independent shops housed in the unchanged, unspoiled terraces.

London is the best place to buy new books, and I nearly always drop into a bookshop when I am there. As I have all the time in the world in this game of Monopoly, I'd browse happily in Daunt Books (wonderful selection of travel books and the most beautiful bookshop interior I know) before going to Foyles to meet the knitting group and spending time and money in the historic café. Then I would stretch my legs and walk over to the wonderfully named and intriguing Lamb's Conduit Street and to Persephone Books to stock up on dove-grey domestic literature.

After the art and culture, I'm ready to hit the shops for little luxuries. If I am fortunate enough to land on Free Parking, I'll be able to take taxis between the Bead Shop, the Button Queen and VV Rouleaux so that I can go from one to the other stocking up on ribbons, sparkles and buttons. With my purchases safely stashed in my car, which is now no longer in danger of being towed, it's time for the department stores.

First I'd stop in at Liberty for quilting fabrics and yarns and a civilized cup of tea in the very beautiful Art Café. Then I'd walk around the corner to John Lewis on Oxford Street and indulge in the pleasures of buying ordinary but indispensable domestic supplies; I always get a huge surge of excitement when I find myself in its basement full of homewares, and nowhere else am I quite as thrilled by the sight of pegs and tea towels and dustpans. When I realize I have bought enough spatulas and cake pans to fill my car, I move on to Selfridges in the hope that its cutting-edge style will rub off on me. I don't mean I go to the fashion department, heavens no: I go to the brilliant food hall for epicurean delights and jelly beans.

It's the afternoon now, and I think it's time for lunch or afternoon tea. Ottolenghi on Upper Street (not far from the Angel, Islington) is a sophisticated destination or, if I'm feeling more bohemian, I'll head for the Soho institutions of Pâtisserie Valerie or Maison Bertaux and read the papers while I eat cake, and then plan the final leg of my game.

I don't have much strength left by this time but, having won the Advance to Jane Asher Cakes card, I scoot over there to pick up a huge, colorful, made-to-order My Monopoly cake to take home to Phoebe, who reads Jane Asher books in bed, and to buy upscale cake-making equipment and sugar roses. Finally, I stop in at my favorite supermarket, Waitrose, for everything I need to fill the fridge and cupboards. And, of course, a chilled magnum of champagne, because I have definitely won this game of Monopoly, even if coming in second in the beauty contest did elude me this time.

* www.mymonopoly.com

Urban Knitter's survival Kit

London, Paris, New York. When I was growing up these three place names possessed an indefinable sophistication. They always came as a threesome on perfumes, shampoos, packaging and advertisements, and it was almost as if there was a single place called Londonparisnewyork that reinforced the limits of my home town of Stockport. I am very fortunate that the unattainable Londonparisnewyork of my youth and imagination has now been broken down into my three favorite cities in the world, and I would be happy to visit any one at the drop of a hat.

After reading *The Dangerous Book for Boys* by Conn and Hal Iggulden, Tom made a brilliantly small but effective boy's survival kit according to the suggestions in the book. It had to contain his best marble, a fish hook, a Band-Aid, some matches and a two-pence coin. He added a penknife, a torch, a pencil and paper. To maintain authenticity, it all went in an old tobacco tin. I marveled at the economy of space and ingenuity of planning, and began to consider what I would put in a kit of my own in preparation for that dropping of a hat.

The boy version is aimed squarely at outdoor and country activities, whereas mine had to be suitable for an older, more sedate, woman in the big city. So it had to contain everything I would need as take-on luggage for that last-minute trip to London, Paris or New York. (I'd be given a toothbrush in first-class, of course.)

My kit would need to be the urban, knitting-and-stitching, candy-eating-and-wine-drinking, quilt-designing-and-toenail-painting version to see me through a stay at Claridge's, the Crillon or the Carlyle.

I'd have a vintage iron-on transfer on fabric, silks and a needle all ready for embroidery. There would be sock yarn, and the coloring pencils (for designing quilts, sketching ideas and coloring in newspaper photos) could double as mini knitting needles. Any completed work would be sewn up with the larger needle.

Should I stray too far from civilization, I could always whittle my own knitting needles from a piece of wood using Simon's Leatherman penknife. Although this is a little on the large size, it would have to be included not only for its scissors, ruler and nail-file, but also for the all-important corkscrew, because I cannot rely on finding screw-cap wines wherever I go.

I would have a piece of watercolor paper for notes and drawings, a business card or two in case I found myself in a formal situation, a few candies to eat when I'm traveling around, and a bottle of nail polish because that's all a girl needs to get ready for a night out.

As I'm a cosmopolitan, metropolitan knitter, I'd need an English pound, a two-euro coin and an American quarter (I'm hoping to strike it lucky in New York . . .). I'd pack a ticket for the metro, a map of the New York subway and a London train timetable, because I'm also a domestic artist on the move. I'd add a stamp to send a postcard home, an antihistamine tablet to stop me sneezing in summer and a flashlight to ensure I can operate in any time zone, day or night. All this fits, with room to spare for a crossword and a good article to read from a newspaper, in Tom's tobacco tin, which measures 4" wide, 3" long and ¾" deep.

And there I am, all set to discover London, Paris or New York. Or even Londonparisnewyork.

JANE BROCKET MA MW

Delight is in the detail

Travel with a grandiose agenda does not appeal to me, and I no longer feel I have to tick off the must-see monuments and sights. Instead, I enjoy the small details and pleasures of a foreign city, the domestic façade rather than the tourist façade. And Paris is the city par excellence of delightful touches, best appreciated by the traveler who simply wanders.

I am the archetypal *flâneur,* a major figure in nineteenth-century culture, first identified in Paris by Charles Baudelaire as someone who wanders or strolls, looking, watching, observing the city and is part of, yet detached from, the crowds. I never encountered the *flâneuse,* the female stroller, in my reading, but discovered recently that she is now being written into history.

I can walk for hours and find that Paris repays this ambulatory approach handsomely. There are glimpses of immaculate courtyards with box knot-gardens filled with pansies; raffish courtyards containing a rusting, turquoise, Citroën 2CV and overgrown geraniums; wonderful, original shop-fronts with gold lettering and ornately decorated mirror panels; intricate stone carvings on buildings and surrounding the huge wooden doors; enormous caryatids apparently supporting entire apartment buildings on their shoulders; small parks where fellow *flâneurs* gently pass the time in the sunshine; brilliant displays of fruit and flowers that spill on to pavements; as well as any number of architectural delights, from the outrageous modern to the sinuous Moderne. I am always impressed that Parisians appear to cherish the city and their specific part of it when so many other cities are in a rush to impose new, improved visions.

Even though I stay only a day or two, I take the time to look as I wander. This way I see Paris at a gentle, domestic pace. In spring I walk through open spaces and down little side streets, sit in cafés, eat when the Parisians eat. In winter I spend time indoors and in shops, looking for bread, buttons, books, macaroons and lovely yarn. In summer I soak up the sun and space of Paris, sit and read and gaze. I see patterns, surfaces, colors and details, and these please me immensely.

One of the few guidebook activities I enjoy is a trip to the Musée d'Orsay, partly because I adore the old station building and cannot conceive of a better place for the flux of visitors to see the incredible collection, and partly because of the art itself. I can find myself overwhelmed by the sheer number of masterpieces, so wander around looking for a handful of less well-known paintings that capture gentle, domestic moments or the fleeting beauty of fruit, vegetables, flowers and weather. I try to fix in my mind a few, simple paintings that celebrate the daily, the ordinary and the human.

I also make a point of going to the top level of the former station and behind the huge clocks through which you can see Paris and the Seine below (see opposite, top left). It's like a tasteful Harold Lloyd film without the dangerous antics of him hanging off a clock hand, or a moody Hitchcock scene with the murderer exposed to the whole of Paris. There's a café set behind one of these enormous, glass faces, so you can sit with a coffee and contemplate the passage of time, which is just perfect for the flâneuse.

See Resources, pages 277–80 and 282, for details of recommended shopping in Paris.

  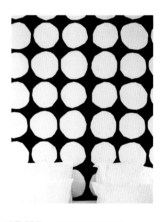

Bag lady

I have never completely mastered the art of traveling light and as a result I have a fair collection of bags. I've improved since my schooldays when I carried a vast, cavernous, canvas bag into which I could put my head and shoulders and still not find my chemistry book, and since my office days when I toted plastic carrier bags, which declared my rebellious, anti-briefcase tendencies. My business travel days were no better, as I lugged an oversize suitcase full of smart clothes because I could never gauge the weather/formality/informality thing. I spent my young mother days looking for the ideal bag to hold all the stuff required for three children to leave the house, so had numerous bags hanging off the back of the stroller, which toppled backwards with great frequency. So, I'm pleased to say that these days I am more reticule than receptacle, but still not quite able to carry everything in my back pocket.

I was never going to be able to deny myself the delightful little bag pictured below made by Alicia Paulson, who is also the brains behind the beautiful and entertaining blog, Posie Gets Cozy (see Resources, page 276). This one is called "Riviera," and I bought it thinking that it could carry me through the English "season" (Ascot, Henley, Wimbledon, back garden) with

poise and style. After all, every girl needs a bag for her lipsticks and nail polish when she's out and about.

When the bag arrived, I posed with it as Grace Kelly might have done in the film *To Catch a Thief,* which is set on the French Riviera and features a very suave and mightily suntanned Cary Grant (see Style, page 143). I even considered repacking it with everything I could possibly need for the moment when Cary sweeps me off my feet, i.e., a toothbrush, train ticket and ten pence for the phone call to say I'm never coming home.

But the sad truth is that I am still an unreconstructed bag lady. I don't actually wear makeup (I had to borrow from my far more sophisticated daughters for the photo below) and, in reality, the bag is perfect for transporting my sock knitting; it's the ideal size and shape, it looks lovely inside and out, and nobody need ever know that I am not really Grace Kelly. That is, until I get on the bus and start twiddling my double-pointed needles, because this is far more likely to be the truth of my travels with this bag. And who knows? Maybe the lady in the head scarf in the painting opposite could have been Grace Kelly if she hadn't become a princess.

On the buses

Pictured above is *The Felixstowe to Ipswich Coach* (c. 1939) by Russell Sidney Reeve. Despite the fact that it depicts quite ordinary coach travel in a quite ordinary part of England, it is full of narrative potential. Which direction is the coach traveling? Is it to the port of Felixstowe and the possibility of exciting European travel? Or is it to the market town of Ipswich and another day of routine? Who are these three people, each quite clearly absorbed in his or her own world? Who will receive the lovely flowers?

Apparently, this is one of the best-loved paintings in the Ipswich Art Gallery, and I can understand why. It's

a comforting picture of local, English travel—the sleeping dog, the blankets to keep legs warm, the bags, books, newspapers and the rather stylish eau-de-Nil and grey interior of the 1930s coach. There is a sense that this is an almost domestic scene and interior, not a means of transport, and that the travelers are journeying further in their imaginations than on the coach.

Of course, I particularly like the fact that the knitting lady stands out with her bright scarf, her flowers, her colorful clothes and her needles. She radiates warmth and brightness on a cold day and is a wonderful role model for all traveling knitters, whatever the size of their bag.

Knit New York

When I was a university student, I used to stand on the threshold of the local Oddbins wine shop and not dare to enter, even though I desperately wanted to. I thought that my ignorance would be exposed and I would leave humiliated and clutching a dreadful bottle of wine. It was this longing to make sense of a huge body of knowledge that pushed me into the wine trade and, eventually, into becoming a Master of Wine.

I used to experience the same mild panic whenever I thought about a visit to New York. How on earth could anyone understand and break down a city of that size and diversity so that they could begin to enjoy it? I was clueless about the different neighborhoods, the subway, the never-ending list of tourist attractions and everything appeared to be one huge, complex, tangled mess of information.

Eventually, I unraveled the mess into smooth threads, like the warp and weft of the city's street system, using a very simple method. Instead of letting myself be overwhelmed by New York, I decided that I would impose my interests on New York. It's not groundbreaking thinking, I know, but it has enabled me to discover a different New York from the one in the guidebook and travel brochures, a New York that is a hub of the gentle arts, a city crammed with domestic treasure.

The first time I went to New York on my own, I decided to "Knit New York." I'd read in blogs that New York was a great knitting destination, and it struck me that this was the perfect way to manage the city. One thread, one focus, one mission. So I researched all the yarn shops I could find on the Internet (printed guidebooks still don't include them) and radiated out from there. If I knew there was a shop on the Upper West Side, for instance, I looked for bookshops, cook shops, delis and bakeries nearby so that I could get to know the whole locality, its character and its flavor.

I visited knitting cafés where you can knit, chat and enjoy a coffee, browsed undisturbed in button shops while dreaming up excuses to buy, ransacked trimmings stores that look like Hollywood sets for Fred Astaire and Ginger Rogers (all those feather boas, rhinestones and satin ribbons . . .), and ate some of the prettiest, sweetest, frosted, pastel cupcakes while sitting on a bench in a little park in SoHo. I went to the American Folk Art Museum to see quilts and "outsider" art, ate wondrous Key Lime Pie at Billy's Bakery on Ninth Avenue while I watched angel cakes being iced and collected armfuls of craft magazines in Barnes & Noble. When the time difference meant I was up before the rest of the city, I would walk to a community garden and marvel at the stubborn ingenuity of gardeners and volunteers who manage to create small, green wonderlands in vacant lots and on busy street corners.

I prefer to walk as much as possible, although the subway is cheap, clean, safe, reliable, entertaining and the best way to get around when distances between yarn shops are too far for my feet. But walking is the only way to experience the intensity of street life in New York, the flux, the energy, the overspill from the small living spaces. It's also the best way to see the city close up, the details, the flashes of color, the humor, the wit, the wonderful patterns of windows in buildings and in windows of shops.

Knit New York works. It also makes me feel at home, because everyone in knitting shops and cafés is happy to chat. Talk is part and parcel of the gentle arts, and I'm more likely to find out how people live in New York, and where the best places are, through discussion of knitting patterns or yarn gauges in a tiny, but dedicated shop, than I ever am when being served in a designer store on Madison Avenue by a sales assistant on commission.

I go back to New York when I can, to indulge my domestic passions and to learn and to be inspired. And, bit by bit, I am weaving new strands into the warp and weft of my own personal, colorful, vibrant tapestry of New York.

Soul food

Every May, Phoebe, Alice and I escape to Whitstable on the north Kent coast for a little nourishment of the soul. We stay in the annex of my friend Marilyn's house, and sleep, live, eat and read in one big room. It's an exercise in creating and enjoying a temporary domesticity, like camping on a grand scale but without the wind and rain in the tent.

We don't aim high. The old-fashioned candy shop, The Sugar Boy, on Harbour Street is our first stop for candy supplies: sour peaches and orange sherbets to match the marigolds that come from Marilyn's garden and silky, striped candies to match Phoebe's cross-stitch. Then the shop where everything costs a pound usually yields something to play with—a skipping rope, a spotted inflatable tube to float in on the sea. Our first meal is at the traditional fish and chip shop with etched glass signs and an old-fashioned wooden partition, which separates the take-out line from the dining room. For treats we go to Morelli's Ices in Broadstairs for ice cream sundaes called Knickerbocker Glories.

Then there's the beach to comb for sea glass or "mermaids' jewels," as Marilyn calls them, and other treasure—smooth pebbles, tiny fossils, iridescent oyster shells. It's not a bucket-and-spade beach, but a shingle one that shelves gently and reveals a great expanse of warm, squelchy mud to wade in when the tide is out.

When the tide is in, we go swimming if it's warm enough. That means Alice and Phoebe swim every time, because their idea of what constitutes warm water does not match mine, and I assist in a purely supervisory, towel-holding and tea-drinking capacity. They do a little synchronized floating before rushing back to the house to warm up with hot chocolate.

Marilyn creates lovely interiors with ever-changing details and touches. The room always contains a little arrangement or still life, like the fabulous floral sushi on a glass plate pictured below left. It's all quite magical, and we fall under the spell every time, and relax into the rhythm of reading and knitting and listening to the waves.

And then, when we have taken in as much as we need, we watch the sky filling with color and then darkening as the sun sets.

Soul food, indeed.

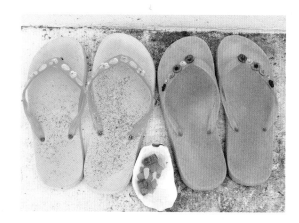

Afterword

When I was young I used to enjoy growing crystals on a piece of string dangling over a salt solution. It took me a while, though, to realize that you can't hurry a crystal and that the longer you left it undisturbed and free to develop, the more beautiful and multifaceted the end result would be.

I recalled these crystals when I was wondering how to explain what I believe is the key to the gentle art of domesticity. For me it is recognition—recognition of the worth of homemaking, of overlooked skills, of ordinary things. Above all it is the recognition of the small but significant moments of pleasure that come with an acceptance and enjoyment of the domestic space. These are the moments that all too often go unnoticed in the general speed and mêlée of daily life. In order to enjoy domesticity, we need to cultivate a habit of stepping back every so often to pause and observe and enjoy, and to allow these moments to crystallize, like my salt crystals, into lovely and long-lasting prisms through which we can view and review our lives.

We should recognize the moments of inspiration or luxury, the delights of domestic nature and style, and allow them to flourish and become a memory, so that we can hold on to them and keep them with us as reminders that although our situations may change, we are always able to recognize the significance and value of domesticity.

My aim in this book has been to celebrate and demonstrate the pleasures and joys of domesticity, and to show just what can be gained when we value and practice the gentle arts. Domesticity is a concept that defies definition, but the mix of pattern, texture, comfort and sharing is common to every creative and fulfilling domestic space, and it is one that I believe is achievable on many different levels if we take the time and make the effort to do so.

Jane Brocket

Resources

GETTING STARTED

The list that follows is by no means comprehensive, but is an eclectic selection of places I know and love and places that come highly recommended by those in the know. Inevitably it is biased toward the United Kingdom, but many of these businesses will ship internationally. When it comes to the United States, I have included my own favorites in New York and gathered some wonderful suggestions from button-buying, chocolate-consuming, quilt-making, knitting friends.

Knitting

Find someone to teach you. There are two websites that can help: Rowan (www.knitrowan.com) for details of knitting workshops and courses and Meetup (www.knitting.meetup.com) to find a knitting group near you.

Read the latest *Vogue Knitting, Interweave Knits,* or *Rowan Knitting & Crochet Magazine* and visit a good yarn store to get ideas and inspiration. Most yarn stores have staff who can offer help and advice.

Begin with something quick and easy like a scarf or cushion cover. Choose a natural fiber yarn in a color or colors that excite you—I would advise something quite thick (aran or chunky weight) so you can see clearly how the stitches are constructed, plus your knitting will grow at an encouraging rate. Use bamboo or metal needles—whatever feels good in your hands—and avoid plastic.

Crochet

If you are confident about teaching yourself, *Simple Crochet* by Erika Knight has excellent photos. Otherwise, you need someone to teach you with practical demonstrations. Check the Meetup website (see above).

A suitable first project is a simple stripy blanket or scarf in double crochet using DK (double knitting) yarn in wool or cotton. This will allow you not only to master the hook and yarn but will also let you have some fun with color.

Interweave Crochet and the *Rowan Knitting & Crochet Magazine* carry crochet patterns and articles, and I would recommend looking at Erika Knight's books if you need to be convinced that crochet can be beautiful (see page 283).

Embroidery

Embroidery is a little easier to master from a book; Mary Norden's books are excellent and they contain some lovely starter projects (see page 281).

A good first project is a small picture that can be framed. You could trace a design or make up your own and fill it with a variety of stitches, or just a couple of favorites. Use DMC or Anchor cotton threads and decent-quality cotton or linen fabric. Alternatively, look at *Colorful Stitchery* by Kristin Nicholas for ideas for bright and cheerful wool embroidery that covers surfaces quickly.

Patchwork and quilting

A simple patchwork of squares using fabrics that delight you is the best way to start. If you need help understanding rotary cutters, self-healing mats, batting, hand- and machine-sewing, it's best to attend a workshop or course.

For me, nothing can beat watching someone and then giving it a try, but if you are confident about learning on your own, I recommend all Kaffe Fassett and Liza Prior Lucy's patchwork and quilting books and magazines for inspiration, diagrams and advice (see page 281).

Baking

Of all the gentle domestic arts, baking is the easiest to learn quickly. Unlike other types of cooking, baking is an exact science, and improvisation does not always improve the end results, so as long as you follow the recipe closely and use the right ingredients, you have an excellent chance of success. You don't need special equipment, although a hand-held electric mixer and some solid metal baking pans are indispensable.

Simple recipes such as cupcakes (see Fairy Buns, pages 208–10), flapjacks (see pages 76–7), oaty biscuits (see page 106) and rock buns (see page 162) are straightforward and can easily be made by complete beginners. For more adventurous recipes, look in books by Delia Smith and Nigel Slater. Nigella Lawson's *How to Be a Domestic Goddess* is the best book on the subject of baking. (See below, for more recommended baking books.)

Blogs

Craft and domestic blogs are an excellent source of inspiration and encouragement to get started. These creative online journals are proof that the gentle art of domesticity is still thriving. Following is a selection of my favorite blogs:
Six and a Half Stitches
    (www.sixandahalfstitches.typepad.com)
Posie Gets Cozy
    (www.rosylittlethings.typepad.com)
Angry Chicken
    (www.angrychicken.typepad.com)
Whip Up (www.whipup.net)

Hop Skip Jump
    (www.hopskipjump.typepad.com)
Wee Wonderfuls
    (www.weewonderfuls.typepad.com)
Knitting Iris (www.knittingiris.typepad.com)
Bella Dia (www.belladia.typepad.com)
Bemused (www.bemused.typepad.com)
Soule Mama (www.soulemama.typepad.com)
Juju Loves Polka Dots
    (www.jujulovespolkadots.typepad.com)
Wise Craft (www.blairpeter.typepad.com)
Mason-Dixon Knitting
    (www.masondixonknitting.com)
Pea Soup
    (www.peasoupoftheday.blogspot.com)
Molly Chicken (www.mollychicken.blogs.com)
Disdressed (www.disdressed.blogspot.com)
Yarn Harlot (www.yarnharlot.ca/blog)
brooklyntweed
    (www.brooklyntweed.blogspot.com)
Julieree (www.julieree.blogspot.com)
Bara Design (www.ohbara.com/weblog.html)
A Ervilha Cor de Rosa
    (www.aervilhacorderosa.com)

BREAD AND BAKING

Shopping for Equipment

New York
Williams-Sonoma
Branches throughout the United States, but the one I visit for unusual cake pans is at
21 East 59th Street
New York, NY 10022
Tel: 917 369 1131
www.williams-sonoma.com

Bridge Kitchenware
711 Third Avenue (entrance on 45th Street)
New York, NY 10017
Tel: 212 688 4220
www.bridgekitchenware.com
Incredible range of baking pans and professional molds.

Broadway Panhandler
65 East 8th Street
New York, NY 10003
Tel: 866 266 5927
www.broadwaypanhandler.com
Colorful and characterful, with the added bonus of a helpful and knowledgeable owner.

Los Angeles
Surfas
8777 Washington Blvd
Culver City, CA 90232

Tel: 310 559 4770
www.surfasonline.com
Surfas has everything the domestic baker could hope for, from a fantastic range of food coloring, to cake pans of every size and shape to a great selection of bannetons for bread-making.

London

Jane Asher Party Cakes and Sugarcraft
22 – 24 Cale Street
London SW3 3QU
Tel: 020 7584 6177
www.janeasher.co.uk
Huge range of high-quality sugarcraft equipment.

Surrey

Squires
Squires House
3 Waverley Lane
Farnham
Surrey GU9 8BB
Tel: 0845 2255671
www.squires-group.co.uk
Online shopping at: www.squires-shop.com
The supplier of the domestic artists' briefcase filled with Squires' food color paste. Also great for baking tins, bun and muffins cases, cake decorations and equipment.

Paris

La Grande Epicerie
38 rue de Sevres
75007 Paris
www.lagrandeepicerie.fr
Part of Le Bon Marché. Huge food hall with magnificent displays. Sells unusual and tasteful cake decorations, sweets and treats. Lovely macaroons, too.

Websites

kitchen-universe.com
Fantastic. An amazing variety of Bundt pans and all shapes of cookie cutters.

de Cuisine
www.decuisine.co.uk
The site for wild cake tins. Stock changes with the season and sells out quickly. Also sells high-quality kitchen equipment.

Cookbook Recommendations

These are the baking books I use over and over again. Some are dedicated to baking, some are more general books that include cake and bread recipes.
    The first two titles are the books that inspired me to bake:
Talking about Cakes, Margaret Bates
Delia Smith's Book of Cakes, Delia Smith

These are the two books that introduced me to pancakes and muffins:

The Fannie Farmer Baking Book, Marion Cunningham
The Breakfast Book, Marion Cunningham

Nigella and Nigel write the sort of cookbooks I'd want to take with me to a deserted island. The following are the best for baking recipes:
How to Eat, Nigella Lawson
How to Be a Domestic Goddess, Nigella Lawson
Nigel Slater's Real Food, Nigel Slater
Appetite, Nigel Slater
The Kitchen Diaries, Nigel Slater

These are all tried-and-tested favorites.
The Baking Book, Linda Collister and Anthony Blake
Baker & Spice Baking with Passion, Dan Lepard and Richard Whittington
The Art of the Tart, Tamasin Day-Lewis
Tamasin's Kitchen Bible, Tamasin Day-Lewis
The River Cottage Family Cookbook, Hugh Fearnley-Whittingstall and Fizz Carr

My favorite books for cake-decorating:
Peggy Porschen's Pretty Party Cakes, Peggy Porschen
Romantic Cakes, Peggy Porschen
Jane Asher's Complete Book of Cake Decorating Ideas, Jane Asher
Cakes for Fun, Jane Asher

Shopping for Cookbooks

New York
Kitchen Arts & Letters
1435 Lexington Avenue
New York, NY 10128
Tel: 212 876 5550
www.kitchenartsandletters.com
A New York institution with a tremendous list of books on food and wine. Check opening times before visiting.

Los Angeles
The Cook's Library
8373 West Third Street
Los Angeles, CA 90048
Tel: 323 655 3141
www.cookslibrary.com
Beautiful shop, beautiful site, beautiful books.

London
Books for Cooks
4 Blenheim Crescent
London W11 1NN
Tel: 020 7221 1992
www.booksforcooks.com
The place for cookbooks.

THE DOMESTIC LIBRARY

This section lists my favorite domestic short stories and novels. (See also Inspiration, pages 26 – 9.) Some are out of print but can be obtained through secondhand sources like abebooks.com or alibris.com.

Short stories
Elizabeth Taylor published four collections of her wonderful short stories, and all have been reprinted by Virago at some point.
The Devastating Boys
The Blush
Hester Lilly
A Dedicated Man

Novels
Jane Eyre, Charlotte Brontë
Cranford, Elizabeth Gaskell
At Mrs. Lippincote's, Elizabeth Taylor
Mrs. Miniver, Jan Struther
The Diary of a Provincial Lady, E. M. Delafield
Family Roundabout, Richmal Crompton
The New House, Lettice Cooper
The Home-Maker, Dorothy Canfield Fisher
They Knew Mr. Knight, Dorothy Whipple
Someone at a Distance, Dorothy Whipple
The Priory, Dorothy Whipple

If you are interested in finding out more about novels on domestic themes, I recommend the illuminating study of women's literature in the first half of the twentieth century by Nicola Beauman, who created Persephone Books.
A Very Great Profession: The Women's Novel 1914 – 39, Nicola Beauman

Shopping for the Domestic Library

London
Persephone Books
59 Lamb's Conduit Street
London WC1N 3NB
Tel: 020 7242 9292
www.persephonebooks.co.uk
Beautifully printed, compact books, each with a carefully chosen endpaper. One of my greatest literary inspirations since I first discovered them a few years ago.

Daunt Books
83 Marylebone High Street
London W1V 4QW
Tel: 020 7224 2295
www.dauntbooks.com
Renowned for its innovative travel section, but also an excellent general bookshop housed in a beautiful Edwardian interior.

Foyles
113–19 Charing Cross Road
London WC2 0EB
www.foyles.co.uk
A London bookselling institution, now
modernized, with a huge range of books.
Great for art and craft books.

FILMS

The *Time Out Film Guide* (updated annually)
is my film-watching companion, even though
it does lack a Kitchen-Table Domestic category. I don't always agree with the reviews, but
they are well-written, informed and pithy.
    See Inspiration, pages 38–41, for reviews
of my favorite domestic films, and Style, pages
142–3, for my top five stylish Cary Grant
films.

Cary Grant

These are two biographies I have enjoyed and
use when I want more information on Cary's
films.
Cary Grant: A Class Apart, Graham McCann
Cary Grant: A Biography, Marc Eliot

And the following title contains the excellent
collection of black-and-white photos that
satisfies my regular requirement for a Cary
style fix.
Cary Grant: A Celebration of Style, Richard
    Torregrossa

BUTTON SHOPS

New York
Tender Buttons
43 East 62nd Street (near Lexington)
New York, NY 10021
Tel: 212 758 7004
The button shop as an art form. Wonderful
shop, wonderful buttons.

Great Buttons
1030 Sixth Avenue (between 38th and 39th)
New York, NY 10018
Tel: 212 869 6811
Every type of button you could imagine in a
scene of organized chaos.

Los Angeles
The Button Store
8344 West Third Street
Los Angeles, CA 90048
Tel: 323 658 5473
www.hushcobuttons.com
A tiny whole-in-the-wall store with a good
range of buttons and buckles, incongruously
placed on one of Los Angeles's chicest shopping streets. A good, old-fashioned button
specialist.

London
The Button Queen
19 Marylebone Lane
London W1V 2NF
Tel: 020 7935 1505
www.thebuttonqueen.co.uk
Not exactly a modern, cutting-edge shop, but
it's full of interesting, often vintage, buttons
and excellent button knowledge.

Yorkshire
Duttons for Buttons
www.duttonsforbuttons.co.uk
This shop comes highly recommended by
readers of the blog. Branches in York,
Harrogate and Ilkley.

Paris
I haven't found any dedicated button shops in
Paris but La Droguerie and L'Entrée des
Fournisseurs both have excellent button
sections (see page 280).

Amsterdam
De Knopenwinkel
Herengracht
1016 Amsterdam
Tel: 020 626 94 72
www.knopenwinkel.net
Large button shop with a lovely button shop-
sign outside so you can't miss it. Brilliant
stock, beautifully laid out.

CHOCOLATES AND EDIBLE INDULGENCES

New York
Jacques Torres
350 Hudson Street (at King Street)
New York, NY 10014
Tel: 212 414 2462
www.mrchocolate.com
New York is Candy City for me, but Jacques
Torres does a very fine line in hot chocolate.

Chicago
Vosges Haut-Chocolat
951 West Armitage Avenue
Chicago, IL 60614
Tel: 773 296 9866
www.vosgeschocolates.com
Vosges is famous for the unexpected flavors
of its truffles, which may include paprika,
green tea or Aztec spices. Spectacular gift
boxes and wonderful brownies and cookies.

Seattle
Fran's Chocolates
2626 NE University Village Street
Seattle, WA 98105
Tel: 206 528 9969
www.franschocolates.com
One of the original high-end chocolatiers in
the United States, Fran's is famous for using

the purest, smoothest chocolate and pairing it
with simple but sublime flavors. Their gift
boxes are beautifully packaged with hand-tied
satin bows, and they sell sublime red satin
heart-shaped boxes of chocolates.

London
Rococo
321 Kings Road
London SW3 5EP
or
45 Marylebone High Street
London W11 5H9
Tel: 020 7353 5857
www.rococochocolates.com

Beautiful, whimsical shops and packaging. The
English Collection features rose, violet,
lavender and geranium creams and should be
eaten while reading *Miss Pettigrew Lives for a
Day* by Winifred Watson.
    You could shop for the little luxuries of
chocolates, ribbons and buttons by combining
a visit to the Marylebone shop with VV
Rouleaux (see page 283) and The Button
Queen (see above), both of which are within
easy walking distance.

Prestat
14 Princes Arcade
Piccadilly
London SW1Y 6DS
Tel: 020 7494 3372
www.prestat.co.uk
Established in 1902 and located in a beautiful,
traditional iron and glass arcade. The red,
heart-shaped, beribboned box of chocs would
be perfect for a day on the chaise longue
watching Cary Grant films.

Charbonnel et Walker
One The Royal Arcade
28 Old Bond Street
London W1S 4BT
Tel: 020 7491 0939
www.charbonnel.co.uk
Established in 1875 and worth a visit just to
see the tiny, glass-fronted shop crammed with
tasteful arrangements of chocolates. Their
violet and rose creams are possibly best
enjoyed while wearing marabou slippers and a
satin dressing-gown. They even do a fabulous floral Theatre Box, which would be just
the thing for *Swan Lake* and fluffy tutus.

Montezuma's
www.montezumas.co.uk
My source of giant milk- and white-chocolate
buttons. Luxury, handmade, organic chocolate
that is made all the more delicious by being
affordable. See website for details of branch
locations.

Paris

Pierre Hermé
72 rue Bonaparte
75006 Paris
Tel: 01 43 54 47 77
185 rue de Vaugirard
75015 Paris
Tel: 01 47 83 89 96
www.pierreherme.com
(and in Tokyo)
Ultra-sophisticated, ultra-minimalist shop that sells ultra-delicious *macarons* in colors and flavors to suit all interiors and tastes. *"Vaut le détour,"* as they say in Michelin guides. Worth the wait, too, they might add.

Pain de Sucre
14 rue de Rambuteau
75003 Paris
Tel: 01 45 74 68 92
Tasteful, contemporary *pâtisserie* that offers modern interpretations of the French classics without sacrificing quality. *Tarte au citron* never tasted *and* looked as good. Dainty, colorful *macarons,* too.

Brussels

Pierre Marcolini
www.marcolini.be
I conducted three years' extensive market research while we lived in Brussels, and I can safely say that there is no *chocolatier* to rival Pierre Marcolini. Take the time to make your own selection and be sure to include the *Coeur Framboise* (Raspberry Heart). The truffles deserve their own separate box. See website for branches in Brussels and other locations in Belgium.

GARDENING
Gardening Book Recommendations

I recommend anything by Sarah Raven, whose courses and books introduced me to a new dimension of gardening with flamboyant colors, extravagant flowers and stunning vegetables.
The Cutting Garden: Growing and Arranging Garden Flowers
The Bold and Brilliant Garden
Grow Your Own Cut Flowers
The Great Vegetable Plot

Monty Don is one of my pinups and writes inspirational books. He is particularly good on the redemptive value of creating a garden and on the appealing attributes of plants.
The Sensuous Garden
Urban Jungle
The Jewel Garden, Monty and Sarah Don

Derek Jarman's Garden, Derek Jarman and Howard Sooley
A beautiful, poetic, haunting story of a garden created on the seashore and seemingly at the end of the world, with delicate, textural photos by Howard Sooley. One of the best explorations of why we garden.

Backyard Bouquets: Growing Great Flowers for Simple Arrangements, Georgeanne Brennan
A lovely book with evocative photos. It takes a similar approach to Sarah Raven's book, but is a little more general and less exuberant.

Creative Vegetable Gardening, Joy Larkom
Full of excellent ideas and advice from a highly respected vegetable expert.

Kitchen Gardens of France, Louisa Jones
A tour of France's vegetable gardens—traditional and modern, simple and grandiose. Beautiful photos.

Planted Junk, Adam Caplin
Urban Eden, Adam and James Caplin
Two enthusiastic, realistic and inventive books full of ideas for growing food and flowers in small spaces.

I also recommend books and articles by Vita Sackville-West, Beverly Nichols and Margery Fish, and writings by Robin Lane-Fox, Beth Chatto and Dan Pearson.

Bulbs

Brent and Becky's Bulbs
7900 Daffodil Lane
Gloucester, VA 23061
877 661 2852
www.brentandbeckysbulbs.com
One of the best resources for bulbs in the United States. Their catalog is the size of a phone book, and is packed with the widest range of unusual and specialty bulbs, including many excellent tulips and precooled hyacinths.

www.oldhousegardens.com
Mail-order source devoted entirely to heirloom bulbs.

Peter Nyssen Ltd
124 Flixton Road
Urmston
Manchester M41 5BG
Tel: 0161 747 4000
I buy most of my bulbs from this no-frills wholesaler, who sends me a box full of bulbs in neatly labeled brown paper bags in September. There is a basic catalog with a few pictures, but the prices, service and flowers themselves more than compensate for the lack of glamour. This is where I buy all of my daffodils, crocuses and alliums, and most of my tulip bulbs.

HABERDASHERY

New York

In the United States "haberdashery" traditionally means a shop selling accessories such as hats and gloves. "Notions" is the closest in meaning to "haberdashery," although I have found that "trimmings" shops in New York are the most delightful places to find unusual extras for your textile creations (see page 283). But there is one New York notions store still standing.

Steinlauf & Stoller
239 West 39th Street
New York, NY 10018
Tel: 212 869 0321
www.steinlaufandstoller.com
This classic notions store/haberdashery in the heart of the Garment District comes highly recommended by Liesl Gibson (www.disdressed.blogspot.com). Judging by the website, the list of practical items stocked is breathtaking.

Boston

Windsor Buttons
35 Temple Place
Boston, MA 02111
617 482 4969
www.windsorbutton.com
One of the best East Coast resources for buttons, sewing and craft notions, Windsor Buttons has just about everything a sewer or quilter could need. Their website isn't extensive, but they are definitely worth a visit if you are in the area.

London

Liberty
Regent Street
London W1B 5AH
Tel: 020 7734 1234
www.liberty.co.uk
Liberty's haberdashery section is still lovely, but these days it is increasingly limited. Paper sewing patterns are no longer sold there, and it's not the place for practical items. Go instead for the beautiful surroundings and frivolous ribbons and feathers.

John Lewis
Oxford Street
London W1A 1EX
Tel: 020 7629 7711
www.johnlewis.com
Branches nationwide. Sewing patterns, scissors, pins and needles, trimmings and notions and much, much more.

MacCulloch & Wallis
25–6 Dering Street
London W1S 1AT
Tel: 020 7629 0311
www.macculloch-wallis.co.uk
Haberdashery, trimmings and fabric in a traditional shop with a magnificent wood and
glass front and gold lettering.

Kleins
5 Noel Street
London W1F 8GD
Tel: 020 7437 6162
www.kleins.co.uk
A seemingly chaotic, but well-stocked Soho
institution.

Paris

La Droguerie
9 & 11 rue du Jour
75001 Paris
Tel: 01 45 08 93 27
www.ladroguerie.com
La Droguerie—branches in many French cities
(check website for details)—has attained holy
grail status for many domestic artists and is,
indeed, a treasure trove of haberdashery, beads
and buttons. But it gets very crowded and the
complicated service and paying systems do
nothing to alleviate the stress. I much prefer
to go to the better-organized concession
Droguerie in Le Bon Marché (where you can
also buy all the Anny Blatt yarn you desire,
visit La Grande Epicerie for some baking accessories and have a coffee and tarte au citron in
one of the super-cool cafés).

La Droguerie
Third Floor
Le Bon Marché
24 rue de Sèvres
75007 Paris
Tel: 01 44 39 80 00
www.lebonmarche.fr

L'Entrée des Fournisseurs
8 rue des Francs Bourgeois (set back from the
road in a courtyard)
75003 Paris
Tel: 01 48 87 58 98
www.entreedesfournisseurs.com
Lovely, light, airy shop in the quirkily fashion-
able Marais, with rack upon rack of beautiful
buttons, ribbons, trimmings and crafty
delights.

HAND-EMBROIDERY
Embroidery Book Recommendations

Teach Yourself Embroidery, Mary Thomas
*Mary Thomas's Dictionary of Embroidery
   Stitches*
Decorative Embroidery, Mary Norden
Embroidery with Wool, Mary Norden
The two Marys are my recommended starting
points for anyone considering taking up hand-
embroidery. Mary T for clear, classic stitch
instructions, and Mary N for simple and
stylish projects.

Colorful Stitchery, Kristin Nicholas
Wonderful, exuberant stitching. Big colors, big
stitches, big personality.

*The Anchor Book of Free-Style Embroidery
   Stitches,* Eva Harlow
Basic stitch dictionary.

Embroidery, Karen Elder
Out of print but worth looking at in the
library—a wide variety of tasteful and imaginative suggestions.

Embroidered Garden Flowers, Diana Lampe
Cottage Garden Embroidery, Judy Newman
These two are both Australian publications.
Diana Lampe's book is perfect for anyone
wanting to recreate an entire stately mixed
border in stitches, while Judy Newman's is
more informal and brings fruit and vegetables
into the garden mix.

The Embroiderer's Garden, Thomasina Beck
The Embroiderer's Flowers, Thomasina Beck
The Embroiderer's Story, Thomasina Beck
*Gardening with Silk and Gold: A History of
   Gardens in Embroidery,* Thomasina Beck
Anything by Thomasina Beck is worth
reading. Her scholarly style underpins a deep
knowledge of embroidery, and her books are
full of wonderful visuals and ideas. Highly
recommended.

Art of Embroidery, Lanto Synge
The best history of embroidery since
Constance Howard's series.

Japanese books

Don't be put off by the fact that these books
are in Japanese. I can think of no other
country that has the same modern, eclectic,
fun, imaginative approach to the traditional
gentle art of embroidery. Without a doubt, the
Japanese publish the very best inspirational
stitching books. The instructions include
excellent illustrations, so it is usually possible
to work it out for yourself.

Bag Embroidery ISBN 978 4 579 10979 1
Fabulous contemporary interpretation of
traditional stitches. Needs high skill level.

Piu Sudo ISBN 978 4 277 31147 4
Whimsical stitched designs for bags, mats,
T-shirts, umbrellas, book covers, slippers.
Includes some appliqué.

Embroidery Works ISBN 978 4 579 11032 3
Beautiful, complex and stylish ideas for
modern "art" embroidery. Fabulous inspiration for less accomplished embroiderers.
Excellent stitch illustrations and instructions.

Point ISBN 978 4 277 31148 2
Simple, sweet, small stitches for household
textiles. Good for beginners. Perfection not
required.

Hand-made Bag ISBN 978 4 579 10792 6
Clever embroidery with beads and ribbons on
small bags.

Charming Bag ISBN 978 4 579 10945 7
Stunning modern takes on classic stitching
techniques create highly desirable handbags.
Worth exploring for stitch and bead inspiration.

Tiny Embroidery Tiny Garden
   ISBN 978 4 277 31144 X
Suggestions for hand- and machine-
embroidered flower and garden pictures
to be framed. Simple and relaxed style,
wonderful detail.

Inspiration

*Thrift to Fantasy: Home Textile Crafts of the
   1930s–1950s,* Rosemary McCleod
The book of the exhibition in New Zealand
in 2005. Fabulously illustrated and well-
researched text about the gentle arts in New
Zealand during the heyday of homemaking.
Beg, steal or borrow a copy.

Magazines

There are many stitching titles on the market,
but only two have a sense of style and moder-
nity that appeals to me.

Selvedge (bimonthly)
www.selvedge.org
Required reading for anyone with an interest
in domestic textiles (although all kinds of
textiles are covered in this beautiful and well-
written magazine).

Embroidery (bimonthly)
www.embroidery.embroiderersguild.com
The magazine of the Embroiderers' Guild
underwent a radical overhaul a little while ago
and is much improved and now full of interesting articles.

I also enjoy vintage magazines such as *Needlewoman* and *Needlewoman and Needlecraft*, which can be found on eBay and in thrift shops and flea markets. You never know when you might need a pattern for a crocheted cottage tea-cozy or a knitted swimsuit.

Thread

Cotton
I buy the widely available Anchor and DMC standard cotton embroidery threads.

Silk
Mulberry Silks
www.mulberrysilks-patriciawood.com
Patricia Wood sells what are possibly the most beautiful silk threads ever. Although you can buy individual colors, she also makes up enticing themed packs. The threads come in three thicknesses and an unbelievable range of colors.

KNITTING AND CROCHET
Knitting Book
Recommendations

I have to admit to owning every issue of the *Rowan Knitting Magazine* (as it was called until recently—it is now *Rowan Knitting & Crochet Magazine*), and it is this publication that has transformed my knitting over the years. Rowan now publishes a wide range of magazines, books and booklets, but I still enjoy the twice-yearly magazine. I also use many of the Rowan Classic books—my source of good tea-cozy and sweater vest patterns.

My knitting was further boosted by my discovery of Debbie Bliss's pattern books when I was knitting baby clothes for Tom and Alice. I've knitted a huge number of Debbie's patterns—adult sweaters, children's cardigans, teddies, rabbits, Fair Isle, cabled, shaped—and can recommend anything by her.

The last few years have been a halcyon period for adventurous knitters. There has been something of a revolution in knitting books led by innovative, imaginative and visually creative American designers, editors and publishers. Every month sees the arrival of some wonderful book on a new theme. Knitters are now spoilt for choice, and not a moment too soon.

The following are my favorite knitting books, the ones I return to and the ones I recommend:

General
Sarah Dallas Knitting, Sarah Dallas
Very English, well-designed and useful.

Weekend Knitting, Melanie Falick
Plenty of inspiration for leisurely knitting.

AlterKnits, Leigh Radford
Excellent, creative, modern approach to the pleasures of knitting.

Last-Minute Knitted Gifts, Joelle Hoverson
Full of wonderful projects and great knitting advice, from the owner of Purl (www.purlsoho.com), my favorite yarn shop.

Greetings from Knit Café, Suzan Mischer
Colorful and charming, written by the owner of a wonderful yarn shop in Los Angeles that I hope to visit one day (www.knitcafe.com).

Mason-Dixon Knitting, Kay Gardiner and Ann Shayne
Enthusiastic, down-to-earth and practical book from the bloggers who have reinvented the knitted dishcloth.

Stitch 'n Bitch: The Knitter's Handbook, Debbie Stoller
Excellent book for beginners and an articulate defense of knitting.

Knits for Barbie Doll, Nicky Epstein
Stylish, perfectly formed tiny knits—coats, sweaters, swimwear, Chanel-style suits and even a wedding dress. Quite brilliant.

For the home
Debbie Bliss Home, Debbie Bliss
Includes the inspiration for the jelly bean cushion cover series.

Comforts of Home, Erika Knight
Simple Knits with a Twist, Erika Knight
Hand Knits for the Home, Caroline Birkett
These three books are full of stylish, textured, modern yet straightforward designs for the home. They cast hand-knitting in a new, sophisticated light.

Techniques and patterns
These are all useful reference books:
The Harmony Guide to Aran and Fair Isle Knitting, ed. Debra Mountford
The Complete Book of Traditional Fair Isle Knitting, Sheila McGregor
Knitting on the Edge, Nicky Epstein
Vogue Knitting Stitchionary Volume One: Knit & Purl
Vogue Knitting Stitchionary Volume Two: Cables

Knitting Website
Knitty
www.knitty.com
An amazing resource for knitters. It is a free, web-only magazine with patterns, articles, technical advice and, crucially, a sense of humor. Knitty is the place to find the pattern for the iconic Clapotis scarf (knitted and worn by many inhabitants of the blogosphere) designed by Kate Gilbert.

Crochet Book
Recommendations

I consider myself a crochet novice without a crochet history—or library. But these books have been invaluable in terms of inspiration and techniques.
Simple Crochet, Erika Knight
Essential Crochet, Erika Knight
200 Ripple Stitch Patterns, Jan Eaton
The Harmony Guides 300 Crochet Stitches Volume 6

And one Japanese book with exquisite ideas for crocheted bags that I may never make, but am happy to know can be made. The title is very misleading:
Knit Work ISBN 978 4 277 17153 2

Shopping for Yarn
New York

New York is a destination city for knitters. I am sure there are other places in the world with an equal concentration of great yarn shops, but I haven't been to them, so New York remains my gold standard.

Purl
137 Sullivan Street (between Prince and Houston)
New York, NY 10012
Tel: 212 420 8796
www.purlsoho.com
My favorite yarn shop of all time is in SoHo. Purl is a small, but concentrated, mass of color, texture, fiber and yarn loveliness, staffed by friendly and knowledgeable knitters. Everything from the window displays to the thick, letterpress-printed address cards speaks of taste, style and creativity. I go to Purl for Koigu, Manos del Uruguay, Alchemy, Artyarns, Joseph Galler Belangor angora, Lorna's Laces and Blue Sky Alpacas, and a good measure of inspiration. There is an enticing café next door called Once Upon a Tart, where you can go if you arrive before the shop has opened or when you need time to plan your purchases.

The Point Café and Yarn Shop
37a Bedford Street
New York, NY 10014
Tel: 212 929 0800
www.thepointnyc.com
New York has several knitting cafés; the mix of food, drink, yarn and socializing is irresistible. I enjoy The Point, which is festooned with colorful hanks of yarn.

Downtown Yarns
45 Avenue A (between 3rd and 4th)
New York, NY 10009
Tel: 212 995 5991
www.downtownyarns.com
For a taste of a real neighborhood yarn shop, the kind that rarely exists these days, go to Downtown Yarns. It is "dedicated to keeping the craft of knitting alive and well among [its] community of knitters"; a laudable aim and one that it fulfills brilliantly with beautiful yarn and sound advice. It's tiny and genuine.

London
Once upon a time, London was blessed with a number of well-stocked yarn shops, but sadly this is no longer the case. Liberty and John Lewis (see page 279) are the only major purveyors of yarn in the capital, and both carry the full range of Rowan yarns. I shop in both.

But London needs more independent shops run by knitting and crochet enthusiasts, such as Loop and Stash Yarns:
Loop
41 Cross Street
London N1 2BB
Tel: 020 7288 1160
www.loop.gb.com

Stash Yarns
213 Upper Richmond Road
London SW15 6SQ
Tel: 020 8246 6666
www.stashyarns.co.uk

Paris
Paris has several independent yarn shops, but I have found all I need in one place—the top floor of Le Bon Marché (see page 280). I go to buy Anny Blatt yarns (the angora, basic merino and Cachmir' Anny are my favorites) and various brands of one hundred percent wool yarn in a wild spectrum of colors.

Yarn Websites
The Internet has enabled small yarn businesses to flourish, and there are now all sorts of specialist mail-order yarn companies selling everything from sock yarn to limited edition, hand-painted yarn. I have used these websites to supplement my yarn shopping:

Sock yarn
www.webofwool.co.uk
Excellent range, including the self-striping Opal and Regia yarns, and great service.

www.simplysockyarn.com
A wonderful list of yarns from all the best producers.

Linen
www.louet.com
For the top-quality Euroflax linen in a wide range of colors.

Unusual
www.colinette.com
Fantastic range of hand-dyed yarns in many fibers and color combinations, which knit up quickly and to great effect.

Cashmere
www.sauveterredesign.com
Axelle de Sauveterre takes hanks of the softest cashmere and hand-paints them in magical colors. The ultimate hot-water-bottle cover can be knitted in Axelle's Mont Blanc double knitting cashmere yarn.

QUILTING AND QUILTS

Quilting Book Recommendations

Inspiration
Glorious Patchwork, Kaffe Fassett with Liza Prior Lucy
Passionate Patchwork, Kaffe Fassett with Liza Prior Lucy
Kaffe Fassett's Museum Quilts, Kaffe Fassett with Liza Prior Lucy
Kaffe Fassett's Quilt Road, Kaffe Fassett
Kaffe Fassett's Kaleidoscope of Quilts, Kaffe Fassett
These are the books I come back to time and again. Kaffe Fassett has an incredible eye for pattern, color and design and, together with Liza Prior Lucy, he creates some of the most stunning quilts I've ever seen. I use his books for ideas, designs, clever and unexpected combinations and as general jumping-off boards. I don't follow them slavishly, but I can think of no one else who can match this pair for sheer creative exuberance and energy.

Supplementary reading
Patchwork, Diana Lodge
The first quilting title I bought and one I still use. A combination of traditional and modern, hand and machine, simple and complex, and a great introduction to this gentle art.

Cotton Candy Quilts, Mary Mashuta
A lovely book written by an experienced and knowledgeable quilter. Informative and full of illustrations of cheerful quilts, both vintage and contemporary. Contains instructions for making some of the quilts. An excellent first-step book and one that confirms that dull and worthy are not necessarily best.

Successful Scrap Quilts from Simple Rectangles, Judy Turner and Margaret Rolfe
An incredibly useful book. All the quilts are made from simple rectangles, and the authors demonstrate just how versatile the blocks can be. I used this to plan my Domestic Front Quilt (see pages 170 – 1).

Quilts, Denyse Schmidt
Written by a talented quilt and fabric designer with a very definite personal aesthetic. Cool and contemporary, apparently simple, but with a subtle quirkiness.

History and reference
American Quilt Classics, Patricia Cox with Maggi McCormick Gordon
The Ultimate Log Cabin Quilt Book, Patricia Cox and Maggi McCormick Gordon
Excellent for visual and historical reference. Both books are full of beautiful, traditional American quilts. The Log Cabin book has a comprehensive section on the many variations on the design.

The Quilts of Gee's Bend, John Beardsley et al. I would urge anyone with even the slightest interest in nonperfect, homemade quilts to look at the quilts made by the women of Gee's Bend. Fascinating history, and amazing quilts that break all the rules and speak volumes about their individual makers. An object lesson in the true meaning of domestic creativity.

Japanese books
Machine-made Patchworks, Suzuko Koseki (2004) ISBN 978 4 579 11020 X
Machine-made Patchworks 02, Suzuko Koseki (2006) ISBN 978 4 579 11082 X
From Quilters Studio, Kumiko Fujita (2005) ISBN 978 4 579 11039 0
(Patchwork) (Quilting), Hiroko Ninagawa (1999) ISBN 978 4 579 10788 8
These are my favorite quilting books from Amazon Japan (www.amazon.co.jp). Brilliant ideas, colors, visuals, inspiration and patterns.

Shopping for Fabric

I write from the perspective of someone living in the UK, where the choice of quilting fabrics is limited and patchwork shops are few and far between.

New York

The City Quilter
133 West 25th Street
New York, NY 10001
Tel: 212 807 0390
Buzzing and busy, excellent fabrics and service, and full of treats for a UK quilter.

Purl Patchwork
147 Sullivan Street
New York, NY 10012
Tel: 212 420 8796
www.purlsoho.com
Purl Patchwork is the sister of Purl, my favorite yarn shop in the world. It is tiny but stocks the most tastefully "edited" selection of quilting fabrics I have seen. Joelle Hoverson, who owns both shops, has an amazing eye, and every fabric she chooses has had to earn its place on the shelf. The biggest problem when visiting is curbing the very understandable desire to take a yard of everything.

B&J Fabrics
525 Seventh Avenue, 2nd Floor
New York, NY 10018
Tel: 212 354 8150
www.bandjfabrics.com
Fabulous array of fabrics and a great source of inspiration.

Mood Designer Fabrics
225 West 37th Street, 3rd Floor
New York, NY 10018
Tel: 212 730 5003
www.moodfabrics.com
Mood is a sprawling fabric store with a fantastic selection of luxurious high-fashion fabrics, trims and buttons. Although it does not have a dedicated quilt fabric section, it is worth a visit just for the colors, textures, patterns and inspiration it offers.

Los Angeles

F and S Fabrics
10629 W Pico Boulevard
Los Angeles, CA 90064
Tel: 310 475 1637
www.fandsfabrics.com
F and S is so big it occupies three different locations on one block. One generous room is devoted to quilt fabric, and has a great selection of Amy Butler and Kaffe Fassett cottons set amongst simple cotton prints.

Mood Fabrics
6151 W Pico Blvd
Los Angeles, CA 90035
Tel: 323 653 6663
www.moodfabrics.com
See description under New York.

Chicago

Vogue Fabrics
718-732 Main Street
Evanston, Illinois 60202
Tel: 847 864 9600
www.myvoguefabrics.com
Vogue Fabrics is a Chicago institution, and its three stores offer a huge range of premium fabric. Their website is a great resource for sewers who don't have a quality fabric store in their neighborhood.

United Kingdom

Liberty
Regent Street
London W1B 5AH
Tel: 020 7734 1234
www.liberty.co.uk
Liberty has recently expanded its Rowan fabric section and now has several walls full of fabrics by designers such as Kaffe Fassett, Amy Butler, Martha Negley, David Wolverson. A lovely place to put together your next quilt, and you can take a breather in the Art Café, where they offer rather special jams with the scones.

The Quilt Room
20 West Street
Dorking
Surrey RH4 1BL
Tel: 01306 877307
www.quiltroom.co.uk
This is my nearest shop with a very good selection of fabrics and the best organic cotton batting I have found.

Websites

Glorious Color
www.gloriouscolor.com
Run by Liza Prior Lucy, it offers what it says—page after page of glorious color. *The* place for Kaffe Fassett and other Rowan designers' fabrics.

eQuilter
www.equilter.com
Amazing array of fabrics, excellent search tool, and a helpful "design board" that allows you to play with thumbnail photos of fabrics.

Cia's Palette
www.ciaspalette.com
A well-chosen selection with a personal touch. Cia has great taste and offers excellent service, too.

RIBBONS AND TRIMMINGS

Many of the shops mentioned in the Haberdashery section (see pages 280–1) carry ribbons and trimmings, but the following are specialist outlets.

The exquisite ribbons by Laura Foster Nicholson (see Luxury, pages 188–9) can be bought on the Internet. Check the website for stockists: www.lfntextiles.com.

New York

The trimmings shops in New York take your breath away with their incredible stock of textile accessories. These are the ones I make a beeline for.

M&J Trimming
1008 Sixth Avenue (between 37th and 38th)
New York, NY 10018
Tel: 800 9 MJTRIM
www.mjtrim.com
M&J Trimming has the best selection I've ever seen of rhinestones, feathers, ribbons, beads, tassels, cords and much more.

Tinsel Trading
47 West 38th Street
New York, NY 10018
Tel: 212 730 1030
www.tinseltrading.com
Tinsel Trading is like stepping into a fairyland of pretty things.

Seattle

Nancy's Sewing Basket
2221 Queen Anne Avenue North
Seattle, WA 98109
Tel: 206 282 9112
www.nancyssewingbasket.com
Nancy's is a shop after my own heart with its wall of buttons, ribbon room, friendly service and useful website.

Atlanta

Nicholas Kneil
290 Hilderbrand Drive, Suite B16
Atlanta GA 30328
Tel: 404·252 8855
www.nicholaskniel.com
Noted for its "fine ribbons and embellishments." A great selection of vintage and hard-to-find European ribbons, with an extensive online catalog.

London

VV Rouleaux
www.vvrouleaux.com
This renowned ribbon specialist also sells exquisite trimmings and passementerie. Fabulous selection of ribbons and wonderful shop interiors. High prices. See website for details of branches in Marylebone Lane and

Sloane Square in London and in Newcastle and Glasgow.

The Cloth House
47 Berwick Street
London W1F 8SJ
Tel: 020 7437 5155
www.clothhouse.com
A small, well-chosen selection of vintage trimmings and buttons in this branch, which also sells a huge range of natural fabrics.

Paris
All the shops in the Parisian Haberdashery section (see page 280) carry extensive ranges of trimmings and ribbons.

SWEET SHOPS

New York
Dylan's Candy Bar
1011 Third Avenue
New York, NY 10021
Tel: 646 735 0078
www.dylanscandybar.com
Open till late and packed at all times. Throw caution to the wind and fill your bags with sour peach, strawberry, grapefruit and cherry candy or buy jelly beans and Skittles in individual colors to match your baking. Check website for details of branches.

Economy Candy
108 Rivington Street
New York, NY 10002
Tel: 800 352 4544
www.economycandy.com
There is no room to blow a gum bubble in here, as it's packed to the rafters with candy. The windows make a sweet patchwork of colors and brand names. Just around the corner from the Sugar Sweet Sunshine bakery and its excellent cupcakes.

Los Angeles
Littlejohn Toffee & Fudge
3rd & Fairfax
Los Angeles CA 90036
Tel: 323 936 5379
www.littlejohnscandies.com
Located in the historic Farmer's Market, Littlejohn's has the richest, creamiest, home-made English style fudge, toffee and caramel.

London
Hope and Greenwood
20 North Cross Road
East Dulwich
London SE22 9EU
Tel: 020 8613 1777
www.hopeandgreenwood.co.uk
A wonderful, deliberately old-fashioned shop with a commitment to quality and enjoyment.

Kent
The Sugar Boy
www.sugarboy.co.uk
The Sugar Boy shops are a delight and stock only the "aristocracy of the confectionery trade," so you know that their rhubarb and custard sweets are the very best. You can sample before you buy. See website for details of branches in Canterbury, Deal and Whitstable.

Website
A Quarter Of
www.aquarterof.co.uk
Our favorite site for classic and modern sweet treats.

TRAVEL GUIDES

I am a great fan of both the Rough Guides and the Time Out Guides and use both (where available) whenever I travel. They may overlap, but they also complement each other. One guide may be better for cafés and hotels, and the other for shopping and history. The Time Out maps are excellent.

The only other books I consult are the Thames & Hudson Style City Guides (London, Paris and New York are all in the series, and I've also used the guide to Amsterdam). These are sophisticated, upmarket and well-researched. They focus on the detail, the esoteric, the quirky and the atmospheric. The books are all beautifully designed, and the photography is stunning. They are also perfect for a little light armchair travel.

Index of Recipes and Projects

thank you

This book is the culmination of years of reading, looking, creating and thinking. There are many people who have contributed to my ideas about domesticity and the gentle arts during this time and, unfortunately, it's not possible to thank everyone here. But I must mention a few.

I've been inspired and encouraged by some wonderful people. Professor Adam Roberts at Royal Holloway College influenced my reading, thinking and writing so fundamentally that the MA (and abandoned PhD) he supervised became a turning point that led to the creation of yarnstorm and, ultimately, this book. Marilyn Phipps has welcomed me into her beautiful home, and Julie Arkell, Linda Miller, Janet Bolton and Juju Vail have all shared their skills and philosophies at workshops. I am indebted to each of them for their inspiration. Nicola Beauman at Persephone Books was the first "literary" person to whom I showed the blog and I am grateful to her not only for encouraging me, but also for publishing books that have sustained and expanded my visions of domesticity. Kaffe Fassett has been an inspiration for twenty years, and his books with Liza Prior Lucy have enabled me to take up quilting after stalling for so long. I would also like to thank Liza for the entertaining and wise emails that enlivened so many days of writing.

Thanks also to some friends: Angela Burdett for encouraging me and asking the right questions, Rachel Merrell for washing-line and recipe talk, Marion Farrell for supplementing (and humoring) my crinoline lady collection, Pauline Wall for organizing our knitting group and everyone who knits at Foyles. And thanks to my mum for turning a blind eye to the creative mess in my teenage bedroom and for sharing her passion for films with me.

There are also some people whom I have never met but must thank. My blog, yarnstorm, has brought me into contact with a community of intelligent, articulate and entertaining readers. Not only do these people contribute to the ongoing conversations about all aspects of creativity and home life, but many of them also write inspirational blogs of their own. In particular I would like to thank Alicia Paulson, Kathy Merrick, Amanda Soule, Jan Burgwinkle, Teresa Parkins, Melanie Dunkley, Jayne Hyslop, Alison Brookbanks, Kay Gardiner, Cassie Kemp, Susan Rees-Osborne, Lisa Congdon, Hillary Lang, Liesl Gibson, Kristin Nicholas, Éireann Lorsung and Blair Stocker.

When I stumbled into the world of publishing, I was immensely fortunate to be taken on firstly by my agent, Jane Graham Maw, and her agency partner, Jennifer Christie, who have both been fantastically helpful, reliable and unflappable, and then by my editor, Sarah Reece. As this is my first book, I have no means of comparison, but I am quite sure that Sarah is a rare gem. Her enthusiasm and commitment go beyond the call of duty, and it has been a great pleasure to work with her. As if this wasn't enough, I was delighted beyond words when it was agreed that STC Craft would publish this book in the US. It is a great privilege to work with Melanie Falick and I am grateful to her for guiding me and my book so carefully and thoughtfully. I am also indebted to Liana Allday for her beady eyes and attention to detail.

I must also thank the team involved in the creation of the book. I am thrilled with the lovely design by Ashley Western, who has captured the essence of yarnstorm and my domestic philosophy, and made them work in print. It is a privilege to have Debi Treloar's beautiful photographs to supplement mine. I had no idea a photo shoot could be so relaxed and enjoyable.

My own domesticity would not be possible without some very special people. Tom, Alice and Phoebe are my muses; they have been brilliantly supportive throughout the yarnstorm and book era (although I think their eyes may roll backwards at their mother permanently someday soon) and I thank them also for their colorful baking contributions to this book. But absolutely none of this—the way of life, the making, the doing, the writing—would have happened without my husband, Simon. He's the best supporter, friend, sounding-board, eating, drinking and laughing partner I could ever have wished for, and I dedicate this book to him.

Picture credits

Hodder & Stoughton would like to thank the following for providing photographs and for permission to reproduce copyright material.

All photographs are taken by, or supplied by, Jane Brocket, with the exception of the following:

Page 2, 9 and 13 bottom right © Debi Treloar; 17 top left Getty Images; 19 by kind permission of the Christopher Wood Gallery, London; 21 top © Manchester City Art Gallery; 21 below Art Archive/Imperial War Museum; 27 private collection, Connaught Brown, London/Bridgeman Art Library; 39 Moviestore; 41 Ronald Grant Archive/Paramount Pictures; 63 Bridgeman Art Library/Aberdeen Art Gallery and Museum, Scotland; 64 Kettle's Yard, Cambridge; 68 and 79 © Debi Treloar; 81 Leeds Museums and Galleries (City Art Gallery), UK, DACS; 85, 88 and 91 © Debi Treloar; 103 private collection/Bridgeman Art Library; 108 top left Art Gallery of New South Wales, Sydney, Australia/The Bridgeman Art Library; 108 below right private collection/Bridgeman Art Library; 109 South African National Gallery, Cape Town, South Africa/Bridgeman Art Library; 114 © Debi Treloar; 122 Bridgeman Art Library/private collection; 127 private collection, Lefevre Fine Art Ltd, London/Bridgeman Art Library; 133 private collection/Bridgeman Art Library; 134–5 © Debi Treloar; 136 and 143 left Kobal Collection; 143 centre Getty Images; 143 right Corbis/John Springer Collection; 148 bottom private collection/Bridgeman Art Library; 159 © Debi Treloar; 160 Getty Images/Time & Life Pictures; 161 left Ashmolean Museum, University of Oxford, UK/Bridgeman Art Library; 163, 192–3, 197 and 198 and 203 © Debi Treloar; 205 Museum of Fine Arts, Houston, Texas, USA © DACS/gift of Audrey Jones Beck/Bridgeman Art Library; 206 © Alfred East Gallery, Kettering, Northamptonshire, UK/Bridgeman Art Library; 209 and 212–13 © Debi Treloar; 215 Getty Images/Time & Life Pictures; 220–1 © Debi Treloar; 223 by kind permission of MacConnal Mason Gallery; 239 private collection/Bridgeman Art Library; 269 Ipswich Borough Council Museums and Galleries, Suffolk, UK/Bridgeman Art Library; endpapers © Debi Treloar.

Every reasonable effort has been made to contact the copyright holders, but if there are any errors or omissions, Hodder & Stoughton will be pleased to insert the appropriate acknowledgment in any subsequent printing of this publication.